SOCIAL POLICY IN TH...

Also by Linda Hantrais

* *From the same publishers*

Social Policy in the European Union

Third Edition

Linda Hantrais

palgrave
macmillan

First edition 1995
Second edition 2000
Third edition 2007

Published by
PALGRAVE MACMILLAN
Houndmills, Basingstoke, Hampshire RG21 6XS and
175 Fifth Avenue, New York, N.Y. 10010
Companies and representatives throughout the world

PALGRAVE MACMILLAN is the global academic imprint of the Palgrave Macmillan division of St. Martin's Press, LLC and of Palgrave Macmillan Ltd. Macmillan® is a registered trademark in the United States, United Kingdom and other countries. Palgrave is a registered trademark in the European Union and other countries.

ISBN-13: 978–0–230–01308–7 hardback
ISBN-10: 0–230–01308–2 hardback
ISBN-13: 978–0–230–01309–4 paperback
ISBN-10: 0–230–01309–0 paperback

This book is printed on paper suitable for recycling and made from fully managed and sustained forest sources. Logging, pulping and manufacturing processes are expected to conform to the environmental regulations of the country of origin.

A catalogue record for this book is available from the British Library.

Library of Congres Catalog Card Number: 2007022295.

10 9 8 7 6 5 4
14 13 12 11 10 09 08 07

Printed in China

Contents

List of Figures and Boxes

FIGURES

BOXES

vii

Preface

The challenges facing the European Union (EU) in the early years of the twenty-first century gave a new salience to social affairs on the policy agenda. The rapid pace of technological, economic, political and socio-demographic change, accelerated by enlargement of the Union on an unprecedented scale to post-Communist countries, intensified pressures on welfare systems. Such momentous change called into question the feasibility and desirability of achieving a common social policy but added a new impetus to the debate about the future shape of the 'European social model'. Softer modes of governance were being introduced to accommodate the ever greater diversity of welfare arrangements while safeguarding the social *acquis*. These events served to strengthen the enduring interest shown in the social dimension of the EU by policy analysts. They justify a new edition of this book, designed to track the development of European social policy over the 50 years since the founding of the European Economic Community in 1957.

As in the first and second editions, the primary aim of this work is to examine the interconnections between social policy formation and implementation at EU, national and subnational level. By analysing the interplay between developments at these different levels, an attempt is made to unravel what is a complex interactive process, while also considering its theoretical underpinnings and implications. Rather than describing national welfare systems one by one and, subsequently, comparing them across member states, a task that would be unmanageable with 27 or more member states, the book is again organized thematically. The chapters examine the main areas of social policy that the Union has addressed, drawing on international comparisons to exemplify the measures introduced in different member states in response to similar social problems. Comparisons across countries enable conceptual variations to be identified in national systems of welfare, in policy processes and modes of delivery of benefits and services. They also provide illustrations of the distinctness of each country and the effects of cultural embedding.

This approach is based on the assumption that students and analysts of comparative social policy are concerned with identifying its socio-cultural determinants and are interested in examining different institutional arrangements, policy options and outcomes. The underlying argument in the book is that national governments in an expanded community continue to differ in their policy responses to common social problems while being increasingly constrained by EU law.

The period between the first and second editions of the book (1995–2000) saw a number of important changes within the Union that had implications for the development of social policy in the early years of the twenty-first century. The new government brought to power in the United Kingdom in 1997 signed up to the Agreement and Protocol on Social Policy, enabling the social chapter to be incorporated into the body of the Union's treaty. Directives in the social area that had long been on the table were finally unblocked. The signing and ratification of the Treaty of Amsterdam in the same year brought formal recognition of the centrality of employment as an issue at EU level, subsequently translated into the European employment strategy, and implemented using the newly developed open method of coordination (OMC). This alternative approach to regulation was soon to be extended to pensions and social inclusion, education, research, social protection, health and immigration. Monitoring progress in the social domain, including the demographic situation, which had been signalled in the Treaty on European Union, became a formal treaty obligation (article 143 in the consolidated EC Treaty). The Commission, and more especially the Directorate-General for Employment, Social Affairs and Equal Opportunities, assisted by Eurostat, the Statistical Office of the European Communities, consequently intensified their information gathering and dissemination efforts. Demographic issues moved to the top of the social agenda and were profiled in a series of policy documents from the Commission.

The countries that were members of the Union by the late 1990s had had to tackle broadly similar issues during the second half of the twentieth century: for example, how to prepare the workforce for rapidly changing labour markets in a context of persistent unemployment and social exclusion; or how to cope with the growing demand for ever higher standards of health and social care, particularly among older people during retirement, in the face of population ageing, changing intergenerational relations, the rising cost of providing services and the need to contain public spending. Analysis shows how perceptions of seemingly common problems, the solutions adopted and their outcomes reflect varying socio-economic conditions as well as differing political ideologies and conceptions of the legitimacy of state intervention.

Enlargement in 2004 to central and east European countries that had undergone fundamental economic and social welfare restructuring and were reporting much lower *per capita* gross domestic product put these concerns into yet another perspective.

The second edition of the book provided an early assessment of the implications socio-demographic change might have for EU social policy in the new millennium. It could not analyse the impact of the OMC on the EU legislative process. Nor did it broach the subject of the Fundamental Treaty of Human Rights, which was adopted at the Nice summit in 2000 and was due to be written into the stalled EU Constitutional Treaty, signed in 2004. The second edition could do no more than speculate about the impact on EU social policy of the accession of the ten countries that met the criteria laid down for membership in 2004. With 27 member states in 2007, the Union's celebration of its first half century provided an opportune moment to take stock of developments in the social policy arena throughout the 50-year period.

Academic and popular interest in the social dimension of the Union has grown markedly since the first edition of the book. Because it draws on methods and insights from a number of disciplines, the subject of social policy, or social welfare, in Europe attracts attention across the spectrum of social science disciplines: from lawyers, political scientists, economists and industrial relations analysts to social policy and labour market specialists. Like the first and second editions, this book refers to a wide variety of disciplinary and methodological approaches to social policy analysis, while remaining as comprehensive as possible in its country coverage. The task has been made more difficult by of the Union's enlargement to the east and by developments in its social policy remit. The present edition has been extended to incorporate new material on membership, legislation and the policy process.

The structure of the book follows the same pattern as earlier editions, but the focus of several of the chapters has been adapted to take account of the increasing concern among member states and in the Commission with demographic issues, (un)employment and the social consequences of enlargement. The centrality of these topics for social policy since the turn of the twenty-first century could have justified restructuring the chapter plan. Rather than substituting the material for existing chapters, the three topics are treated as leitmotivs or transversal themes throughout the book.

The first chapter provides insights into the factors shaping European social policy by charting the Union's social remit over half a century. A major obstacle to effective social policy making at EU level has been the lack of a common understanding of central concepts and the societal contexts within which social policy is formulated and implemented. Both the first and second chapters therefore raise a number of questions about the changing status of social policy in the Union and the desirability and feasibility of harmonization and coordination of national social protection systems. Why did the Union develop a social policy? How have its aims, objectives and competences changed over time? What is the relationship between economic, employment and social policy? How has enlargement affected the social dimension? In seeking to answer these questions the first chapter revisits the debate about citizenship versus workers' rights, equalization, competition and social cohesion, following the latest wave of enlargement, which has given a new salience to discussion about the notions of social dumping, social inclusion and the ubiquitous European social model.

The social protection systems of the six original EEC member states can be considered as variants of what is known as the continental model of welfare. Successive waves of membership in the 1970s, 1980s, 1990s and, more especially, in the early years of the twenty-first century brought together countries that did not share the same welfare histories. While the goal of harmonizing social protection seemed to have become more pressing in the 1990s with the move towards the Single European Market (SEM) in 1993 and the launching of EMU in 1999, doubts were increasingly expressed about the feasibility and desirability of harmonizing such very different welfare systems. The second chapter examines this diversity as an obstacle to social union and a common social policy. In tracking the shift away from the original aim of harmonizing national systems, the chapter charts the route through coordination, cooperation, cohesion, mutual recognition and convergence, leading on to an analysis of the OMC as a means of spreading good practice and achieving common goals, while respecting diversity. The overview of national systems is organized in relation to the different waves of membership, thereby documenting the extent to which diversity can be accommodated within a shared social model.

Education and training provide a good example of the shift towards a more pragmatic approach to convergence. After many years of work comparing the content and level of qualifications across the Community in an attempt to reach agreement over transferability from one member state to another, general directives were issued on the mutual recognition of the equivalence of diplomas. Measures of output suggest, however, that recognition does not mean vocational and educational training has been standardized. The third chapter reviews the lengthy process leading to the mutual recognition directive and initiatives at Community level to encourage mobility among students and young workers. It then compares developments in the educational and training systems of individual member states, including national responses to the Lisbon strategy and the Bologna process, and their impact on labour market opportunities for young people and on lifelong learning.

Several articles in the EEC Treaty were devoted to the improvement of living and working conditions as a means of equalizing opportunities and promoting mobility. Despite the early interest shown by the Community, comparisons of working conditions and health and safety at work, as governed by national labour law, demonstrate that member states are far from sharing common standards. The fourth chapter explores the relationship between European law and national policies for health and safety at work, spilling over to working time arrangements and public health, a topic that was incorporated into the revised EC Treaty and has since developed as an important area of interest for multilevel governance.

Since family policy is only indirectly affected by workers' rights, it is an area where member states have been reluctant to seek agreement on a common policy, and where the Commission, like many national governments, has limited itself to monitoring the situation rather than trying to prescribe family policy measures. Although some convergence in family patterns may be occurring spontaneously, due to similar demographic trends, member states have continued to hold differing views on what constitutes the 'benefit' family and on the aims and objectives of family policy. The fifth chapter examines changing family structures and the responses of national governments in line with the growing concern at EU level about socio-demographic issues.

The employment model of welfare that has been dominant in the Union put women at a disadvantage in access to social protection. The directives on equal pay for work of equal value, equal treatment and employment-related social insurance rights sought to redress the balance for women who are economically active for the greater part of their working lives. The 1990s saw further development of measures to assist both women and men in combining paid and unpaid work, and also the incorporation of the concept of mainstreaming into the European agenda. The sixth chapter analyses changing gender relations at EU and national level with reference to the situation of women as both policy actors and recipients of social policies. Specific reference is made to efforts at EU level to promote reconciliation of family life and paid work and, subsequently, work–life balance as policy objectives in

1   Developing European Social Policy

When the Treaty establishing the European Economic Community (EEC) was signed in Rome in 1957 [1.2], the dominant political philosophy was market driven. The six original EEC member states – Belgium, France, the Federal Republic of Germany, Italy, Luxembourg and the Netherlands – believed that, if enterprises were allowed to compete on equal terms, the distribution of resources would be optimized, enabling untrammelled economic growth, which would automatically result in social development. Upward social harmonization was seen as an end product of economic integration rather than a prerequisite. For these reasons, the social provisions in the treaty did not define precise social policy objectives; EEC responsibility was limited to promoting cooperation (Collins, 1975; Shanks, 1977). Member states did recognize the need to establish a social fund to help declining areas of the economy, but it was to operate on a very small scale.

As the optimistic assumptions of the founder members proved to be ill conceived, and as Denmark, Ireland and the United Kingdom joined the European Community (EC) in 1973, a more active approach to social reform was advocated on the grounds that the unevenness created by giving free rein to market forces was unacceptable and not in the long-term interests of member states. For the following decades, this philosophy underpinned the growing commitment, at least in principle, to the social dimension as a component of European integration and a necessary complement to economic policy.

This chapter provides a brief overview of the historical development of Europe's social dimension within the context of its treaties, charters, social action programmes and social policy agendas. Several of the central concepts underlying European social policy are introduced, including social space, social dialogue, social plinth, subsidiarity, proportionality and social dumping. As well as exploring why and how the social dimension became a concern for member states, the chapter seeks to identify and track the changing aims, objectives and nature of the European social policy-making process over half a century.

THE SOCIAL DIMENSION OF EUROPEAN POLICY

In many respects, the Treaty of Paris, which set up the European Coal and Steel Community (ECSC) in 1951 [1.1], and the Treaty establishing the European Atomic Energy Community (EAEC) in 1957 [1.3] were more interested in social policy than the EEC Treaty. The ECSC had to deal with the social impact of structural change in two major industries and was endowed with funds to cover the resettlement of displaced workers. It also conferred responsibility for looking into the living and working conditions of miners and steel workers. The EAEC laid down basic standards for the health and protection of workers and the general public, as well as procedures for monitoring and checking their implementation. The EEC Treaty had a limited, albeit specific, social remit, for example in its commitment to raising standards of living (article 2), the provision of a social fund (3 §i) and the task of promoting close cooperation in the social field (118). It did not set the framework for a fully developed European social policy, as did the Council of Europe in 1961 with its social charter, which was later to serve as a source of inspiration for the Community Charter of the Fundamental Social Rights of Workers [1.12]. This section tracks the development of social provisions through European legislation and policy statements over the 50 years since the signing of the EEC Treaty [1.26].

Social policy in the EEC Treaty

Twelve of the 248 articles in the founding treaty were devoted explicitly to social policy (articles 117–28). Since the aim of the treaty was to create an economic union, the relatively low priority given to social affairs was logical. Justification for the inclusion of any reference to the social dimension can be found in the overriding principle that distortion of the rules of competition was to be avoided at all costs. In the negotiations leading up to the signing of the treaty, the French had argued that the high social charges the state imposed on employers and employees in France in the best interests of the workforce, combined with the principle of equal pay for men and women, which was written into the French constitution, would put France at a competitive disadvantage. Consequently, they advocated harmonization of provision in these areas. The Germans countered the French case by arguing that social charges were a result of the operation of market forces and should not, therefore, be subject to regulation under EEC law. A compromise solution, creating an enduring precedent, was eventually a situation where gender has become only one among several areas targeted by equality and anti-discrimination legislation.

Since greater life expectancy has been accompanied by heavy demands on health and care services, member states have grown increasingly concerned, individually and collectively, about the effects of population ageing on social protection systems. The seventh chapter focuses on different forms of provision for older and disabled people, including maintenance and caring arrangements, attempts to ensure the sustainability of pension and incapacity schemes, and the overall impact of policy on living standards and intergenerational relations.

The effects of economic recession, rising unemployment and demographic ageing in the 1970s were offset to some extent by the Community's structural funds. The core–periphery debate intensified, however, as the problem of poverty moved onto the policy agenda. The Commission responded by developing a series of action programmes to combat poverty and social exclusion. The eighth chapter examines these issues with reference to the attempts to define and measure poverty, and the initiatives taken at EU level to combat social exclusion and promote social inclusion through activation policies and economic integration. This topic gained new salience with eastern enlargement and serves as a prime example of the OMC in operation.

Coordination of social protection systems, mutual recognition of qualifications, the general improvement of living and working conditions, monitoring of family policy, directives on equality of access to social benefits and measures at EU level to reduce poverty were all justified, at least in part, as a means of breaking down barriers to the free movement of workers within the Union. Information about intra-European mobility suggests that, despite changes in the pattern of labour flows, net mobility has remained at a relatively low level. Even if the Union's policies on the recognition of qualifications or the coordination of social protection systems may have had some impact on formal obstacles to mobility, other difficulties associated with linguistic and cultural traditions would seem to be more resistant to EU social policy initiatives. The ninth chapter considers these issues with regard to both intra-European and non-European mobility (2006 was nominated as European year of mobility). Greater emphasis than in previous editions is placed on the question of economic migration within the Union following enlargement to the east and on the issue of the transportability of social security rights.

The final chapter tracks the progress of the Union's social dimension across the topics that are identified in the introductory chapters and recur throughout the book in the discussion of different areas of social policy. It examines the changing parameters of European social policy as mediated by the relationship between the economic and social dimensions of the Community and Union, and by the centrality of workers' compared with citizenship rights. An attempt is made to assess the extent to which the Union has developed its own social policy competence in the face of the constraints arising from strong national interests, the threat posed to national sovereignty and the persistence of diversity in welfare systems and practices. This concluding chapter looks at the signs of a shift towards a more broadly based European social policy, made all the more necessary by enlargement eastwards.

Although the chapters in the book are linked by common themes and approaches so as to provide a cumulative and wide-ranging overview of social policy in the Union and its member states, each of Chapters 3 to 9 can be studied independently by readers wishing to explore any one policy area in isolation. To supplement the References, which cover works cited throughout the book, separate lists have been compiled of legislation and the key policy documents relevant to each chapter. References in square brackets in the text indicate the EU documents cited in the boxes at the end of chapters. They include materials produced by the Commission as COM documents or published in the *Official Journal of the European Communities* (abbreviated to *OJ*), as well as publications by the Office for Official Publications of the European Communities in Luxembourg (abbreviated to OOPEC). The boxes also contain website addresses for internet sources, where many of the materials cited are readily accessible.

My thanks are due to all those who have given generously of their time to provide feedback on the three editions of this book and, in particular, to Jo Campling for her valuable advice and support. Sadly, she died before completion of this third edition. I am grateful also to the Centre for International Studies at the London School of Economics, where I held a Visiting Fellowship during the period when this edition of the book was being completed. Steen Mangen, Eric Marlier and anonymous readers are to be thanked for their comments on drafts of the text.

LINDA HANTRAIS

reached whereby the treaty included a section on social policy (title III) without stipulating how most of the provisions should be implemented. Article 118, for example, specified that the Commission should promote close cooperation between member states in matters relating to training, employment, labour law and working conditions, social security and collective bargaining, but without specifying the form such cooperation should take (see Chapters 3 and 4). Article 119, which defined the equal pay principle in response to the demands of the French (see Chapter 6), and article 121, which was concerned with implementing common social security measures for migrant workers (see Chapter 9), were more explicit. Similarly, articles 123–8 set out specific arrangements for operating the European Social Fund. The ESF was intended to make the employment and re-employment of workers easier and to encourage geographical and occupational mobility within the EEC by providing assistance with the cost of vocational retraining and resettlement allowances (see Chapters 3, 8 and 9).

When discrepancies between the laws and practices of member states were deemed to be distorting competition, article 101 of the treaty allowed for directives to eliminate any differences. The EEC was, however, premised on the principle that rules avoiding distortion of competition would make it unnecessary to interfere with redistributive benefits, which should remain a matter for individual states (Collins, 1975, p. 9). Provision was made for equal pay, the improvement of standards of living and social harmonization only insofar as they supported the goal of economic integration (see Chapter 2).

A second justification for the 'social' concerns of the original member states was free movement of labour, which was a fundamental aim of the EEC Treaty. In addition to the establishment of the ESF, provision was made in the two chapters of the treaty on the free movement of persons, services and capital for issuing directives or adopting other measures to facilitate the mobility of workers (articles 48–51) and the right of establishment (52–8).The chapters covered information on job availability in other countries, arrangements for mobile workers to retain social security entitlements and the recognition of professional qualifications (see Chapters 3 and 9).

Although the signatories to the treaty had flagged their interest in the social dimension of the EEC, the compromise that resulted from their failure to agree about objectives and to set up mechanisms for achieving them led to what could be described as a modest, cautious and narrowly focused social policy. The treaty merging the ECSC, EEC and EAEC in 1965 [1.4] to constitute a single Council and a single

Commission of the European Communities did not bring any formal changes in the social policy field, although the clear social protection remit of the two other treaties may have had some impact on the subsequent development of European social policy, particularly in the area of health and safety at work (see Chapter 4).

The 1974 Community social action programme

Whereas the EEC's approach to social policy was cautious, the Council of Europe was much more explicit and affirmative in the social charter it adopted in 1961, heralded as the economic and social counterpart of its 1950 Convention on Human Rights. The charter established a comprehensive and coherent set of policy objectives, guaranteeing fundamental rights for workers and citizens. It referred explicitly to the rights of families, mothers and children to social, legal and economic protection. The charter did not have the same legally binding status as the convention, but it did offer a prototype for the European Community.

Signs of a growing political commitment to social legislation and to a more positive and interventionist social policy within the EEC can be found more than a decade after the Council of Europe's social charter in the Commission's social action programme. In 1974, a resolution from the Council of Ministers (subsequently referred to as the Council) 'concerning a social action programme' [1.11] noted that economic expansion was not to be seen as an end in itself but should result in an improvement of the quality of life. The programme provided for action in three areas, primarily concerned with the working environment. It set out to achieve several broadly based objectives: the attainment of full and better employment; the improvement of living and working conditions; the increased involvement of management and labour in economic and social decisions, and of workers in the life of undertakings.

The Council's view of Community competence in the area of social policy at that time was presented in cautious terms, foreshadowing the concept of subsidiarity, which was to remain prominent in statements on social policy through to the end of the century:

> [The Council] considers that the Community social policy has an individual role to play and should make an essential contribution to achieving the aforementioned objectives by means of Community measures or the definition by the Community of objectives for national social policies, without however seeking a standard solution to all social problems or attempting to transfer to Community level any responsibilities which are assumed more effectively at other levels. [1.11, p. 2]

Since the EEC Treaty did not require a social programme, and the Community did not have direct powers of intervention, its responsibility being confined to promoting cooperation between member states, action had to be justified on political rather than legal grounds. The resolution expressed the 'political will' [1.11, p. 2] to adopt the measures required. In keeping with the priorities of the treaty, the principles of free movement of labour and equalization of competitive conditions between enterprises were stressed, and the importance of the ESF was reiterated as a means of palliating the uneven effects of economic growth on weaker sectors of the population.

The social action programme thus set the scene for the development of the Community's social policy over the next decade. The 1970s saw a spate of action in the areas of education and training, health and safety at work, workers' and women's rights and poverty, leading to the establishment of a number of European networks and observatories to stimulate action and monitor progress in the social field.

The social dimension and the Single European Act

By the mid-1980s, pressure was building up for a more regulatory social policy. The idea of creating a social space (*espace social*), put forward by the French President, François Mitterrand, in 1981, was taken up by Jacques Delors when he became president of the Commission in 1985. The social space was first mooted during the French presidency of the Community at a time when the revitalization of social policy was still very much associated with economic performance (Beretta, 1989, p. 5). In line with the policy-making stance adopted by France's left-wing government, employment was placed at the heart of proposals for European social policy, the dialogue between management and labour was intensified, and cooperation and consultation on social protection were strongly advocated. Social policy was promoted as the means of strengthening economic cohesion, to be developed on the same basis as economic, monetary and industrial policy. According to this neo-functionalist logic, 'Community social policy grows as a functional prerequisite of economic integration' (Room, 1994, p. 21).

In an approach influenced by social democratic and social catholic theory, Delors (1985, p. xviii) made clear his own commitment to the social space: 'The European social dimension is what allows competition to flourish between undertakings and individuals on a reasonable and fair basis... Any attempt to give new depth to the Common Market which neglected this social dimension would be doomed to failure.' For

Delors, the social space was a natural complement to the completion of the internal market and a means of resolving the stalemate that had arisen over previous endeavours to establish the social dimension of the Community through legislation. Some member states opposed the legislative route on the grounds that it would go against national provision, but without legislation European social policy was not binding. By referring to a social space, Delors appeared to be seeking to introduce an equivalence of standards, which would be agreed by both sides of industry through social dialogue, a concept central to his thinking. The social dialogue was intended to make trade unions and employers act as the initiators of social policy, on the understanding that, in return, the Commission would refrain from developing new initiatives itself. The social partners would thus be concerned with principles and objectives, leaving member states to implement them within existing industrial relations frameworks, thereby achieving 'convergence in the employment and labour policy goals of the member states, rather than the standardisation of industrial relations institutions and processes' (Teague, 1989, p. 70).

A series of discussions on socio-economic issues was organized at Val Duchesse (a castle in Belgium) in 1985 to secure the involvement of the social partners, represented by the European Trade Union Confederation (ETUC), and the two employers' organisations: the Union of Industries of the European Communities (UNICE) and the European Centre of Public Enterprises (CEEP). Although the talks fulfilled the objective of encouraging social dialogue between management and workers' representatives, the employers refused to sign the final texts unless Delors gave an undertaking that the Commission would not use the joint opinions as a basis for legislation, thereby preventing the outcome that he had been seeking to engineer. A more positive result was the renewed emphasis on social cohesion, involving closer coordination of the ESF's activities to direct aid towards the poorer member states.

When the Single European Act (SEA) [1.5] was signed in 1986 by the then 12 member states, relatively little progress had been made towards building social policy into the legislative framework of the Community, although significant changes were introduced to speed up and facilitate the social policy-making process. A new article 118a, a supplement to article 118 of the EEC Treaty, stressed the importance of the working environment and the health and safety of workers, providing for decisions to be taken in this area by qualified majority voting (see Chapter 4). By extending the use of this form of voting to health and safety at work, and by introducing a new cooperation procedure,

which imposed time limits for the passage of legislation and strengthened the role of the European Parliament, the SEA gave the Council an
opportunity to tackle more controversial issues in areas of social policy
where agreement had previously been difficult to reach.

Another new 118 article (118b) placed emphasis on the idea of a
social dialogue at EC level, as initiated in the Val Duchesse talks in
1985. Article 100 on the approximation of laws was modified by 100a
to enable decisions to be taken by qualified majority voting for the
approximation of provisions aimed at the establishment and functioning
of the internal market. Fiscal provisions, free movement of people and
workers' rights continued to be governed by the unanimity rule. Under
subsection IV, a new title V was added on economic and social cohesion (articles 130a–e). Article 130b aimed to strengthen economic and
social cohesion, particularly through closer coordination of the structural funds, namely the European Social Fund, the European Agricultural Guidance and Guarantee Fund, and the European Regional
Development Fund (see Chapter 8).

Despite these changes, the SEA left the issue of the social space
largely unresolved. Interest in the proposal was revived by the Belgian
government during its presidency in the second half of 1987, when the
idea was developed of a social policy based on a 'plinth' (*socle social*)
of social rights that would not undermine established statutory guarantees for workers (Teague, 1989, p. 76). Belgium's Minister for Labour
spoke of the need 'to establish a platform [*socle* in the French version]
of basic rights which would give the two sides of industry a stable,
common basis from which they could negotiate to guarantee that the
internal market has a real social dimension' (Soisson, 1990, p. 10). In
1988, before the ETUC, Delors had stressed the need for a 'revival' of
social policy, advocating a 'minimum platform of guaranteed social
rights with a view to the implementation of the single European market
of 1992'. Echoing the words of the Belgian minister, he explained that:
'This mandatory platform could be negotiated between the two sides of
industry and then incorporated into Community legislation. It would
serve as a basis for the social dialogue and for strengthening European
cohesion.' (cited in Soisson, 1990, p. 10)

The Community Charter of the Fundamental Social Rights of Workers

Although the SEA did not provide a blueprint for European social policy, the preamble offered a statement of principle in which the signatories agreed to work together to promote fundamental rights as laid

down in the Council of Europe's Convention on Human Rights and its social charter. Meeting in Strasbourg on 8–9 December 1989, the heads of all member states, with the exception of the United Kingdom, adopted the Community Charter of the Fundamental Social Rights of Workers [1.12], heralded as the social dimension of the SEA. The preamble to the charter stated resolutely that 'the same importance must be attached to the social aspects as to the economic aspects and..., therefore, they must be developed in a balanced manner'. Preliminary drafts of the charter had referred to 'citizens' rather than 'workers'. Significantly, the final version did not define rights in terms of citizenship. Most clauses in the charter referred implicitly or explicitly to workers, a focus that was clearly identified in the title and in the section devoted to employment and remuneration, whereas the Council of Europe's social charter had included the right to social and medical assistance and social services without linking them to employment.

Like the Council of Europe's social charter, the Community charter did not have force of law and was not binding on its signatories. As 'soft' law (Hervey, 1998, pp. 49–50), it took the form of a solemn declaration, leaving decisions on implementation procedures to individual member states. The social plinth had been an attempt to ensure that the areas to be covered by social protection would be accepted throughout the Community. Much of the debate about the charter focused on a related issue: whether the Community and its member states were aiming for a maximum or minimum level of social provision. Should equalization be based on an average, the highest or lowest level in the Community? States intent on defending what they considered as a higher level of social protection feared that the internal market would result in a downward alignment of social security allowances and benefits towards the lowest common denominator in a race to the bottom.

The nebulous terms 'adequate', 'sufficient', 'appropriate' and 'satisfactory', used in the charter to refer to the levels to be achieved, are indicative of the problems of reaching agreement over the definition of targets. They reflect the Council's reluctance to impose standards by regulation, the most binding form of legislation (Gormley, 1998, pp. 324–6). This lack of precision left open the possibility that some states would seek competitive advantage by not offering the same level of social protection to their workers, resulting in what has come to be known as 'social dumping', whereby companies decide to move to countries with lower labour and social costs. The term 'dumping' was used in article 91 of the EEC Treaty, in the economic context, to describe the practice of differential pricing of goods with no economic justification. In the case of social dumping, disparities in social protection between member states may also serve as an obstacle to mobility of labour and capital. It has been argued that firms will not invest in low social wage countries unless other factors, for example infrastructure and productivity, justify such investments, and that economic integration may lead rather 'to a more gradual and indirect process of social policy erosion' (Leibfried and Pierson, 1992, p. 350).

Another metaphor frequently found in this context is the 'level playing field' of competition, implying that everybody should be playing by the same rules and with equal chances of success in the market place. Accordingly, a higher level of social spending should be sought across member states to avoid putting national governments that do want to introduce more generous provisions at a competitive disadvantage.

These concepts were not invented with the SEA and the Community charter. Fears of social dumping and the creation of an unlevel playing field were, however, exacerbated when Greece joined the Community in 1981, and Portugal and Spain in 1986, since they were all countries with less developed social protection systems than in both the original EEC member states and countries that became members in the 1970s. The same fears resurfaced with even greater intensity as the new wave of members from central and eastern Europe joined the Union in the early twenty-first century (see Chapter 2).

Although the charter may not have produced any innovations in the area of social protection, crucially the surrounding debate drew attention to a number of issues regarding the social dimension of the Single European Market (SEM), or internal market, which came into operation on 1 January 1993. The different bodies of opinion that emerged over the interventionist role of the Community in social policy and the basis on which it should be founded were symptomatic of the diverging principles underlying systems of social protection in the 12 member states. They also signalled the concern felt in several countries about the possibility of losing national sovereignty and being forced to take action in areas where national governments may be reluctant to intervene.

In the absence of any direct legal means of enforcement, provision was made in the Community charter for an action programme. Under §28, the Council invited the Commission to prepare initiatives with a view to the adoption of legal instruments for the effective implementation of rights that fall within the Community's area of competence. The Commission responded with an action programme containing 47 initiatives for developing the social dimension of the SEM [1.13]. The first annual report set out the dual aims of the programme: 'to establish a sound base of minimum provisions, having regard on the one hand to the need to avoid any distortion of competition, and on the other to support moves to strengthen economic and social cohesion and contribute to the creation of jobs, which is the prime concern of completion of the internal market' [1.13, p. 5].

The measures proposed were wide ranging, covering all the topics dealt with in the charter and adding a chapter on the labour market. The methods to be used for implementing the action programme relied heavily on the consultation process, mediated by advisory committees and the social dialogue.

The report reiterated the point raised at the Luxembourg Council meeting in June 1991 that the achievements made in implementing the SEM programme had not been accompanied by comparable progress in the field of social policy [1.13, p. 22]. This and subsequent annual reports stressed the importance of maintaining a balance between the three fundamental principles underlying the Commission's initiatives: subsidiarity, diversity of national systems, cultures and practices, and the preservation of the competitiveness of undertakings. The reports thereby defined the parameters for subsequent developments in the field of social policy, while, for the time being, reaffirming the secondary status of the social dimension in European treaties.

It has been argued that the SEA added nothing new in the field of social welfare, which remained no more than an area of indirect and limited competence for the Community (Berghman, 1990, p. 9). Some coordination of national social security systems was needed to ensure free movement of workers, but these contingencies had already been covered in the early 1970s by relatively uncontroversial legislation on the application of social security schemes to employed persons and to members of their families moving within the Community (see Chapter 9). In all the policy areas covered by the charter, action had been initiated before 1989, but, importantly, the charter did provide an impetus for a more concerted and coherent approach to social affairs.

The social chapter in the Maastricht Treaty

The principles set out in the Community charter were taken up in the Agreement on Social Policy annexed to the Treaty on European Union, signed in Maastricht on 7 February 1992 [1.6]. The Maastricht summit again illustrated the difficulty of reaching agreement over the social chapter, which, on the insistence of the United Kingdom, was removed from the body of the treaty. By including a separate Protocol on Social

Policy, the other 11 member states could proceed with the Community charter and make decisions without taking account of British views.

Article 1 of the Agreement on Social Policy amended article 117 of the EEC Treaty by removing the references to harmonization of social systems and to the belief that improvements would naturally ensue from the functioning of the common market and the approximation of provisions. Instead, it identified specific objectives, covering: 'the promotion of employment, improved living and working conditions, proper social protection, dialogue between management and labour, the development of human resources with a view to lasting high employment and the combating of exclusion'. Significantly, these objectives were to be achieved through measures that 'take account of the diverse forms of national practices, in particular in the field of contractual relations, and the need to maintain the competitiveness of the Community economy' [1.6, Agreement on Social Policy, article 1].

Article 2 of the agreement assigned a complementary role to the Community in the areas of health and safety at work, working conditions, information and consultation of workers, equality between women and men, and the integration of persons excluded from the labour market. It empowered the Council to act in the area of social affairs to adopt, 'by means of directives, minimum requirements for gradual implementation, having regard to the conditions and technical rules obtaining in each of the Member States'. Any constraints that might impede the creation and development of small and medium-sized enterprises, seen as the new engine for growth, were to be avoided. Issues still requiring unanimous voting by the 11 signatories to the protocol were social security and social protection of workers, protection of workers made redundant, representation and collective defence of workers and employers, conditions of employment for third-country nationals, and financial contributions for job promotion. The distinction between the areas subject to qualified majority and unanimous voting was important, since it was later to dictate the social agenda, limiting it to topics where a considerable degree of consensus already existed.

As in article 118 of the EEC Treaty, the agreement stressed that the Commission's role was to monitor the social situation (article 7), consult, encourage cooperation and facilitate policy coordination (5). Member states were not to be prevented from introducing their own measures over and above those required at EU level (2 §5, 6 §3). Action was, in any case, constrained by subsidiarity, as laid down by article 3b in the body of the Maastricht Treaty, one of the three principles regarded as 'cardinal' by the Commission. The principle of subsidiarity was set out in a communication in 1992 [1.14] and was later respecified in Protocol No. 30 of the consolidated EC Treaty [1.8].

The treaty emphasized three related issues: greater democratic control, more transparency in European legislation and respect of the principle of subsidiarity, which was important in determining how the Union exercised its competences. By virtue of the subsidiarity principle, the Union is empowered to act when its aims can be more effectively achieved at EU rather than national level; for example in establishing minimum standards for member states to introduce, or in allowing them to maintain higher standards when this is not incompatible with the treaty. The burden of proof is on the Union's institutions to demonstrate a need to legislate at EU level and at the intensity proposed, with recourse to the most binding instruments as a last resort. Accordingly, wherever possible, preference should be given to support measures and framework directives rather than to detailed rules and regulations. The Union should only intervene if, and insofar as, the objectives of the proposed action cannot be satisfactorily achieved by member states themselves, assessed by comparative efficiency and value added. Intervention by supranational agencies may be justified only if the benefits sought cannot be obtained by other means (Spicker, 1991, p. 5).

The choice of the most appropriate policy instrument is made on the basis of the principles of both subsidiarity and proportionality. According to the principle of proportionality, the means employed should be commensurate with the objectives pursued. Decisions should be taken as closely as possible to the citizens themselves, without endangering the advantages to be gained from common action at the level of the Union as a whole, and without changing the institutional balance.

These constraints on action at EU level were to some extent offset by the new powers that the Agreement on Social Policy gave to management and labour. Article 3 confirmed the commitment to the social dialogue by requiring the Commission to 'consult management and labour on the possible direction of Community action' (§2) and the content of proposals (§3), as well as enabling the social partners to forward an opinion or recommendation to the Commission and to initiate agreements with the Community (§4). Social dialogue was recognized as a key component in the developing European social model.

The green and white papers on European social policy

Although, together, the Community charter of 1989, the action programmes and the Agreement on Social Policy in the Maastricht Treaty provided a clearer statement of thinking on social policy at EU level than was present in the EEC Treaty drawn up in the 1950s, they did not signal a strong commitment to social affairs as an objective in its own right, or on a par with economic union. Nor did they put in place the administrative structures needed for producing a common European social policy. By incorporating the principle of subsidiarity in the Maastricht Treaty, member states seemed to be confirming their continued reluctance to develop an overarching social policy that might impinge on national sovereignty. In 1993, however, the Commission published a consultative document, which demonstrated that the issue of a European social policy remained firmly on the agenda. The green paper on European social policy [1.15] announced a wide-ranging review of social policy in the Union, the *acquis communautaire* (legal attainments) and the areas where further action was needed. Government departments, social partners, the European Parliament, the Economic and Social Committee and other organizations and individuals were invited to assist the Commission in preparing the next phase of the Union's social policy. The green paper sought views on the objectives, targets and measures that would be acceptable to member states and social partners in the areas of the labour market, social protection and exclusion, equal opportunities and training, thereby reaffirming the wide range of issues that fell within the Union's competence. It also demonstrated that the Commission wanted to be seen to take account of the opinions expressed by other social actors.

The white paper on European social policy [1.15], published eight months later in 1994, aimed to preserve and develop a European social model, based on a set of shared values, held together by the conviction that economic and social progress must go hand in hand. The introduction described the 'vital part' social policy had to play 'in underpinning the process of change', by building on past achievements and putting forward new proposals for the future, so that the people of Europe benefit from 'the unique blend of economic well-being, social cohesiveness and high overall quality of life which was achieved in the postwar period' [1.15, p. 7]. The white paper set the scene for European social policy through to the end of the decade by providing a comprehensive statement of policy directions and goals. Future policy was to be broadly based: although jobs would remain at the top of the agenda, categories of people who were not in work should also be taken into account, with a view to establishing 'the fundamental social rights of citizens as a constitutional element of the European Union' [1.15, p. 69], a task that the Community charter had failed to accomplish.

The social action programmes for 1995–2000

The white paper offered a long-awaited framework for the management of change and for action through to the end of the century. The Commission quickly took advantage of the momentum by launching a medium-term social action programme for 1995–97 [1.16]. The first progress report opened with the statement that it was based on the concept of social policy as 'a productive factor facilitating change and progress, rather than a burden on the economy or an obstacle to growth' [1.16], reflecting the Commission's increasingly proactive approach. Pointing to the growing importance of multilevel governance, the report stressed the role played by the dialogue between political (member states), social (employers and unions) and civil (non-governmental organizations) actors in enabling successful implementation of the programme.

The messages of the social action programme were reiterated in communications from the Commission on the modernization and improvement of social protection in 1997 and 1999 [1.17], and in the summary of the 1997 report on social protection in Europe, subtitled 'modernising social protection and adapting systems to change' [2.2]. Highly developed social protection systems were presented in the 1997 communication as a 'fundamental component and a distinguishing feature of the European model of society' [1.17, p. 1]. The main challenge the Union faced was how to adapt social protection to sustain high standards of provision in a context of population ageing, changing family structures, a new gender balance and enlargement, without abandoning the values of solidarity and cohesion. Acting as the Union's conscience, the Commission was seeking to justify supranational intervention by formulating objectives and proposing policy instruments, without infringing the principles of subsidiarity and proportionality.

The 1998–2000 social action programme maintained the pressure for recognizing the importance of the social dimension in responding to the major social challenges the Union was facing at the turn of the twenty-first century [1.19]. On the one hand, Economic and Monetary Union (EMU) was creating the economic conditions needed to underpin social progress. On the other, population ageing and, more especially, the ageing of the workforce were raising concerns about the implications of demographic trends for employment and social protection systems in Europe. In addition, the prospect of enlargement was fuelling debates about the role that social policy could play in the transition to a market economy in candidate countries, raising questions about how they would bring their social legislation into line with other member states and develop adequate systems of social protection. Echoing article 2 of the Treaty on European Union and the white paper on social policy, the programme took as its basic premise that 'economic and social progress go hand in hand'. Social policy was to play a more proactive role at the close of the century and beyond, aimed at promoting 'a decent quality of life and standard of living for all in an active, inclusive and healthy society that encourages access to employment, good working conditions, and equality of opportunity' [1.19, p. 8].

The social dimension and the amended treaties

The Treaty of Amsterdam [1.7], signed on 2 October 1997, amended the Treaty on European Union and the Treaties establishing the European Communities. A consolidated version renumbering the articles in the original EEC Treaty was published in the same year [1.8]. Following the British opt-in, the Agreement on Social Policy was incorporated into the main body of the consolidated treaty under title XI on social policy, education, vocational training and youth, thereby endorsing the commitment of member states to the development of the social dimension as an important component in the process of European integration. Reflecting public concern about unemployment across the Union, the reference to 'a high level of employment and of social protection', which had been introduced into the Treaty on European Union in article 2 of the principles in part I, moved into second place in the list of priority areas at the beginning of the amended EC Treaty. In line with the Union's policy on mainstreaming, 'equality between men and women' was inserted in third position before 'sustainable and non-inflationary growth'. On the insistence of the Germans, Dutch and British, the reference to 'convergence of economic performance' was amended to include 'competitiveness'. The reference to the environment was expanded to cover 'a high level of protection and improvement of the quality of the environment'. A new article 13 extended action against discrimination to encompass 'sex, racial or ethnic origin, religion or belief, disability, age or sexual orientation'.

Under the new title XI, the original EEC Treaty articles 117–28 on social provisions and the European Social Fund were replaced by renumbered articles 136–50, incorporating the text of the Agreement on Social Policy. The first article (136) in the chapter on social provisions opened with a reference to the charters of both the Council of Europe and the Community. In other respects, it was an amalgam of article 117 in the EEC Treaty and article 1 of the Agreement on Social Policy.

Articles 137–9 reproduced articles 2–4 in the agreement, while article 140 conflated EEC article 118 and article 5 in the agreement. A new paragraph was added to article 141 (EEC article 119) on equal pay, endowing the Council with the authority to act to ensure the application of measures on equal opportunities, treatment and pay, thereby giving this policy area a specific legal base. The reference in article 6 §3 of the agreement to member states not being prevented from taking specific measures to assist women was amended to read 'the under-represented sex' in article 141. Article 7 of the agreement became article 143, and EEC Treaty articles 120–2, unchanged except for the reference to the European Parliament, became articles 142 and 144–5.

A shortened chapter on the European Social Fund (renumbered articles 146–8) retained an amendment, added in the Maastricht Treaty, referring to the role of vocational training and retraining as a means of helping workers to adapt to industrial and technological change. A third chapter from Maastricht, replacing EEC 126–8, on education, vocational training and youth became articles 149–50.

Title XIII introduced article 152 on public health. Here, a number of insertions reinforced the complementary role attributed to the Union at the same time as the need to respect the responsibilities of member states in the organization and delivery of health services and medical care. Paragraphs were added stressing the importance of high standards of quality and safety, justifying EU involvement in an area of topical concern. Whereas the new title XVII on economic and social cohesion and title XIX on the environment focused largely on economic aspects, reference was made, in both cases, to the role of the Cohesion Fund in contributing to environmental projects. The link with the concern about public health was confirmed in article 174. The status of environment issues was also formalized in a new article 6 in the first part of the treaty, requiring environmental protection to be integrated into the definition and implementation of all Community policies and activities.

Few alterations were made to the chapters on the free movement of workers (articles 39–48), but a new and much disputed title IV (articles 61–9) was inserted covering visas, asylum, immigration and other policies related to free movement of persons across the Union's external borders. Many of the provisions covered issues of security and administrative procedures. They were relevant to the social dimension insofar as they concerned living conditions and issues of racial equality.

Arguably, the most significant change to the treaty, at least at the symbolic level, was the addition of title VIII on employment (articles 125–30), which set out the objectives and responsibilities of member states and the Union, calling for cooperation and coordinated action. Despite the efforts by the French to try and persuade the other heads of government to attribute a more interventionist role to the Union and to commit additional funds (Duff, 1997, p. 64), as in other social policy areas the treaty reaffirmed that Community action was to be confined to a supportive and complementary role (article 127). In article 128, the Council and Commission were assigned the tasks of reporting on the employment situation, drawing up guidelines and examining the measures taken by national governments as well as their implementation. Article 129 provided for initiatives to encourage cooperation between member states in developing the exchange of information and best practice, and for the evaluation of experience.

The Treaty of Nice [1.9], adopted at the European Council meeting in December 2000, introduced revisions to the decision-making procedures that were to have implications for social policy development. In paving the way for enlargement, the treaty proposed a re-weighting of votes to ensure that the influence of the smaller countries would not become disproportionate to their size, the extension of qualified majority voting and application of the codecision procedure with the European Parliament to anti-discrimination measures, mobility and specific actions for economic and social cohesion. The Commission's role in social affairs was reinforced by establishing a Social Protection Committee to monitor the social situation, promote exchange of information and prepare reports and opinions. The Presidency Conclusions [1.20, §IV A.13] stressed the 'indissoluble link between economic performance and social progress', characteristic of the European social model.

The Charter of Fundamental Rights of the European Union [1.21], finalized during the Nice summit in 2000, provided a clear statement of the rights of Europeans. With due regard to the principles of subsidiarity and proportionality, the charter extended the boundaries of social policy beyond the workplace to the reconciliation of family and professional life, the protection and care of children and older people, social and housing assistance, preventive health care, and religious belief and practice. The aim was to consolidate the Union's commitment to the values of human dignity, freedom, equality and solidarity, while continuing to respect the diversity of cultures and traditions. Like the social charter, the human rights charter again took the form of a solemn proclamation, which meant that it was not legally binding. However, the Convention set up at the Laeken European Council meeting in 2001 [1.20] to prepare for enlargement to the east proposed incorporating the entire charter into the Constitutional Treaty for Europe [1.10]. The draft treaty was submitted at the European Council meeting in Rome in 2003, and signed on 29 October 2004 by the 25 member states and three candidate countries, but was then blocked when the French and the Dutch failed to ratify it in referenda held in May and June 2005.

The draft treaty distinguished areas where the Union would have exclusive competence (monetary policy, customs union, common commercial and fisheries policy) from those where it should have shared competence, including social policy, economic, social and territorial cohesion, and common safety concerns in public health matters (part I, title III, articles 12–13). For economic and employment policies, the Convention (article 14) proposed that the Union should adopt measures to ensure coordination between member states by issuing guidelines, as specified in the Amsterdam Treaty. The same article (§3) stipulated that 'The Union may adopt initiatives to ensure coordination of Member States' social policies'. A further category of supporting, coordinating or complementary actions covered improvement of human health, education, vocational training, youth and sport, and culture (article 16), with the proviso that, in this case, any legally binding acts may not entail harmonization of national laws and regulations.

The Constitutional Treaty thus restated the limits of Union competence in the social policy field. Although unanimous voting would apply only when the Constitution does not provide the necessary powers to attain the Union's objectives, several areas of social policy would remain within the unanimity rule: social security and social protection of workers, workers whose employment contract is terminated, representation and collective defence of the interests of workers and employers, and conditions of employment for third-country nationals residing in Union territory (article III-99). Except in areas falling within the Union's exclusive competence, power to act would still be governed by the principles of subsidiarity and proportionality (article 9). The right of member states to define the fundamental principles of their social security systems and ensure their financial equilibrium was to be left intact.

The development of soft law as a social policy instrument

The Union's legal sources include primary legislation in the form of treaties and secondary legislation, ranging from regulations, directives and decisions, the most binding instruments used to create uniform rules that all member states are obliged to implement, to recommendations, resolutions and opinions, which are advisory, or communications and memoranda used to signal initial thinking on issues. Relatively few regulations have been introduced in the social field; notable exceptions concern the structural funds and freedom of movement for workers (see Chapters 8 and 9). Directives, which lay down objectives for legislation but leave individual states to select the most suitable form of implementation, have been exploited to considerable effect in the areas of health and safety at work and equal treatment (see Chapters 4 and 6). Recommendations have played an important role in developing a framework for concerted action and convergence of social policy (see Chapter 2).

Several references have already been made in this chapter to the ways in which some of the softer alternatives helped prepare the ground for subsequent hard law, for example the social charter. The Lisbon summit of 2000 [1.20] formalized another 'softer' alternative to binding forms of governance. The priority given to employment in the consolidated treaty had dominated the social scene in the late 1990s. The extraordinary European Council meeting on employment in November 1997 in Luxembourg [1.20] had already gone much further than the treaty in agreeing an overall strategy and a common approach with regard to objectives, targets and means. The Council identified four main areas for action, retained as the four pillars to be incorporated into national action plans: improving employability; developing entrepreneurship; encouraging adaptability in businesses and their employees; and strengthening policies for equal opportunities. The guidelines confirmed the shift towards more active employability measures, emphasizing training and setting out the means for encouraging job creation. The social partners were invited to modernize work organization by negotiating over flexibility and removing barriers to employment.

At the Lisbon summit, member states pledged to make Europe the most competitive knowledge-based economy in the world by 2010, while maintaining a commitment to solidarity and equality. The open method of coordination (OMC), which had been developed during the 1990s and applied in the employment guidelines, was promoted as a means of achieving these goals. The method was based on the principles of subsidiarity, convergence through concerted action, mutual learning, an integrated approach and management by objectives (Adnett and Hardy, 2005, p. 28). National governments were to cooperate in agreeing guidelines, setting common targets based on indicators and benchmarks, developing national action plans and exchanging best practice. The method relied on regular monitoring of progress to meet the targets set, allowing member states to compare their efforts and learn from the experience of others, without incurring formal sanctions for non-compliance; naming and shaming are a sufficient incentive. The

2001 white paper on governance argued that the OMC added value at EU level when little scope existed for legislative solutions [1.23, p. 18]. The employment strategy was relaunched in Brussels in March 2005 [1.20]. By 2006, a streamlined version of the OMC had been extended to social protection systems, social ex/inclusion, education, research, immigration, pensions, health and long-term care. This new instrument for tackling social concerns, described as 'third way' social policy (Roberts and Springer, 2001, p. 3), was to serve as both a supplement to hard law and a substitute for it (Trubek and Trubek, 2005, p. 363), capable of supporting 'system adaptation' (Ferrera, 2005, p. 247).

Setting the social agenda in the twenty-first century

The challenges and strategic goals identified at the Lisbon summit framed the social agendas for the first decade of the century. The preface to the Commission's communication on the social policy agenda for 2000–05 [1.22] announced an integrated approach designed to 'ensure the positive and dynamic interaction of economic, employment and social policy' in modernizing the European social model. Social policy was again presented as a productive factor, and the combination of good social conditions, high productivity and high quality goods and services as key features of the social model. The actions planned for 2000–05 focused on three topics central to the Lisbon strategy: realizing Europe's full employment potential by creating more and better jobs, with emphasis on quality of work and mobility; modernizing social protection systems so as to promote social inclusion, strengthen gender equality, reinforce fundamental rights and combat discrimination; and preparing for enlargement, the promotion of international cooperation and the social dialogue. The communication stated unequivocally that the social policy agenda was not seeking to harmonize social policies and did not require additional funding. Rather, the aim was 'to work towards common European objectives and increase coordination of social policies in the context of the internal market and the single currency', while seeking the 'redirection of public expenditure to improve efficiency and investment in people' [1.24, p. 7].

The social agenda [1.24], adopted in 2005, for the remainder of the decade aimed to strengthen further the social dimension of the Lisbon strategy, following the realization that sustained efforts were needed to adapt to the economic and social changes resulting from globalization and ageing of Europe's populations. This last topic was highlighted in a green paper published in 2005, entitled 'Confronting demographic change', followed in 2006 by a communication on 'The demographic future of Europe – from challenge to opportunity' [1.25]. The agenda, which adopted as its motto 'A social Europe in the global economy: jobs and opportunities for all', contained a 'roadmap for European social policy up to 2010', based on the conviction that the Union cannot deliver on social policy goals without more growth and jobs [1.24, p. 9]. Building on the 2000–05 agenda, the roadmap focused on what had become perennial topics: full employment, the key role of social dialogue, a European labour market, the promotion of social cohesion and social inclusion, diversity and non-discrimination.

EU SOCIAL POLICY FOR THE TWENTY-FIRST CENTURY

The overview in this chapter of 50 years of social policy development at EU level goes some way towards answering the questions as to why and how the Union progressively, but cautiously, extended its intervention in social affairs. It provides an indication of the philosophy underlying EU social policy and possible interconnections between EU and national level. This relationship is explored more fully in subsequent chapters with reference to specific policy areas. In conclusion to the present chapter, an initial assessment is attempted of the extent to which the development of social policy prepared the Union to meet the challenges of the twenty-first century.

Many of the early policy statements cited in the chapter were based on a conception of social policy as a handmaiden to economic objectives, and as a spillover from economic policies. By the 1990s, due in no small part to the efforts of the Commission, under the leadership of Delors between 1985 and 1994, the social dimension had moved up the agenda. Since, by definition, economic policy was the justification for the original EEC Treaty and those that followed, social policy was still cast in a supporting role. If social affairs had become a more central concern of the Union and its member states, nowhere was the economic justification difficult to find. Just as the French had insisted on provision for equal pay between men and women in the founding treaty to prevent distortion of competition, the principle of guaranteed access to adequate social protection in the 1989 Community charter and to a high level of social protection in the Lisbon strategy was also justified on economic grounds. The development of a large European internal market based on free trade and economic progress dictated the continuing priority given to the Union's economic objectives.

Unfaltering commitment to the principles of subsidiarity and pro-portionality meant that areas of Union competence in the social field remained difficult to demarcate. The need for a common approach to social policy, based on shared values, became a topical issue in the 1990s when the Union was facing major social problems as a result of slow economic growth and persisting long-term unemployment, popu-lation ageing, the increasing cost of providing social protection, pres-sures to meet the targets for EMU and the prospect of further enlarge-ment. The decision to write employment into the Treaty of Amsterdam in response to public concern about widespread unemployment marked another turning point for the social dimension, foreshadowing a more proactive and concerted approach to reform, and a readiness to apply alternative methods of governance, better suited to an enlarged Union. The 1998 employment guidelines [1.18] began the task of setting quan-tifiable targets for policy within the framework of the OMC.

Statements produced by the Commission from the mid-1990s had prepared the way for an upgrading of the social dimension, on the grounds that economic progress and a high level of social protection are interdependent. The Lisbon strategy was premised on the Union becom-ing the most competitive knowledge-based economy in the world, but-tressed by the European social model, based on advanced systems of social protection and agreed targets [1.20, §31]. The 2000–05 social policy agenda presented high social standards as a key element in the competitive formula and a factor contributing to the efficiency of Euro-pean society, justifying the need for 'the positive and dynamic interac-tion of economic, employment and social policy' to convert the politi-cal commitments made at Lisbon into concrete action [1.22, preface].

Despite the Commission's insistence on the interactive and recipro-cal relationship between the three policy areas, achieving full employ-ment and a more cohesive society were identified as the two priorities for 2005–10 [1.24]. Even if the Charter of Fundamental Rights of the European Union [1.21] went some way towards redressing the balance and extending the reach of social policy, the main reference point for social policy documents undisputedly became the employment situa-tion. The modernization of the European social model was being advo-cated 'to underpin economic dynamism and pursue employment-generating reforms', on the grounds that '[w]ell-targeted social protec-tion is essential for adapting the economy to change and providing for an efficient and well-trained labour force', while '[m]ore and better employment in a dynamic and competitive economy strengthens social cohesion' [1.22, pp. 6–7].

Box 1   Legislation and official publications relating to the development of European social policy

PRIMARY LEGISLATION

1.1   Treaty establishing the European Coal and Steel Community (ECSC), signed in Paris on 18 April 1951.

1.2   Treaty establishing the European Economic Community (EEC), signed in Rome on 25 March 1957.

1.3   Treaty establishing the European Atomic Energy Community (EAEC), signed in Rome on 25 March 1957.

1.4   Treaty of 8 April 1965 establishing a Single Council and a Single Commission of the European Communities (the Merger Treaty).

1.5   Single European Act (SEA), signed in Luxembourg on 17 February 1986 and at The Hague on 28 February 1986.

1.6   Treaty on European Union, signed in Maastricht on 7 February 1992; Protocol and Agreement on Social Policy, concluded between the member states of the European Community, with the exception of the United Kingdom.

1.7   Treaty of Amsterdam amending the Treaty on European Union, the Treaties establishing the European Communities and certain related acts, signed in Amsterdam on 2 October 1997.

1.8   European Union consolidated version of the EU and EC Treaties, incorporating the changes made by the Treaty of Amsterdam, 1997.

1.9   Treaty of Nice, adopted on 11 December 2000, ratified in 2002, and brought into force on 1 February 2003.

1.10 Constitutional Treaty for Europe, signed on 29 October 2004, not ratified by 1 November 2006, *OJ* C 310 47/1 16.12.2004.

SECONDARY LEGISLATION AND OFFICIAL PUBLICATIONS

1.11 Council Resolution of 21 January 1974 concerning a social action programme, *OJ* C 13/1 12.2.1974.

1.12 Community Charter of the Fundamental Social Rights of Workers, adopted in Strasbourg on 9 December 1989 by the member states, with the exception of the United Kingdom.

1.13 Communication from the Commission concerning its action programme relating to the implementation of the Community Charter of Basic Social Rights for Workers, COM(89) 568 final, 29.11.1989; Commission of the European Communities, First report on the application of the Community Charter of the Fundamental Social Rights of Workers, COM(91) 511 final, 5.12.1991.

1.14 Communication of the Commission, The principle of subsidiarity, SEC(92) 1990 final, 27.10.1992.

1.15 Commission of the European Communities, European Social Policy: options for the Union, Green paper, COM(93) 551, 17.11.1993,

OOPEC, 1993; European Commission, European Social Policy: a way forward for the Union, White paper, COM(94) 333 final, 27.7.1994, OOPEC, 1994.

1.16 European Commission, Medium-term social action programme 1995–97, *Social Europe*, 1/95; Progress report on the implementation of the medium-term social action programme 1995–97, *Social Europe Supplement*, 4/96.

1.17 Communication from the Commission, Modernising and improving social protection in the European Union, COM(97) 102 final, 12.3.1997; Communication from the Commission, A concerted strategy for modernising social protection, COM(99) 347 final, 14.7.1999; Council Conclusions of 17 December 1999 on the strengthening of cooperation for modernising and improving social protection, *OJ* C 8/05 12.1.2000.

1.18 Council Resolution of 15 December 1997 on the 1998 employment guidelines, *OJ* C30/1 28.1.1998; followed by annual, then biennial guidelines.

1.19 European Commission, Social action programme 1998–2000, COM(1998) 259 final, 29.4.1998, OOPEC, 1998.

1.20 European Council Presidency Conclusions: Copenhagen, 21–22 June 1993; Extraordinary meeting on employment Luxembourg, 20–21 November 1997 (DOC/97/23); Lisbon, 23–24 March 2000; Nice, 7–9 December 2000; Stockholm, 23–24 March 2001; Göteborg, 15–16 June 2001; Laeken, 14–15 December 2001; Barcelona, 15–16 March 2002; Brussels, 22–23 March 2005, available on-line: http://europa.eu/european_council/conclusions/index_en.htm

1.21 Charter of Fundamental Rights of the European Union, 2000, *OJ* C 364/1 7.12.2000.

1.22 Communication from the Commission, Social policy agenda, COM(2000) 379 final, 28.6.2000.

1.23 European Commission, European Governance, White paper, COM(2001) 428 final, *OJ* C 287/1 12.10.2001.

1.24 European Commission, Social agenda 2005–2010: a social Europe in the global economy, jobs and opportunities for all, incorporating the Communication from the Commission on the social agenda, COM(2005) 33 final, 9.2.2005, OOPEC, 2005.

1.25 Communication from the Commission, Confronting demographic change: a new solidarity between the generations, Green paper, COM(2005) 94 final, 16.3.2005, OOPEC, 2005; Commission Communication, The demographic future of Europe – from challenge to opportunity, COM(2006) 571 final, 12.10.2006.

1.26 Home page for internet access to information about European social affairs: http://europa.eu.int/comm/employment_social/index_en.htm

2 Towards a European Social Model

The intention in the Treaty establishing the European Economic Community (EEC) [1.2], signed in 1957, was to remove barriers to mobility and ensure that no one nation would be at a competitive advantage or disadvantage because of its social provisions. Under the section on social policy, article 117 introduced the principle of harmonization of social systems across the six original member states, implying that their welfare arrangements would ultimately converge. Although the first paragraph of article 117 was expanded, redrafted and renumbered following the signing of the Treaty of Amsterdam [1.7] in 1997, the original reference to the term 'harmonization' was neither removed nor amended. Article 136 of the consolidated EC Treaty [1.8] set out the objective of both the Community and member states to promote improved living and working conditions 'so as to make possible their harmonisation while the improvement is being maintained'. As in the original EEC Treaty, such a development was expected to 'ensue not only from the functioning of the common market, which will favour the harmonisation of social systems, but also from the procedures provided for in this Treaty and from the approximation of provisions laid down by law, regulation or administrative action'.

The founder members – Belgium, France, the Federal Republic of Germany, Italy, Luxembourg and the Netherlands – had developed social protection systems that can be considered as variants of a 'continental' welfare model, based on corporatist rights and income-related insurance contributions. This shared tradition did not mean that the six member states would find harmonization easy to achieve, since each country had its own particular brand of social protection in terms of the political principles underlying the system and the policy-making process. Each wave of membership brought with it different welfare models, making harmonization more difficult to achieve. The social protection systems in the Nordic/Anglo-Saxon countries that joined the Community in 1973 – Denmark, Ireland and the United Kingdom – had developed in line with the principle of universal coverage of risks, funded from taxation. The southern European countries, sometimes described as the Latin rim, which became members in the 1980s – Greece in 1981, Portugal and Spain in 1986 – had much more limited welfare systems. They still relied heavily on family, community and religious support in dealing with social problems (Guillén and Álvarez, 2001). Of the states that joined in 1995, Austria was closer to the continental model. Finland and, especially, Sweden belonged to the universalistic tax-based welfare variant, previously exemplified by Denmark.

The goal of harmonizing social protection had been made more pressing, but also more complex, by the preparations for Economic and Monetary Union (EMU), and by the need to maintain the principle of freedom of movement within an enlarged Community. Over the years, however, doubts were expressed increasingly about the feasibility, or even desirability, of harmonization. Although the Community Charter of the Fundamental Social Rights of Workers used the term in three contexts [1.12, §3, §8, §19], the Agreement on Social Policy, concluded by 11 of the 12 member states and annexed to the Maastricht Treaty [1.6], made no reference to harmonizing social protection systems across the Union. Instead, it stated unambiguously that account should be taken of the 'diverse forms of national practices, in particular in the field of contractual relations' (article 1), stressing the need to maintain the competitiveness of the Community's economy. While reinstating the reference to harmonization cited above, the second paragraph of article 136 in the consolidated EC Treaty retained the amendment in the agreement, thereby juxtaposing harmonization and diversity.

The two island states, Cyprus and Malta, which joined the Union in 2004, had adopted welfare systems similar to those in existing member states. Enlargement to the east – Czech Republic, Estonia, Hungary, Latvia, Lithuania, Poland, Slovakia and Slovenia in 2004, and Bulgaria and Romania in 2007 – brought further diversity to the social protection arrangements in the Union by adding countries that were, after many decades of Communist rule, in the process of restructuring their economies and welfare systems. As for previous waves of enlargement, they were expected to adopt the Union's social *acquis* as a condition of membership. The Copenhagen criteria [1.20] drawn up by the European Council in 1993 covered the establishment of democratic principles and structures; the development of a functioning market economy; and acceptance and transposition into national law of the EU legal *acquis*, requiring adherence to the political, economic and monetary aims of the Union, including social and employment standards. However, social protection reform was low on the list of priorities for these new member states, and it was no coincidence that, during the pre-accession period, the Union was introducing softer alternatives to regulations and directives, such as the open method of coordination (OMC), which left member states to find the most appropriate means for implementing social policies formulated at EU level.

This chapter examines the shifting focus between two seemingly irreconcilable objectives: harmonization of social protection systems and respect for national diversity and specificity. Firstly, the concepts of approximation, harmonization, coordination, cooperation, cohesion and convergence are introduced and located in relation to the development of the Union's social dimension. The characteristics of national welfare systems, which are deeply embedded in national cultural traditions, are then explored with reference to the concept of welfare models or regimes. Finally, in the absence of a harmonized European social protection system applicable to all citizens of the Union, an attempt is made to assess the extent to which the European social model is being successful in reconciling shared values with diversity.

HARMONIZING NATIONAL SOCIAL POLICIES

The EEC Treaty [1.2] carried conflicting messages about harmonization of social policy. The establishment and functioning of the common market were founded on the principle that provisions should be approximated (article 100). Approximation as laid down by law, regulation or administrative action was intended to affect the establishment and functioning of the common market, thereby favouring 'the harmonisation of social systems' (article 117). From the outset social policy was, however, primarily a matter for individual member states to determine, except for migrant workers (articles 51, 121). Article 118 required the Commission to 'act in close contact with Member States by making studies, delivering opinions and arranging consultations both on problems arising at national level and on those of concern to international organisations', but it was under no compulsion to propose legislation. It has been argued that article 117 did no more 'than direct attention to the need to consider the removal of artificial restrictions which have grown up over the years as part of national policies', and that the close collaboration referred to in article 118 'did not imply the necessity for subsequent action'. Rather, the EEC Treaty could be seen as 'broadly educational and promotional', leaving member states to define their own approaches to social policy (Collins, 1975, pp. 22–23, 31).

The coordination of national systems, with the intention of safeguarding social security arrangements for migrant workers and their dependants, figured among the very first regulations adopted by the Council of Ministers in 1958 (see Chapter 9). Elsewhere the treaty was less prescriptive about how harmonization, or approximation, of social systems was to be achieved. Article 122 required the Commission to report annually on social developments within the Community and gave it the ill-defined brief of drawing up reports on 'any particular problems concerning social conditions'. This section examines more closely progress towards the goal of achieving harmonization of social protection systems by charting the shift towards the concept of convergence of objectives while pursuing subsidiarity in implementation.

From harmonization...

Harmonization of social protection, as written into the EEC Treaty, implied that member states should work together and adapt their own social security systems to bring them into line with one another through a change in the substance of national laws. It goes further than coordination, which involves linking separate legal systems at supranational level and accepting certain common principles and standards without changing the content, the aim being to minimize loss of rights by migrant workers (Holloway, 1981, pp. 11–12). It falls short, however, of unification (as applied to East Germany in 1990), which requires a fundamental reshaping of existing systems.

Controversy over the desirability and feasibility of harmonization continued almost unabated through to the 1990s, with individual member states taking up entrenched positions in defence of national sovereignty, concerned that the welfare arrangements of individual member states might have to be extended or reduced. The debate was reactivated each time new treaty amendments were being negotiated. At the outset, the French government had argued that, if the overriding aim of the Community was to avoid distortion of competition by evening out labour costs, harmonization of social protection, particularly in terms of funding, was a desirable objective and even a precondition for fair competition. Some countries used economic arguments against harmonization. For the Germans, indirect labour costs were only one of a number of elements determining competitiveness. Other factors, such as the taxation system, geographical location, labour productivity, the climate of labour relations, had to be taken into account and needed to be kept roughly in balance. Accordingly, any attempts to harmonize national social security arrangements at Community level might upset the balance, thereby obstructing competition. British governments also argued strongly against any approximation of welfare systems on economic grounds. They vehemently opposed European legislation that might encroach on national social space and present a threat to competitiveness in a global economy. For the southern European countries, harmonization implied a heavy cost they could ill afford, whereas the Swedes were concerned that approximation would mean levelling down their high standards once they joined the Union.

The early member states feared not only that social dumping (see Chapter 1) would become a widespread practice but also that welfare, or social, tourism might develop if some countries offered more attractive living and working conditions, and benefits than others (see Chapter 9). Welfare tourism, or shopping, describes the process whereby older, unemployed and poor people may be induced to seek refuge in the countries and regions within the Union affording the most generous systems of social protection. In these circumstances, measures to encourage harmonization were considered necessary to prevent welfare systems from becoming a bargaining counter between member states.

Another argument in support of the harmonization of social security systems was that the move towards the Single European Market (SEM), in combination with the greater diversity of the 12 member states compared with the original six, created a new set of conditions. On the grounds that marked differences in the funding of social security, as well as direct or indirect subsidies, can distort competition, harmonization of national social security systems was seen as imperative when other components of labour costs and other factors determining competitiveness were converging, notably through approximation in the area of fiscal and employment law, improved infrastructures and standards of education and training (Pieters, 1991, p. 182). As far as the Commission was concerned, by 1992 harmonization of social protection systems was no longer on the agenda. Rather, it recognized the diversity of national systems, 'firmly anchored to specific cultures, traditions and models' [2.1, 5/92, p. 9].

...through coherence, social cohesion and convergence...

When Jacques Delors became President of the Commission in 1985 in the period leading up to the signing of the Single European Act (SEA), he was looking for the best way to introduce a social dimension. He was aware that legislation requiring harmonization would be opposed

by member states unwilling to adapt national systems but, without
legislative controls, states would not be bound to respond. Delors' plan
represented a compromise. He rejected the idea that the social dimension implied uniformity or unification and, instead, advocated 'coherence' (Delors, 1985, p. xviii). His plan involved a social dialogue,
whereby unions and employers would become the initiators of policy in
the social field, rather than the Commission (see Chapter 1).

The SEA confirmed the shift away from harmonization towards
respect for national systems. While still referring to the 'harmonisation
of conditions', the new article 118a stressed that directives should be
adopted setting out 'minimum requirements for gradual implementation, having regard to the conditions and technical rules obtaining in
each of the Member States'. The SEA (title V) also introduced the
concept of 'cohesion', subsequently incorporated into the consolidated
EC Treaty (articles 158–62). Member states were encouraged to work
together to bring about greater economic and social cohesion between
the regions. The structural funds were identified as the main instrument
available to compensate for possible losses arising as a result of economic integration, and to enhance social cohesion (Hannequart, 1992).

A more pragmatic and less legalistic approach was pursued during
the preparatory phase of the Community Charter of the Fundamental
Social Rights of Workers [1.12] in the late 1980s. After more than 30
years of operation, the Community was directing its efforts towards
encouraging national policies to converge over a number of precisely
defined common objectives without encroaching on systems that have
developed from different traditions. The Community charter took some
account of this change in approach. The term 'harmonization' was
retained in the context of freedom of movement with the object of harmonizing the conditions of residence in all member states (§3); the
duration of paid leave was to be harmonized (§8); and measures were to
be taken to achieve further harmonization of conditions for safety at the
workplace (§19). Member states undertook, however, to recognize
national differences in social protection systems. Reference was made
to the need to act in accordance with national practices (§8) and the
arrangements applying in each country (§9).

The action programme for the implementation of the Community
charter [1.13, §4] stated that the diversity of national practices should
be retained as a positive input. At the same time, a balance was to be
sought between economic and social measures to protect the competitiveness of business. Member states were given responsibility for guaranteeing the social rights embodied in the charter and for implementing

the necessary social measures to ensure the smooth operation of the internal market, but the Commission invited them to submit initiatives with a view to the adoption of appropriate legal instruments. These conflicting objectives were to be reconciled by observing the principle of subsidiarity, whereby the most appropriate minimum level of involvement by the Union's institutions is applied, be it harmonization, coordination, convergence or cooperation (see Chapter 1). In other words, the Community should intervene only where necessary, and where measures cannot be better put into effect at national level, so that the rules established do not prevent member states from acting in accordance with their own circumstances.

The Agreement on Social Policy, annexed to the Maastricht Treaty [1.6], mentioned neither harmonization nor approximation. Instead, it reaffirmed the intention to respect national specificity, recommending that its terms should not prevent member states from either maintaining or introducing their own more extensive measures (articles 2, 6). The Commission's role was limited to encouraging cooperation between member states and facilitating the coordination of their action in all the social policy fields covered by the agreement (article 5). In line with the Delors approach, social dialogue and consultation were to be essential components in the process.

The term 'convergence' was introduced into title II article 2 of the Maastricht Treaty in the context of economic performance. At the time when the treaty was signed, a Council recommendation was being prepared 'on the convergence of social protection objectives and policies' [2.1]. On the grounds that differences in social security cover might act as a serious brake to the free movement of workers and exacerbate regional imbalances, particularly between the north and south of the Community, the Council proposed that 'a strategy be promoted for the convergence of Member States' policies in this field, underpinned by objectives established in common, making it possible to overcome such disadvantages' [2.1, p. 49]. The Community's strategy was designed to be flexible in nature, progressive and non-binding [2.1, 5/92, p. 7]. Any *de facto* convergence that was occurring as the result of common trends leading to common problems was to be further promoted, by establishing common objectives, based on the principles of equal treatment and fairness, to guide national policies and avoid all forms of discrimination and disadvantage. The recommendation did not clarify how these principles should be operationalized, stating only that social protection systems were to be adapted and developed as necessary, and administered with maximum efficiency and effectiveness [2.1, p. 51].

...to cooperation, coordination and dialogue

The consolidated version of the EC Treaty [1.8] retained the reference to convergence of economic performance in article 2 but did not extend it to the social area. Title VIII on employment referred to a 'coordinated strategy for employment' (article 125), described as a topic of 'common concern' (article 126 §2). Member states were, however, left to formulate their own employment policies 'in a way consistent with the broad guidelines...of the Member States and of the Community' (article 126 §1), respectful of national competences (article 127 §1). The Council was empowered to make recommendations to member states, but only within well-defined circumstances (article 128 §4). Article 129 allowed for incentive measures to be adopted encouraging cooperation, but it explicitly excluded the harmonization of national laws and regulations.

The same exclusion is found in the chapters on education, vocational training and youth (article 150 §4), culture (article 151 §5), and public health (article 152 §4c), while cooperation and complementarity became key concepts. Article 136 in the chapter on social provisions retained the reference to harmonization from article 117 in the EEC treaty where it was presented as a possibility rather than an obligation. The most binding use of the concept can be found in title XIX article 174 §2 on the environment but, even here, a safeguard clause allowed member states to take provisional measures for non-economic environmental reasons, subject to Community inspection procedures.

As in other social policy areas, the social chapter in the consolidated version of the EC Treaty observed the conciliatory tone already present in the Agreement on Social Policy, stressing the subsidiarity principle and the supportive role of the Union. It was playing down the treaty commitment to achieve a strongly interventionist European social policy based on harmonizing social protection systems. However, while national governments appeared to be vacillating, the Commission was actively cultivating a consensual approach in shaping the social policy agenda. The 1994 white paper on European social policy had defined the characteristic features of a European social model, while reiterating that total harmonization of social policies was no longer being sought [1.15, pp. 7, 12]. By setting common objectives, different national systems would be able to coexist and progress in harmony towards shared goals. The Commission was looking for ways of modernizing and improving social protection. While taking care to observe the subsidiarity principle and acknowledging that member states remained responsible for framing, organizing and financing their social protection systems, the Union assumed responsibility for the coordination of national social security schemes for mobile workers [1.15, pp. 36–7].

By the late 1990s, the Commission was confidently promoting the convergence of employment policies 'towards jointly set, verifiable, regularly updated targets' [1.18, 1998, p. 1], requiring proactive strategies, as a complement to the convergence required by EMU. At the turn of the twenty-first century, a further incentive to find practical mechanisms for achieving the Lisbon strategy [1.20] was impending enlargement to the east, which made the prospect of convergence of social welfare systems become ever more remote. However, in its conclusions to the Nice summit [1.20, §II 5], the Council was 'pleased to see that the principle of differentiation, based on each candidate country's own merits, and allowance of scope for catching up' had been reaffirmed.

In the same year, the provisions of the long-awaited Charter of Fundamental Rights of the European Union [1.21] left no doubt about the importance of national jurisdiction, including in areas of social policy that had hitherto received less attention. While the right of workers to information and consultation (II-27), collective bargaining and action (II-28), and protection in the case of unjustified dismissal (II-30) fall within the conditions provided for by EU law, the charter acknowledged that they are also dependent on national laws and practices. In addition, the charter unambiguously stated that the right to marry and found a family (II-9), the right to conscientious objection (II-10) and to education (II-14) should be in accordance with national laws.

The social policy agenda for 2000–05, which set the tone for the twenty-first century, made no reference to harmonization except to confirm that the aim was not to harmonize social policies. Rather, it advocated coordination of social polices, as well as economic and employment policies, in the context of the internal market [1.22, p. 7]. Social protection thus remained the competence of member states, while cooperation at EU level was intended to 'facilitate collective reflection on how best to address the challenges in modernising and improving the various social protection systems' [1.22, pp. 11–12]

The social agenda for 2005–10 [1.24] confirmed that cooperation between EU institutions, member states and the other parties involved, coordination of social security schemes and other areas of social policy through the OMC, and the exchange of good practice between member states were to be key concepts for social policy in the twenty-first century. The agenda made a point, however, of restating that the social dialogue would continue to be premised on the Commission respecting the autonomy of the social partners [1.24, p. 24].

RECOGNIZING NATIONAL DIVERSITY

The amended version of the treaties had left the way open for cooperation and coordination based on recognition and tolerance of diversity. If
the result of policies happens to be convergence of national social protection systems, at least as far as the treaties are concerned, such an
outcome is incidental rather than being actively and explicitly sought.
Emphasis is on agreement over targets and goals, and shared objectives,
leaving member states to implement policies in accordance with national laws and practices. Many of the problems associated with adopting a common approach to social provisions, as well as resistance to
harmonization in the social area and reluctance to develop quantifiable
targets for social convergence, except with regard to employment, can
be attributed to the different starting points of member states. Postwar
welfare statism may, it is argued, have contained the same ingredients
across countries, but the mix was very different (Jones Finer, 1999, p.
17; Alcock, 2001, p. 3). National governments have remained alert to
what they stood to lose if a uniform system, guaranteeing a minimum
level of provision, was universally applied. This section explores different models of welfare, represented by the five waves of EU membership over 50 years. The aim is to identify areas of common concern,
similarities and differences in approaches to social issues within the
framework of a European social model.

Models of welfare

In the 1960s and 1970s, proponents of convergence theory argued that
welfare states in industrial societies were a logical outcome of industri-
alization, and that attitudes towards social problems were converging as
similar conclusions were reached about how to resolve them. The convergence thesis was countered by other writers who criticized it for
being too deterministic and for oversimplifying patterns of development
in social policy. Such critics (for example Mishra, 1977, pp. 33–42)
stressed the persistence of diversity in welfare patterns in advanced
industrial societies, where the influence of technology was only one
among a number of factors shaping social policy, as exemplified by the
mix between state and occupational welfare provision. In the early
1980s, the diffusion of welfare systems was partly attributed to countries imitating and adopting innovative pioneering institutions from
elsewhere, but internal socio-economic problems and political mobili-
zation also needed to be to taken into account (Flora and Alber, 1981,

pp. 60–3). Although none of these theories referred specifically to the EEC or the possible influence of policy formulated in Brussels on the convergence of welfare systems, arguments about economic forces driving social policy had a strong resonance in the context of EMU.

Concurrently with the debate over convergence, several attempts were made to identify typologies that might help to describe and explain the diffusion of different patterns of welfare and their diversity. In the 1960s, again without reference to the EEC, Richard Titmuss (1974, pp. 30–1) had developed a conceptual approach to the analysis of welfare, which distinguished between three models. In the residual model, social welfare institutions came into play when the private market and family support broke down, thereby limiting state intervention to marginal and deserving groups. According to the industrial achievement–performance model, social welfare institutions were adjuncts of the economy, and social needs were met on the basis of merit, work performance and productivity. Under the third, institutional redistributive, model, social welfare was seen as a major integrated institution in society, operating to provide services universally outside the market.

Residual, industrial and institutional interpretations thus represented very different conceptions of welfare: minimum, targeted provision, performance-related and optimum universal provision. The residual concept of social policy has also been extended to describe welfare as a 'residual luxury' supported by economic surpluses (Heclo, 1981, p. 403). When, in the 1970s, an economic surplus could no longer be assured, welfare states were criticized as a drain on resources. Governments adopted crisis containment measures. The postwar welfare capitalist consensus was challenged, and fundamental questions were raised about the relationship between economic and social policy (Pierson, 1991, p. 222), an issue that assumed ever greater salience as member states moved towards EMU and further enlargement (Pieters, 1998).

The reactions to the challenges of the 1980s highlighted both quantitative and qualitative differences between welfare states in terms of ends and means (Jones Finer, 1999, p. 23). In the early 1990s, renewed interest in analysing models of welfare as an alternative to convergence theory led to several proposals for typologies based on the different ways in which welfare is organized in relation to social structures, political interests and market forces. The three welfare regimes proposed by Gøsta Esping-Andersen (1990, subsequently revisited in 1999) for the capitalist nations were widely discussed and provoked a number of alternative proposals (reviewed by Arts and Gelissen, 2002). Liberal welfare states, according to Esping-Andersen, could be exemplified by the Anglo-Saxon countries. As in the Titmuss residual model, in the absence of a class alliance, selective welfare was targeted at the poor, a dual system of private and occupational services provision was available for the middle classes, and an attempt was made to minimize direct intervention by the state to give free rein to market forces. As in the Titmuss industrial achievement–performance model, Esping-Andersen's conservative corporatist regime applied to countries, such as Germany, where conservative central government had developed systems of occupational social insurance welfare, shaped in no small measure by the influence of the Church, and predicated on the subsidiarity principle, in an effort to ensure support from the working and middle classes. His social democratic regime corresponded to the Titmuss institutional redistributive model, as represented by Scandinavian countries, especially Sweden, where the welfare state, responding to the solidarity of the working and middle classes, ensured universal provision of services, premised on equal opportunities and full employment.

In Esping-Andersen's (1990, p. 74) classification, based on data from the 1970s and 1980s, Austria, Belgium, France, Germany and Italy were rated high on conservative attributes, with Ireland and the Netherlands obtaining a medium score. Denmark, Finland, the Netherlands and Sweden were rated high on social democratic criteria, with Belgium, Germany and the United Kingdom in the medium band. None of the member states was found to record a high degree of liberalism. The United Kingdom was awarded a medium rating in this category, but so too were Denmark, France, Germany, Italy and the Netherlands.

The southern European member states and the central and east European countries were not included in Esping-Andersen's analysis. Proponents of the logic of industrialism thesis might have argued that Greece, Portugal and Spain would in time develop the same level of welfare provision as their more advanced wealthier neighbours through a catching-up process. Since they already relied heavily on social insurance, mainly funded by employers' contributions well above the European average, a strong case could be made for expecting their systems to develop in line with the continental model. It has also been argued (Rhodes, 1997; Guillén and Álvarez, 2001, p. 106) that these countries constitute a distinct southern European welfare model, characterized by a mix of Bismarckian income maintenance policies and social democratic traditions of universal provision for health and education. Another distinguishing feature of the model, at least in comparison with their northern neighbours, is the relatively slow development of social assistance and personal welfare services.

The central and east European candidate countries were forced to revise their approach to welfare provision following the collapse of state socialism in 1989. Under Communism, their social protection systems had in common their bureaucratic state collectivist origins. They were, according to Esping-Andersen's terminology, highly de-commodified in that welfare was essentially provided by the state, but they were also openly redistributive, like the social democratic regimes. Since they reserved special treatment for the party state apparatus, they contained elements of corporatist conservative arrangements.

Observers predicted that these postsocialist welfare systems would be shaped by variables such as institutional legacies, the nature and character of the 1989 revolution, economic transformation during the 1990s, the political impact of transnational agencies and, not least, the criteria laid down for membership of the Union (Deacon, 1993, pp. 190–7; Nielsen, 1996, pp. 206–11). In the early 1990s, the signs were that they were reacting to the perceived failures of the previous system by becoming highly commodified and were placing greater reliance on the market place, which was generating inequalities. By the end of the decade, despite internal differentiation, three trends were identified in welfare policies: an almost ubiquitous neo-liberal tendency, character-ized by market deregulation, the drive to reduce direct and indirect labour cost, privatization and marketization of former public goods and services, accompanied by efforts to strengthen self-reliance and self-provisioning; a shift towards conservatism, with Church, family and nation as core values; the legacy of the past, or path dependency, which proved difficult to counter in the short term (Ferge, 2001, pp. 129–31). In the immediate pre-accession period, it was thought most likely that the neo-liberal, residualist welfare strategy would be pursued (Ferge, 2001, p. 150). The fact that this 'extreme model' of social protection is not based on the principles of solidarity, universality and social dia-logue raised fears that the new member states might even undermine or weaken the European social model, leading to a lowering of standards and casting doubts on the effectiveness of the OMC as an instrument for delivering EU policy (Vaughan-Whitehead, 2003, pp. 162–3).

Characterizing welfare states in the European Union

In this chapter, it has been argued that the different waves of member-ship of the European Community and Union made harmonization of social protection systems a more distant goal. Each wave of member-ship was accompanied by a fall in *per capita* gross domestic product

(GDP). Enlargement to the east from 2004 brought an unprecedented reduction in *per capita* GDP, beyond that resulting from all previous enlargements [8.12, vol. 2, p. 22], thereby exacerbating the severe strains already placed on social protection by the drive towards EMU. In taking stock of developments in social protection systems across the Union, the intention in this section is to test the argument that, at the very least, the expansion of the Community complicated the harmonization process and made prospects for achieving it more distant. EMU had been expected to make convergence of social policies more likely, if not more necessary; enlargement to the east made even target setting, as provided for in the OMC, more difficult to realize.

Financing social protection

During the 1980s and through to the early 1990s when Austria, Finland and Sweden joined the Union, *per capita* spending on social protection increased by more than 40 per cent across EU15, largely due to slow economic growth and high unemployment. Despite fluctuations during the decade, as a proportion of GDP, in 2003 expenditure in EU15 was close to the level reached in 1993 at around 28 per cent. In the early 2000s, EU15 member states were experiencing faster growth in social protection expenditure than in GDP, whereas, in the countries that joined the Union in 2004, spending on social protection as a proportion of GDP was decreasing due to faster growth in GDP [2.5, 14/2006].

Figure 2.1 shows the classification of countries by wave of membership in terms of social protection expenditure in 2003, both in relation to GDP and *per capita*. The figure brings out the contrast, for the percentage of GDP, between the countries in waves 1, 2 and 4 of membership, which were almost all close to, or above, the EU25 average, with the notable exceptions of Luxembourg and Ireland, and those in waves 3 and 5, which were consistently at or below the EU25 average.

In Figure 2.1, the difference between the high and the low spenders is even more marked for *per capita* expenditure, measured in purchasing power standards (PPS). For this indicator, Luxembourg was far above the EU25 average in 2003. It was spending nearly three times more on social protection than Portugal, the EU15 member state with the lowest level of expenditure on this budget head, and nine times more than Latvia, which had the lowest level of all. Social spending in PPS *per capita* for fifth-wave member states fell far below the EU25 average in the early 2000s. It was also relatively low in Ireland and the southern European countries.

Figure 2.1 Social protection expenditure in EU member states, as a % of
GDP and *per capita* in PPS, 2003

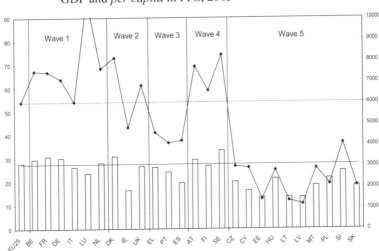

Source: Data from Eurostat, *Statistics in Focus*, 14/2006, table 1, figure 2.

Figure 2.2 The structure of social protection receipts in EU member
states, as a % of total receipts, 2003

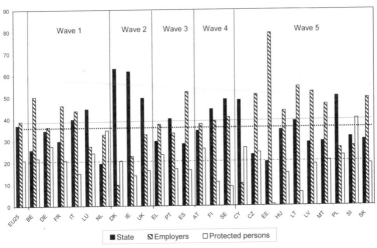

Source: Data from Eurostat, *Statistics in Focus*, 14/2006, table 6.
Note: 2002 data for Cyprus; no data for Bulgaria and Romania.

Figure 2.2 shows how social protection was financed across member states in the early 2000s. The second-wave countries – Denmark, Ireland and the United Kingdom – relied most heavily on tax-funded government subsidies. The contribution from the state also reached over 40 per cent of total receipts in Luxembourg, Finland, Sweden, Cyprus and Poland, but fell below 25 per cent in the Netherlands, the Czech Republic and Estonia. The preference in most of the fifth-wave countries was to shift away from state financing in favour of social insurance contributions, oriented towards the needs of workers, with the main burden falling on employers. Social contributions from employers reached almost 80 per cent in Estonia. Employers were also responsible for more than 50 per cent of total receipts in Belgium, Spain, the Czech Republic, Latvia and Lithuania. In 2003, the implicit tax rate (taxes and social contributions as a percentage of labour costs) was highest (in order) in Sweden, Belgium, Finland, Italy, the Czech Republic and France, and lowest in Malta, Cyprus, the United Kingdom and Ireland (Eurostat, 2006, table II-3.1). Protected persons contributed more than a third of receipts in the Netherlands and Slovenia. Receipts from other sources, such as occupational pensions, user charges and voluntary insurance premiums (not shown in the figure) accounted for over 13 per cent of receipts in Cyprus and nearly 15 per cent in the Netherlands.

Administration and structure of welfare systems

The legal basis and administrative structures of national systems vary across the Union [2.4]. The founder members of the EEC shared a certain similarity of approach to welfare in that their social protection systems were mainly derived from the Bismarckian statist corporatist model, in accordance with the principle that workers are guaranteed benefits and a substitute income related to their previous earnings through contractual insurance schemes (Clasen and Freeman, 1994). The 'continental' insurance model was based on the assumption that employment qualified individuals for welfare benefits as well as wages, and that benefits should be funded primarily, if not exclusively, from contributions paid by employers and employees as part of labour costs.

The conservative-corporatist model of social policy, which developed from the Roman legal tradition, relied on substantive and procedural codes, favouring regulation rather than markets and contracts (Adnett and Hardy, 2005, p. 22). The resulting welfare model was intrinsically non-egalitarian insofar as access to employment varied with age, gender, ethnic origins and qualifications, among other factors (see Chapters 3, 6, 7, 8, 9). Over the postwar period, schemes were perpetuated that offered different arrangements to different categories of workers, ensuring horizontal distribution of income over the lifetime of individuals. They were less concerned with vertical redistribution from one sector to another within society.

The original schemes in Bismarckian Germany, such as that instituted in 1889 for old age pensions, were targeted at industrial workers and provided compensation for loss of income, calculated on the basis of earnings, rather than a minimum income. They thereby reproduced in retirement the inequalities of income earned from employment. Provision for public sector workers was particularly generous and constituted an additional source of inequality. These schemes were underpinned by a highly structured and corporatist industrial relations system. Labour unions and employers' associations were strong social partners bound by law to cooperate in the codetermination process and collective bargaining over working conditions (Roberts and Springer, 2001, pp. 58–63). Belgium, France, Italy, Luxembourg and the Netherlands followed a similar principle to Germany in creating employment-related social insurance schemes.

In most of the founder member states, social protection was first introduced in the areas of industrial injuries and occupational diseases at the end of the nineteenth century, followed by invalidity, sickness and maternity benefits, unemployment, then old age, survivors' and family benefits [2.4]. The provision of health care was also based on insurance contributions, although Italy established a national health service in 1978. They had all developed some form of non-contributory minimum social assistance as a safety net, subsidized by the state from general taxation (see Chapter 8). Where social assistance is organized at regional or local level, considerable variations can be found in coverage, both between and within countries, for example between the north and south of Italy, or between the old and new *Länder* in Germany.

The six countries display commonality in the underlying principles and organizational structures of their social protection systems. They also have in common that *per capita* spending on social welfare is above the EU25 average (see Figure 2.1). Although they share several of the broad characteristics of the continental welfare model, the social protection systems in the founder member states are far from being uniform, either structurally or in terms of their funding arrangements. The social costs of labour are, for example, likely to be much higher in Belgium, France and Italy where contributions fall heavily on employers (see Figure 2.2). While the Italian national health service shifts some of the burden to the state, reforms in the 1990s were moving in the direction of a partial withdrawal of the state in favour of quasi-markets to improve quality and efficiency [2.2, 1997, pp. 138–9].

By contrast, the three states that joined the Community in 1973 – Denmark, Ireland and the United Kingdom – shared a general conception of social protection closer to what can be described as the citizenship or welfare model. According to the Beveridge scheme for social welfare in Britain and to the Scandinavian, or social democratic, model (Esping-Andersen, 1990), which developed in Denmark, the right to a pension, health care and family allowances was granted on the basis of social citizenship. The assumption was that employment provided a living wage, whereas welfare benefits were distributed through taxation to all citizens on equal terms, irrespective of their employment status.

The social security systems in these three countries continue to be distinguished from the 'continental' model by their marked preference for fiscal resources and by universal provision of health care, rather than insurance-based contributions and income-related benefits. In Denmark, emphasis was placed on income maintenance, whereas in Ireland and the United Kingdom the aim was to ensure subsistence by providing low flat-rate payments or means-tested benefits, which may help to explain the difference in the lower overall level of *per capita* spending on social protection. The Anglo-Irish approach to welfare was based on common law and judicial discretion. Under Thatcherism in the United Kingdom, it resulted in deregulated flexible labour markets characterized by relatively low labour costs. By the late 1980s, despite their voluntarist and adversarial labour relations traditions, the much weakened British trade unions were finding a useful ally in Brussels.

Greece, Portugal and Spain, which joined the Community in the 1980s, were characterized by less advanced and less coherent social security systems compared with most of the earlier members. Apart from the core labour market, they relied heavily on traditional forms of support through family and kinship networks and the Church, with discretionary provision at local level. All three countries had to rebuild their industrial relations systems following regime change in the 1970s, leaving them receptive to the influence of EU directives (Roberts and Springer, 2001, pp. 78–83). These three social protection systems are today broadly based on corporatism, as in the continental model, with employers carrying the major burden of the cost of delivering benefits in Spain. In 2005, Greece was still distinguished by the lack of a general social assistance scheme. Health care was provided in both Portugal and Spain by a national health service, largely funded from taxation.

While the EU membership of Austria in 1995 further reinforced the dominant continental model of welfare, Finland and Sweden strengthened the tax-based, social democratic regime (Esping-Andersen, 1990), hitherto represented by Denmark. Here, the right to a pension, health care and family allowances is granted on the basis of social citizenship, with the state as the main funding source (see Figure 2.2). Their *per capita* spending on social protection was well above the EU25 average in 2003 (see Figure 2.1). The industrial relations systems supporting this welfare model were based on strong labour unions, centralized employers' associations, collective bargaining, a hands-off relationship with government and relatively high levels of employee participation, particularly in Sweden (Roberts and Springer, 2001, pp. 73–6).

Despite their shared tradition of state socialism, when the central and east European countries joined the Union, they did not constitute a homogeneous grouping corresponding to one of the welfare regime types outlined above. Each country has chosen its own way of organizing and administering welfare funding (see Figure 2.2). Given their low levels of GDP and persistent economic problems during the 1990s, the fifth wave of eastern rim member states initially followed the more residual pattern of welfare provision characteristic of the southern European countries. Their social protection systems were redesigned rather than being radically changed [2.3, p. 249], although some governments carried out far-reaching structural reforms of pension systems.

During the 1990s, the central and east European countries had introduced a system of independent non-state regional health insurance bodies, based mainly on the Bismarckian model. For the countries of the former Austro-Hungarian empire, this represented a return to the social health insurance principle before the centralized, integrated state model introduced in the early 1950s. Provider capacity was reduced through privatization and transfer from central to local government, and it was not unusual for patients to have to make informal payments to obtain treatment [2.3, pp. 105–9].

Most governments introduced earnings-related rather than flat-rate social benefits, although at a relatively low level of support due to fiscal restraints. Universalism was largely replaced by means-testing, and workfare was promoted in preference to welfare. The effect was that the relationship between contributions and benefits was not apparent for the protected person, to the extent that employers developed strategies to avoid paying their contributions [2.3, p. 237]. Private and semi-private solutions were adopted, with a minimal safety net subject to local discretion, putting the onus on family solidarity to fill gaps in provision.

Social dialogue, collective bargaining and worker participation were weak in the central and east European countries. Industrial relations relied heavily on the state and were governed by complex and burdensome legal regulations, but without an adequate system for monitoring labour practices or enforcing legislation. The new member states were not, therefore, well equipped to implement the principles of solidarity, universality and social dialogue held to underpin European social protection systems (Vaughan-Whitehead, 2003, pp. 162, 272–3).

CONSOLIDATING THE EUROPEAN SOCIAL MODEL

The social protection systems examined in this chapter share a common core, both in terms of the risks they cover and the general administrative arrangements set up to deal with contingencies. However, closer scrutiny reveals numerous differences within and between groups of countries with regard to the legal status of social protection, funding mechanisms, the distribution of responsibilities and sectors of the population covered by contributory and non-contributory schemes [2.2; 2.3; 2.4]. Each country has developed its own peculiar brand of social protection as a result of a long process reflecting idiosyncratic socio-economic, political and cultural traditions, which would seem to give the lie to the thesis of the logic of industrialism, at least as far as administrative and financial structures are concerned.

In line with convergence theory, it could be argued that disparities in systems might be due to the stage of socio-economic development reached by each country. Accordingly, the countries in southern, central and eastern Europe might be expected to learn from, and imitate, their more advanced neighbours, stimulated in the 2000s by the OMC. While evidence can be found to suggest that innovatory schemes may be used as models, as was the case with the Bismarckian and Beveridgian social security schemes, the economic and political conditions in which these two groupings of countries were developing their social protection systems when they joined the Community were very different from those pertaining in the 1960s and 1970s, even if the structural funds did enable some upwards levelling.

Over the second half of the twentieth century, all welfare regimes were forced to adapt in response to changing socio-economic and political circumstances. During the 1990s, most governments were engaging in welfare retrenchment, even if the level of expenditure did not decline significantly. The result was a mixed economy of welfare, or welfare pluralism, in which the employment-insurance model had become predominant. The corporate welfare systems, based on employers' and workers' contributions and income-related benefits, had not entirely replaced occupational and voluntary schemes, which were increasingly being called upon to provide cover for contingencies such as old age (see Chapter 7). Although this model of welfare served the Union's economic interests, at the social level it was moving member states away from a more redistributive conception of welfare citizenship, reinforcing differentiation, segregation and polarization. While the market could be expected to take care of workers in regular employment, those unable to enter or re-enter the labour force ran the risk of being marginalized. The corporatist principle that rights are derived from employment and paid work is the primary means of achieving social integration became the hallmark of the early years of the twenty-first century. Emphasis had shifted towards more active labour market policies designed to move unemployed people off benefits and into work, as institutionalized in the Lisbon strategy [1.18].

Evidence can also be found for the development of a welfare mix in member states that had initially based their social protection systems on universal state provision of health care and flat-rate benefits for other contingencies. Schemes for earnings-related payments and occupationally-based pensions, and private health care were progressively extended to other sectors of the working population. Universality still depended on a high degree of involvement of public sector institutions in Denmark and Sweden, but here too pressure was increasingly being exerted by public opinion and government to turn to market and civil society solutions as a means of reducing the tax burden.

A certain amount of involuntary or spontaneous, rather than intended or planned, convergence may thus have taken place under the influence of the market forces and economic imperatives driving social policy. The actual welfare mix continued, however, to depend on the political context and the human and social processes involved in policy development at national level. Just as industrial technology and state intervention in social affairs were not considered sufficiently powerful to bring about convergence of social policy in the past (Mishra, 1977, p. 40), the economic factors that are a major force behind welfare pluralism may not necessarily suffice to overcome differences in national welfare state ideologies, as recognized in documents issued by the Commission in the early years of the twenty-first century.

If diversity appears to have been accepted in the Union's treaties and charters, the explanation may lie, at least partly, in the fact that member states are broadly in agreement about the overriding objectives of social policy. The Commission has described highly developed social protection systems as a 'fundamental component and a distinguishing feature of the European model of society' [1.17, 1997. p. 1]. In the absence of harmonization of the administrative and financial structures delivering welfare, a more powerful unifying force, which was developing outside the regulatory framework, was the shared belief among EU member states in the core values of such a model and the desire to preserve them. These values included 'democracy and individual rights, free collective bargaining, the market economy, equality of opportunity for all and social welfare and solidarity' [1.15, 1994, p. 9].

Social progress was identified as a key element in the model, aimed at achieving high levels of employment and of social protection, raising the standard of living and quality of life, and promoting economic and social cohesion, while striking a balance between social justice and economic efficiency. The fear being expressed within the Union at the turn of the twenty-first century was that fifth-wave member states would be unable to conform to the European social model, resulting in it becoming unsustainable in the context of enlargement, and prompting some observers to articulate their concern that the risks involved might endanger its very survival (Vaughan-Whitehead, 2003, p. 493). The shortcomings of the new member states in social protection and labour relations presented a significant challenge to the European social model, and were being used to justify the setting of minimum, rather than the same, social standards (Adnett and Hardy, 2005, p. 28–9).

Box 2   Secondary legislation and official publications relating to the development of a European social model

2.1   Council Recommendation of 27 July 1992 on the convergence of social protection objectives and policies, 92/442/EEC, *OJ* L 245/49 26.8.1992; Commission of the European Communities, The convergence of social protection objectives and policies, *Social Europe Supplement*, 5/92.

2.2   European Commission, *Social Protection in Europe*, OOPEC (biennial, 1993–2001).

2.3   European Commission, *Social Protection in the 13 Candidate Countries: a comparative analysis*, OOPEC, 2003.

2.4   European Commission, Missoc, *Social Protection in the Member States of the European Union* (annual), available on-line [1.26].

2.5   Eurostat, *Statistics in Focus, Population and Social Conditions*, available on-line: http://ec.europa.eu/eurostat

3 Education, Training and Employability

In the Community's and Union's treaties and charter, most legislative provisions in the area of social policy refer to the protection of workers under labour law and in social security systems, where the basis for entitlements is derived primarily from employment. When the Treaty establishing the European Economic Community (EEC) [1.2] was signed in 1957, the six member states were concerned with social provisions only insofar as differences in national systems might impede freedom of movement for workers within the Community or distort competition. For the EEC founder members, education and training were, therefore, of only indirect interest.

If social policy is defined in a broad sense as the collective provision of particular services to meet the basic social needs of citizens (Alcock, 2001, p. 1), and as government interventions with the aim of shaping society (Kleinman, 2002, pp. 1–7), covering both non-economic and economic objectives (Titmuss, 1974, p. 29), education and training are legitimate areas for intervention by European institutions. As its social remit was gradually extended, and as the promotion of high levels of employment moved onto the agenda (see Chapter 1), education and training became a recognized policy area for the Union. An agreed set of objectives was formulated, and administrative measures were prepared for their implementation, albeit with due regard for the principles of subsidiarity and the need to respect diversity and ensure the relevance of education and training to employability.

This triangular relationship is addressed throughout the chapter. Education and training are first located within the wider context of European social policy development, including a review of the concept of educational space, the mutual recognition of qualifications and Community programmes in the field of education, training and research. Data are then compared on access to education, training and employment in member states. In conclusion, consideration is given to the possible impact on national systems of action initiated by the Union in a policy area of growing importance.

THE LEGAL FRAMEWORK FOR EDUCATION AND TRAINING

The interests of the Union have been bound up primarily with economic concerns, as argued in previous chapters. The issue of competition for labour was relevant when the Community was established, since employers were expected to seek to poach well-qualified workers and to compete in offering the most favourable terms of employment in an effort to attract appropriate skills in areas of labour shortage (see Chapter 9). Since the 1970s, another labour market-related reason for interest in vocational training has been the growing problem of unemployment, particularly among young people. Improvement in the quality and skills of the labour force has been promoted to further the goal of economic cohesion (see Chapter 8). In the 1994 white paper on growth, competitiveness and employment, attention turned towards the adaptation of education and training systems, with the aim of 'stimulating growth and restoring competitiveness and a socially acceptable level of employment in the Community' [3.8, p. 133]. The European employment strategy of the late 1990s was premised on the achievement of a high level of employability. This section considers the development of the Union's remit and action in the area of education and training with reference to vocational training, mobility, the mutual recognition of qualifications, and as important components in active labour market policies.

Developing a European education area

Article 118 of the EEC Treaty gave the Commission the task of 'promoting close cooperation between Member States'. In the area of basic and advanced vocational training, the treaty did not explicitly address the subject of education. Article 128 provided for the establishment of a 'common vocational policy capable of contributing to the harmonious development both of the national economies and of the common market'. The first phase of a programme for the exchange of young workers was launched in 1964, setting a pattern for a series of initiatives designed to encourage mobility during training. Under the section on the right of establishment, article 57 §1 empowered the Council to 'issue directives for the mutual recognition of diplomas, certificates and other evidence of formal qualifications', the purpose being to make it easier for self-employed workers to pursue activities in another member state.

    When, ten years later in 1974, the Commission signalled an interest in the social dimension of Europe through its social action programme [1.11], education was already on the agenda (Corbett, 2005). A resolution of the Council in 1976 'comprising an action programme in the field of education' [3.1] identified a number of priorities, including improved facilities for education and training, closer relations between educational systems, improved statistics on education, greater coopera-tion between member states in the field of higher education, covering recognition of qualifications and periods of study abroad, and the pro-motion of foreign language teaching and equal opportunities in access to education. The programme addressed the questions of unemployment among young people, the educational needs of the children of migrants, the preparation of young people for work and the smooth transition from education to working life. European Social Fund rules were later recast to give priority to the under-25s, and a number of measures were introduced that had implications for employment. The programme thus prepared the ground for subsequent action.

While the final stages of the Community Charter of the Fundamen-tal Social Rights of Workers [1.12] were being negotiated, the Commis-sion issued a communication 'on education and training in the Euro-pean Community', setting out medium-term perspectives for education over the period 1989–92 [3.3]. The communication provided a clear statement of the Community's objectives and initiatives in this area. The introduction spoke of the need to create an 'educational space for mobility and interchange', analogous to Jacques Delors' 'social space' (see Chapter 1). The same document stressed the broad consensus reached over the pivotal role that education and training would be called upon to play in the Community's overall development strategy, spearheading its commitment to invest in people. The communication suggested, moreover, that human resources could provide 'an essential bridge between economic and social policies' [3.3, p. 1].

The Commission's views on the subject were to some extent incor-porated into the 1989 Community charter. Under the heading for the protection of children and adolescents, the rights of young people in-cluded a minimum working age, which 'must not be lower than the minimum school-leaving age and, in any case, not lower than 15 years' (§20). Vocational training was mentioned in five of the 12 sections of the charter, indicating the priority being given to this area of social policy insofar as it had immediate relevance for workers. As in the EEC Treaty with regard to vocational training, the charter reiterated the need to eliminate obstacles arising from the non-recognition of qualifications (§3). Emphasis was placed on the right of workers to vocational train-ing and retraining throughout their working lives, without discrimina-tion on grounds of nationality. The aim was to help workers improve or extend their skills, 'particularly in the light of technical developments' (§15). Young people were to be entitled to receive 'initial vocational training of a sufficient duration to enable them to adapt to the requirements of their future working life', and such training was to take place during working hours (§23). The right of men and women to equal treatment was to extend beyond access to employment, remuneration, working conditions and social protection to equality in access to education, training and career development (§16). The section on health protection and safety at the workplace included the need for training (§19) and the entitlement of disabled persons to vocational training to improve 'their social and professional integration' (§26).

Following on from the Community charter, the Council issued a series of conclusions, recommendations and resolutions in the early 1990s setting out EU policy for education and training. While the economic motivation of encouraging freedom of movement of workers continued to dictate policy, the concept of an educational space was gaining acceptance. Emphasis was gradually shifting towards more qualitative objectives, with mobility being presented as a source of mutual enrichment and cultural interchange, rather than an end in itself. In 1991, a Commission memorandum on higher education clearly set out the Community's policy objectives for post-compulsory education and training. It referred to the 'wider responsibilities of higher education institutions for maintaining, developing and transmitting the cultural heritage of Europe and its Member States and for mobilising the creativity of people to advance the boundaries of knowledge, in the humanities as well as in science and technology' [3.4, pp. 1–2]. A number of factors were identified in the same document as influencing higher education in the Community: the increasing pace of European integration and labour mobility following the completion of the internal market, and progress towards monetary and political union; the impact of scientific and technological advances for economic and daily life; the enlargement of the Community; and increasing opportunities for co-operation, partnership and mutual support both within Europe and on the world scene. These changes were expected to have an impact on the level and mix of skills required by the workforce, and thus on the form that education and training took, if skill shortages were to be avoided, and competitiveness was to be maintained. The conclusions of a meeting of the Council and ministers for education in 1993 'on furthering an open European space for cooperation within higher education' [3.6] stressed the demands greater mobility would place on education policy and the key role of access, quality and relevance of studies.

Rather than relegating it to the Protocol and Agreement on Social Policy like many other areas of social affairs, the Treaty on European Union [1.6] addressed the issue of education and training directly, thereby signalling its relevance for international competitiveness. Title VIII chapter 3 in the main body of the treaty was devoted to education, vocational training and youth, becoming part of title XI in the consolidated EC Treaty [1.8]. Article 128 in the original EEC Treaty was replaced by two new articles (149 and 150) in the EC Treaty. The articles set out the Community's commitment to encouraging quality education through cooperation between member states, and reaffirmed that individual member states were to retain responsibility for the content of programmes and the organization of their educational and vocational systems. Cultural and linguistic diversity were also to be respected and promoted according to a new title XII on culture under article 151, an aim subsequently taken up in a Council resolution in 2002 [3.17].

The aims expressed were wide ranging: to develop the European dimension in education through language teaching and dissemination; to encourage the mobility of students and teachers, including the recognition of qualifications and periods of study in another country; to promote cooperation between educational institutions; to develop the exchange of information and experience on common issues relating to young people and socio-educational instructors, and on distance learning (article 149). In addition, vocational training policy was intended to ease the process of adaptation to industrial change, and to improve initial and continuing training, with a view to assisting entry and re-entry into the labour market and access to training, while stimulating cooperation among training establishments, or between them and firms (article 150). Both articles allowed for the Council to act in shaping policy content, in the case of article 149 by adopting incentive measures and recommendations, and in the case of article 150 by adopting measures to contribute to the achievement of its objectives. The wording of article 123 of the original EEC Treaty on the European Social Fund was also revised (article 146 in the consolidated EC Treaty), by adding a reference to vocational training and retraining as the means of helping workers to adapt to industrial change. The treaty revisions in these three articles thus provided a legal framework for proposing cooperative actions in education and training, supported by financial incentives.

A green paper on the European dimension of education [3.7], issued in 1993 shortly before the treaty came into force, seized the opportunity to stimulate discussion about future action. Areas were identified where the Union could complement the efforts of member states and bring added value to the development of quality in education. The 1994 white paper on European social policy further demonstrated the Commission's commitment to investing in education and training as 'one of the essential requirements for the competitiveness of the Union as well as for the cohesion of our societies' [1.15, p. 23].

The white paper on growth, competitiveness and employment, published in the same year, recognized that education and training alone could not provide the answer to the immediate challenges facing the Union, but they were presented as a significant element in the emergence of a new development model in the longer term [3.8, p. 133]. Member states saw training, both initial and continuing, as an instrument of active labour market policy. Investment in human resources through lifelong learning was needed to increase competitiveness. The white paper recommended that member states should develop training policies involving public authorities, business and the social partners, and that fiscal incentives should be used to reallocate resources from unemployment compensation to training. Action was to be promoted at Community level to extend existing programmes and regulations, with a view to developing the European dimension of education. Emphasis was placed on the need for innovation, exchange of experience and information on good practice, mutual recognition of qualifications and skills, as well as the process of lifelong learning [3.8, pp. 135–8].

The momentum was maintained and reinforced by the 1995 white paper on education and training [3.9], which stressed their value to both individuals and society. It argued strongly for a European approach to education in the context of globalization, the spread of new technologies and enlargement, as a means of preserving diversity and providing a focal point for cooperation between the Union and member states. The white paper set out guidelines for building a learning society on the basis that education and training are vital for the Union's competitiveness, to preserve its social model and avoid social divisiveness between those with and without knowledge. Special emphasis was placed on the need to promote the European dimension 'to avoid the risk of a watered-down European society' [3.9, p. 29]. To this end, the white paper identified five main objectives, and presented proposals for achieving them: encouraging the acquisition of new knowledge; bringing schools and the business sector closer together; combating exclusion; developing proficiency in three European languages; and treating capital investment and investment in training on an equal basis [3.9, p. I].

The white paper opened by stating that education and training have 'emerged as the latest means for tackling the employment problem'

[3.9, p. 1], but it also commented that they cannot solve the problem alone. Whereas article 125 under title VIII on employment in the consolidated version of the EC Treaty [1.8] referred simply to the importance of promoting a 'skilled and trained and adaptable workforce', the Council's 1998 employment guidelines [1.18] made training a central plank in the strategy for improving employability, and for easing both the transition from school to work and the return to work.

A Commission communication issued in 1997, entitled 'Towards a Europe of knowledge' [3.11] reiterated that education and training were strongly anchored in treaty commitments underpinning the economic goals of European union. When the terms of the Community charter are read in conjunction with the revised and renumbered articles 149 and 150 of the consolidated version of the EC Treaty, clearly education and training policies, while firmly on the agenda, were being handled with the usual caution characteristic of the Council's approach to social affairs. The Union continued to be concerned primarily with promoting cooperation between member states through programmes aimed at encouraging mobility and the exchange of information. According to the treaty, the intention was not to interfere with national education systems, nor to use the legislative channel to bring pressure to bear on member states to persuade them to harmonize systems. Provision was, however, made for incentives to encourage member states to achieve the Union's objective of building a dynamic European education area.

The Commission was aware that many obstacles remained to transnational mobility [3.10]. Regulatory and administrative deficiencies falling within its competence were thought to be discouraging free movement. Examples could be quoted of countries that had not transposed European law into national legislation. Other barriers identified included territorial restrictions on student grants, the lack of recognition of vocational qualifications acquired in another member state, the loss of rights to unemployment benefit and social security for job-seekers undergoing training of more than three months in another member state, and the problems of classifying voluntary work.

In the Bologna declaration of 19 June 1999 [3.12], the ministers of education in the 15 EU member states and candidate countries affirmed their commitment to building upon and strengthening Europe's intellectual, cultural, social, scientific and technological dimensions. They recognized the importance of 'awareness of shared values and belonging to a common social and cultural space', and stressed that education is paramount in developing 'stable, peaceful and democratic societies' [3.12, p. 1]. The declaration set out to enhance the international competitiveness of European higher education by adopting a system of easily comprehensible and comparable degrees at undergraduate and graduate level: undergraduate training lasting a minimum of three years, leading to a qualification relevant to the European labour market; and graduate training to masters and/or doctorate level. They advocated using a system of credits to encourage student mobility, combined with ready access to study and training opportunities, and related services. The proposals for greater European cooperation covered quality assurance, based on the development of comparable criteria and methodologies, curricular development, integrated programmes of study, training and research. Without referring to higher education, the Charter of Fundamental Rights of the European Union [1.21, article II-14], signed in 2000, affirmed the right to education and access to vocational and continuing training, extending to free compulsory education.

The Lisbon European Council in the same year set out the strategic goal of making Europe into 'the most competitive and dynamic knowledge-based economy in the world, capable of sustainable economic growth with more and better jobs and greater social cohesion' [1.20]. In 2001, the Commission issued a report 'on the concrete future objectives of education and training systems' [3.14]. Rather than advocating a common policy, the report outlined a comprehensive, consistent and coherent approach for national policies on education in EU member states, designed to make Europe's education systems a 'world quality' reference point by 2010. The report, which was to be implemented using the open method of coordination (OMC), had three main objectives, accompanied by indicators for measuring progress: to improve the quality and effectiveness of education and training systems in the EU; to facilitate access to lifelong education and training; and to open up education and training systems to the wider world. The targets set included halving the number of 18 to 24-year-olds with only lower-secondary level education by 2010, ensuring internet access, increasing *per capita* investment in human resources, encouraging language acquisition and mobility of students, teachers, trainers and researchers.

Mutual recognition of qualifications

As in other areas of social policy, over the years the focus of interest in education and training shifted progressively from harmonization to cooperation and exchange of information and experience, but not before much effort had been expended comparing the content and level of qualifications across the Community in an attempt to reach agreement over their transferability between member states. The overall shift in education and training policy did not mean the original aim of achieving mutual recognition of qualifications had been forgotten. Although the 1989 charter on workers' rights specified that the intention was not to harmonize the content and duration of education and training systems across member states, it reiterated the EEC Treaty's initial objective by proposing that obstacles to mobility due to non-recognition of diplomas or equivalent occupational qualifications should be eliminated [1.12, §3]. Actions such as the mutual recognition of qualifications were, however, expected 'to stimulate movements towards convergence in the training for particular professions' [3.4, §20].

Whereas the completion of the internal market was heralded as marking the advent of a new era of enhanced mobility of human capital and labour, harmonization and convergence within the Community, most of the measures resulting from the Single European Act (SEA) [1.5] regarding recognition of qualifications had already been initiated by 1986. A number of directives relevant to the harmonization of the professions had become statutory. Since 1964, about 60 sectoral directives had been adopted, ensuring the mutual recognition of conditions for access to particular occupations, many of which sought to enable recognition of work experience acquired in another member state.

Between 1964 and 1982, directives were issued covering industry and crafts, the retail trade, personal services, such as restaurants, bars and hotels, food industries and drinks production, the wholesale trade in coal, trade in toxic products, itinerant activities, insurance agents and brokers, transport agents and hairdressers. Occupations involving road transport of goods or passengers were granted freedom of establishment and freedom to provide services, as stipulated in the EEC Treaty.

Occupations such as the health professions needed a more complex set of measures to cover the conditions under which they were exercised. Two directives were required for each occupation: the first to coordinate and harmonize training, covering quality (content) and quantity (number of years and hours of study); the second to establish the automatic recognition of diplomas conforming to Community norms. Minimum standards were imposed, leaving each country to determine and enforce additional expectations. The directives were binding but to allow for flexibility did not specify the details of provision.

Coordination and mutual recognition directives were issued between 1976 and 1985, covering doctors, nurses, dentists, veterinary surgeons, midwives, accountants, architects and pharmacists. Seventeen years of negotiations were needed before architects with specified diplomas were granted the right to exercise their profession in another member state. Professionals in regulated activities were given the right to establish themselves in another member state, subject to fulfilling the requirements of the host country, by undertaking a period of adaptation or undergoing aptitude tests. For lawyers, recognition concerned the status of lawyer as recognized in the country of origin. The directive also laid down conditions for the provision of services.

These lengthy attempts at harmonization for individual professions progressively gave way to a more global approach, as exemplified by Council Directive 89/48/EEC 'on a general system for the recognition of higher-education diplomas awarded on completion of professional education and training of at least three years' duration' [3.2], which came into force in 1991. The directive applied to all diplomas not covered by sectoral directives involving higher education and training of at least three years. The same principle was adopted in Directive 92/51/EEC issued in 1992, which extended recognition to other previously excluded post-secondary qualifications and training courses. It was then supplemented by Directive 95/43/EC [3.5]. Ten years later, Directive 2005/36/EC on the recognition of professional qualifications [3.19] aimed to ensure freedom to provide regulated services, contingent upon the possession of appropriate qualifications. The new directive, which was due to be transposed into national legislation by 2007, consolidated 12 sectoral directives and three general system directives.

Whereas equivalence was generally understood to refer to a detailed comparison of the individual elements of programmes of study, recognition involved a more global evaluation of the whole of a student's education, taking account of the function and overall level of academic study for the purposes of admission to further study or employment. The directives were intended to operate on a case-by-case basis, relying on mutual confidence between member states and assuming comparability between levels of education and training. By the early 2000s, the extensive legislative framework put in place was expected to remove educational obstacles to free movement of persons and services.

COMMUNITY INITIATIVES ON EDUCATION AND TRAINING

Statements from the Council and the Commission on education and training have constantly emphasized the importance of the European dimension and of broadening the understanding of other cultures. A number of programmes have been implemented since the 1970s to encourage mobility of young people, students and researchers in Europe, with a view to providing opportunities for exposure to different languages and cultures as part of the learning experience. Mobility of scholars within Europe is not a new idea. Of all institutions, universities have one of the longest traditions of cooperation dating back to the Middle Ages, when they shared a *lingua franca* (Latin), and the itinerant scholar was a common phenomenon. Yet, over the centuries, national higher education systems have tended to diverge, with the effect that they display quite marked differences in their aims and objectives, structures, programmes and qualifications.

Having again formally recognized that 'blanket harmonisation or standardization of the educational system is entirely undesirable' [3.3, p. 4], the Union set as its objective 'to improve the overall quality of educational provision by bringing the different systems into a long-term process of contact, cooperation and concertation and by avoiding unnecessary divergences which would otherwise impede the free movement of persons and ideas' [3.3, pp. 4–5]. Cooperation was seen as essential in developing a commitment to lifelong learning based on quality and solidarity [3.16]. One means of achieving closer cooperation has been by devising arrangements whereby educational reforms and restructuring within member states are carried out in full awareness of the wealth of experience accumulated across the Union.

The aim of improving opportunities for vocational training has resulted in programmes to encourage the mobility of students, with the explicit objectives of promoting shared democratic values, increasing the understanding of the multicultural dimension of the Community and preparing young people for European citizenship [3.3, p. 5]. In the late 1980s, education was presented as the 'binding force for cooperation and partnership in all other sectors', emphasizing the importance of 'mutual understanding' and the 'capacity to work together', which Community programmes were intended to stimulate (Jones, 1990, p. 9).

The programmes launched over the years can be divided into four main overlapping categories, outlined in more detail below, covering the objectives contained in the amended EC Treaty: to collect and disseminate information about education and training arrangements across the Union, thereby providing a better understanding of other national systems; to encourage mobility of students and young people, and promote cooperation between educational institutions in different member states, with a view to extending knowledge of Europe and its languages, and adding a European dimension to education and training; to provide work experience and vocational training in another national setting, designed to enhance social and economic integration and promote co-operation between educational institutions and industry; to assist member states in adapting to new technologies and to extend opportunities for collaboration in research and development.

Information on education and training

In 1975, the Council set up a special agency, the European Centre for the Development of Vocational Training (Cedefop), originally located in Berlin, as an information network to increase and improve the circulation of information on education policy [3.23]. Following a decision by national governments in 1993, it was moved to Thessaloniki. The Eurydice education information network was launched a few years later and came into operation in 1981, with responsibility for developing a data bank on education and training. While recognizing the diversity of education systems in member states, the Council wanted to ensure that it would not become an obstacle to the free movement of people. Cedefop was charged with providing information in all the Community languages, involving a costly and laborious process. The decision in the 1980s to pursue the recognition of vocational qualifications for occupations through a more general directive, similar to that for professional occupations, can be seen as a means of avoiding the problems of trying to standardize different national practices for qualifications and training. A network of National Academic Recognition Information Centres (Naric) was established in 1984, subsequently coordinated by the Erasmus bureau, to provide information on the recognition of qualifications across member states and of periods of study in other countries.

In its 1989 communication on education and training, the Commission noted that national governments were continuing to implement major educational reforms without systematic reference to practices in other member states and without adequate consideration of the implications for different systems. It therefore recommended that arrangements should be made to ensure a regular flow of information on experience across the Community and that a forum should be provided for coordinating discussion of policy issues, with technical assistance from Eurydice [3.3, p. 15]. To meet this commitment, Eurostat, the Union's statistical agency, was required to publish regular updates of indicators on education, and Cedefop and Eurydice were given the task of compiling information on the structure of education and initial training systems for young people across EU member states [3.24; 3.25]. To facilitate educational mobility, in 2004 the European Parliament and Council adopted a common European format for a *curriculum vitae*, implemented by Cedefop, providing a simple, efficient and transparent presentation of individual qualifications and skills, in combination with a Europass, or passport, indicating the knowledge and experience that had been acquired through formal and informal training [3.18].

Mobility and cooperation between institutions

In compliance with article 50 of the EEC Treaty, the 1964 programme for the exchange of young workers was one of the earliest Community actions [3.21]. The Community's programme for the Vocational Training of Young People and their Preparation for Adult and Working Life (Petra), set up in 1988, was another response to this particular need. It involved placements or exchanges for young people undergoing training and a network of transnational partnerships and initiatives.

In the late 1980s, programmes, such as the European community action scheme for the mobility of university students, named after the sixteenth-century humanist scholar and priest Desiderius Erasmus, were designed to foster cooperation without requiring harmonization. Awarding bodies were called upon to recognize formally periods of training in another member state, but each country remained free to decide on the content and organization of its own programmes in respect of the principle of subsidiarity, as reaffirmed in the treaties. The European Community course credit transfer system (Ects) was set up in 1989/90 to enable students to undertake all or part of their higher education in another member state. The Trans-European Mobility Scheme for University Studies (Tempus) extended exchanges to central and eastern Europe from 1991.

The aim of the Youth for Europe programme was to extend opportunities provided by Erasmus to countries or categories of young people that were under-represented in student exchanges or whose language was less widely spoken. Phase III of Youth for Europe for the period 1995–99, covering young people aged 15 to 25, extended the scope of earlier measures, while at the same time providing positive action for disadvantaged young people. Five main areas of action were identified: intra-Community activities directly involving young people; youth workers; cooperation between member states over the exchange of experience; exchanges with non-member countries; and information for young people and youth research.

The Socrates programme was launched in 1995 to build on the previous generation of programmes. The first phase ran from 1995 to

1999, and the second from 2000 to 2004. The aim of Socrates was to strengthen the European dimension of education at all levels, in particular through the development of language learning; the promotion of cooperation through exchanges; the removal of obstacles to mobility by recognizing diplomas and periods of study abroad; and the encouragement of innovation, particularly in the field of new technologies.

Within the programme, various elements were identified, each targeting a specific activity or level of education. For example, in phase II, Comenius was concerned with the European dimension of school education, covering transnational partnerships between schools, the education of the children of migrant workers and teacher training activities. Erasmus continued to deal with exchanges in higher education. Grundtvig focused on European cooperation in relation to educational pathways for young people without formal educational qualifications. The Lingua programme was designed to support linguistic diversity. It had been introduced by the Commission in response to the realization that foreign languages should be an essential part of European education and training, and that inadequate knowledge of languages was a major obstacle to mobility as well as a handicap in international trade. Atlas covered open and distance learning and the use of new technologies in language learning. Provision was also made for accompanying measures, such as information campaigns and dissemination activities.

One of the aims of the youth programme for 2000–06 was to encourage debate between member states on drafting a proper youth policy. With the prospect of the number of young Europeans reaching 75 million in 2004, the 2001 white paper 'on a new impetus for European youth' [3.15] was a response to the strong disaffection among young people with traditional forms of participation in public life and an attempt to promote active citizenship. The white paper advocated increasing cooperation between member states and taking greater account of the youth factor in sectoral policies, using the OMC to stimulate the information flow and exchange of ideas and good practices.

In 2005, the Commission announced a new generation of European programmes for education and training, culture and youth for 2007–13 [3.21]. The Youth in Action programme, with a budget of 915 million euros, was intended to develop a sense of personal responsibility, initiative, concern for others, citizenship and active involvement at local, national and EU level among young people, while improving support systems for youth activities. An integrated action programme in lifelong learning with a budget of 13.62 billion euros was designed to combine school education (Comenius), higher education (Erasmus), vocational training (Leonardo da Vinci), adult education (Grundtvig), and the Jean Monnet programme, which addressed European integration [3.20].

When they were first introduced, Erasmus, Lingua and Youth for Europe were promoted as the Community's 'flagship' programmes [3.3, p. 3]. Together, they represented a substantial input of resources, but most of the schemes proved administratively onerous to operate, and their success is difficult to assess, especially where the intention was to heighten awareness of other cultures. In quantitative terms, the total number of beneficiaries was small in relation to the number of potential clients and the target figures. The target initially set for student mobility was that 10 per cent of all students should experience a period of training abroad. An estimated 127,000 students in the Union (representing less than 1 per cent of the student population in higher education) and EFTA countries and over 10,000 teachers participated every year in mobility programmes. By 2005, an estimated 1 million students had taken advantage of the Erasmus scheme. Another 40,000 young people participated in young people's exchange schemes under the Youth for Europe programme. Within its integrated programme, the Commission's target for its education and training programmes was that Comenius should involve at least 5 per cent of EU school pupils in joint activities by 2011, and that Erasmus should provide opportunities to study abroad for 3 million university students [3.20, articles 17, 21].

While the number of students undertaking part of their studies in another member state had been increasing over the years, so too had the total student population in the Union. It is not known to what extent various programmes have encouraged longer-term study in another country. In the early 2000s, approximately 5.5 per cent of all students in EU member states were citizens of a country other than the one where they had been studying for at least a year, but only about 2 per cent were from elsewhere in the Union. The countries with the largest proportions of their student population studying abroad were Cyprus (52 per cent) and Luxembourg (66 per cent), although numbers were declining as these countries increased their own provision. The United Kingdom recorded the smallest proportion of British students studying elsewhere in the Union (under 1 per cent), while being a popular destination for students from other member states [3.24, 2005, figure C20].

Training in new technologies and cooperation with industry

Several action programmes were created in response to the need for the workforce to master technological change through partnerships between education and industry. A programme in the field of vocational training and technological change (Eurotecnet) was set up in 1985 and formalized in 1990. The programme on cooperation between universities and enterprises providing for training in the field of technology (Comett), another of the Community's flagship programmes, was launched in 1986. Both programmes recognized the blurring of the boundaries between jobs under the pressures of technological change, as well as the need to introduce young people to new technologies while they are in full-time compulsory education and once they begin initial training.

The 1991 action programme for the development of continuing vocational training in the European Community (Force) was designed to encourage information exchange and good practices. In recognition of the problems that women have in gaining access to training, a European network of vocational training projects for women (Iris) was set up in 1988 to meet their specific needs. The aim was to develop a methodology on women's vocational training and evaluation tools. The new opportunities for women (Now) initiative, included in the third medium-term Community action programme on equal opportunities for women and men [6.10] in 1991, offered member states opportunities to co-fund actions. All the action programmes implemented in the 1990s contained an equal opportunities statement. However, most applicants' guidelines did not (Rees, 1998, pp. 132–3).

Drawing on the experience gained from implementing earlier programmes, the Commission launched phase I of a new initiative on vocational training in 1994, called Leonardo da Vinci, combining Force, Petra, Eurotecnet and Lingua. Developed in conjunction with EU structural funds, Leonardo was designed to rationalize and streamline existing actions and improve their effectiveness on the basis of a common vocational training policy. The aim was to promote the social and occupational integration of young people by enhancing their employability, while expanding and developing access to high quality continuing training and lifelong skills. In keeping with the principle of subsidiarity and in recognition of the diversity of systems, the action programme took account of the need to ensure that, within a common framework of objectives, member states would be free to choose means appropriate to their situation. The measures proposed were intended to support national systems, arrangements and policies, innovative actions for the training market and the development of a European dimension in training, while encouraging the dissemination of best practice.

The Leonardo programme was expected to assist about 80,000 young people per year by the end of the programme to enable them to undergo initial training or employment in enterprises. The Grundtvig scheme was intended to help at least 7000 adult education students per year to benefit from studying abroad in an attempt to stimulate the development of lifelong learning [3.20, articles 25, 29].

The European research area

EU-funded research and technological development have also become an important area of cooperation and mobility between member states. Since 1984, the Commission has managed a series of framework programmes (FPs), designed to strengthen the scientific and technological base of European industry, and improve the European economy's competitiveness in the world market, by coordinating transnational research partnerships, disseminating and utilizing research findings [3.22].

In January 2000, a communication from the Commission set out the parameters for a 'European research area' [3.13], which was to be a driving force for economic growth, capable of competing with the United States and Japan. An important component of the strategic goal set at the Lisbon European Council in preparing for the transition to a knowledge-based economy was an improved research and development policy [1.20]. Member states were required to apply the OMC with a view to developing appropriate mechanisms for networking national and joint research programmes, designed to have a structuring effect on research activities conducted in Europe. The Commission's Community framework programme for research activities in 2002–06 had the express aim of contributing to the creation of the European research area by introducing new instruments (networks of excellence, integrated projects) and by encouraging Community participation in national programmes carried out jointly under article 169 of the EC Treaty.

A specifically social dimension was, progressively, been built into the general objectives of the FPs, aimed at 'improving the human research potential and the socio-economic knowledge base', and gaining a better understanding of the 'social and economic challenges' confronting Europe [3.22]. The FPs were also designed to enhance the career development of researchers through training and mobility, thereby adding European value by increasing the quality and quantity of the Union's scientific potential, and strengthening its competitive edge. The budget allocated to training and career development for 2007–13 amounted to 4.7 billion euros, compared with 610 million for research in socio-economics and the humanities, thereby confirming the Union's strong commitment to intra-European training and mobility.

NATIONAL TRENDS IN EDUCATION AND TRAINING

Although directives on the mutual recognition of vocational and professional qualifications involved examining their content, crucially European policy on education and training has not sought to influence national education systems, except indirectly by exposing educators and trainers to different approaches through exchange and mobility programmes, and by recognizing the equivalence of qualifications and of studies of the same duration. The consolidated version of the EC Treaty [1.8, articles 149–50] explicitly ruled out all attempts to harmonize national legislation or to interfere with national practices. This non-interventionist stance may be attributed to two factors in particular. Firstly, member states have resisted supranational legislation in areas where they consider national sovereignty to be paramount. Secondly, the experience of seeking to harmonize qualifications showed how difficult and counterproductive it would be to attempt to standardize educational systems leading to different qualifications. This section examines the main trends in education and training arrangements across member states to determine whether national policies in this area are showing signs of convergence in line with economic integration.

Participation in national education and training schemes

In keeping with the spirit of European policy, all member states have been investing more heavily in the education and training of their young people. In the early 2000s, at any one time, over 100 million pupils were enrolled in an educational institution across EU25, and around 17 million were in tertiary education. Despite the fall in the proportion of younger people in the population due to lower birth rates, the percentage in education rose steadily during the 1980s and 1990s, reaching about a quarter of total population in 2002. The number of graduates had risen to 3.1 million by 2003, an increase of more that 30 per cent in five years [2.5, 10/2005, table 1; 19/2005, p. 1].

Differences remain between member states with regard to the length of compulsory schooling and levels of participation at the beginning and end of the compulsory period. In the early 2000s, compulsory schooling began at the age of four in Luxembourg and Northern Ireland, but at seven in Bulgaria, Denmark, Estonia, Finland and Sweden [3.24, 2005, figure B1]. In Belgium, France, Italy and Spain, pre-primary schooling was standard practice at the age of three and covered close to 100 per cent of the age group. The proportion of three-year-olds in education was over 50 per cent except in Austria, Cyprus, Finland, Lithuania and Poland. It was close to zero in Ireland and the Netherlands. By age four, the proportion of children in education had risen to almost 90 per cent or more in the Czech Republic, Denmark, Hungary, Malta and the United Kingdom. It fell below 50 per cent only in Finland, Ireland and Poland [2.5, 10/2005, table 1]. More than 90 per cent of pupils in primary schools had access to before- and after-school childcare in France, Hungary, Slovenia and Sweden, compared with between 45 and 50 per cent in Cyprus and Greece, and less than a 33 per cent in the United Kingdom, 22 per cent in Romania and only 13 per cent in the Netherlands [3.24, 2005, figure B12].

All EU member states were moving towards 16 as the standard school-leaving age. In the early 2000s, full-time compulsory schooling ended at 16 in the majority of countries. After that age, young people were obliged to remain in education and training for one year (part-time) in the Netherlands, two years in Belgium and Poland (full-time or part-time) and Hungary (full-time), and three years in Germany. An additional year was possible in Denmark and Sweden, and education could be continued in a vocational training institution in Lithuania from the age of 14 and in Latvia from 15 [3.24, 2005, p. 62].

In the early 2000s, the extension of schooling and vocational training meant that, at age 18, across the Union as a whole, only 24 per cent of young people were not in some form of education. However, in the United Kingdom, only 55 per cent of young people aged 18 were in education. Lower rates were found only in Malta (43 per cent) and Cyprus (28 per cent). At the other end of the scale, the level reached over 90 per cent in Finland and Sweden. At age 24, almost 20 per cent of Europeans were still in education, with Finland recording the highest rate at nearly 40 per cent, followed by Denmark and Sweden with around 30 per cent. The rates for Malta, Ireland, the United Kingdom and Cyprus were closer to 10 per cent [2.5, 10/2005, table 1].

The British education system has long been distinguished in Northern Europe by relatively early selection of the transition routes determining later participation rates and early exit. The Nordic states provide an example of late entry and late exit. The net effect of differences in the length and timing of studies on the age distribution of students in tertiary education is that more than 15 per cent of students were aged over 31 in Denmark, Germany and Sweden, while half of all students were under 20 in Belgium, Cyprus, Malta, Ireland and the United Kingdom [3.24, 2005, p. 155]. In the early 2000s, the age on entry to tertiary education was most widely dispersed in the United Kingdom, ranging from 19 to 40 years, and from 21 to 39 years in Sweden. In Cyprus, France, Greece, Poland and Slovakia, 70 per cent of all student entries were between the ages of 18 and 25 or 19 and 26 [2.5, 19/2005, p. 3].

With longer tertiary education and training, the gender balance has shifted: participation at this level has been increasing at a faster rate for women than for men, with the result that, on average 110 women were enrolled in tertiary education for every 100 men in 2002. They outnumbered men everywhere except Germany. In the Baltic states, 160 women were enrolled for 100 men. The higher rates for women may be explained to some extent by the tendency for boys to opt strategically for vocational upper secondary education, whereas girls more often obtained general educational qualifications at this level and, therefore, needed to pursue tertiary education to gain more occupationally relevant qualifications [3.24, 2005, pp. 153].

Gender differences are reflected in the subjects studied. Despite efforts at EU level to promote technical subjects among women, in the early 2000s they were still more likely than men to study subjects in the humanities, applied arts, education, health and welfare. In the social sciences, business studies and law, women were in the majority except in Denmark, Germany and the Netherlands. Men were more strongly represented in science, mathematics and computing, although the numbers of women enrolling in these subjects had grown at a faster rate than the increase in the proportion of women in tertiary education. Parity had already been achieved in Italy, and women were in the majority in Bulgaria, Portugal and Romania. The disparity in favour of men remained most marked for engineering, manufacturing and construction, especially in Cyprus and the Netherlands. In Bulgaria, Denmark, Estonia, Lithuania and Sweden, however, women accounted for around 30 per cent of students in these subjects [3.24, 2005, p. 156].

Despite the Council directive recognizing qualifications based on three years of higher education after the school-leaving certificate as equivalent throughout the Community [3.2], and the Bologna declaration [3.12] promoting greater standardization of the duration of tertiary education, marked differences in the arrangements for upper secondary level education and training, combined with disparities in the nature, structure and content of university higher education, made it difficult for employers to interpret qualifications obtained in another country. While British students, for example, routinely graduated after three years, and left higher education by the age of 21 or 22 with a qualification recognized in the United Kingdom as an indication of general intellectual and academic ability, in the early 2000s more than 60 per cent of students in Italy, Austria, the Czech Republic, Slovakia, Poland, France, Germany and Spain completed at least five-year programmes, often for specialist tertiary qualifications [2.5, 19/2005, figure 10].

Vocational training and employability

Many attempts have been made to construct typologies portraying the relationship between education and the labour market. The linkage that has developed between schools, firms and labour markets can take a number of different forms. It may be market led and industry based as was long the case in Italy and the United Kingdom. It may be training led and school based as in Belgium, Denmark, France, the Netherlands and Sweden. Or it may be training led and industry based as in Austria and Germany. These interlinkages have arisen as the result of elaborate historical trade-offs between social partners, central and regional government, different pressure groups, taxpayers and workers themselves, each with their own objectives and time horizons (Drake, 1994). The outcome is that the effectiveness of initial vocational and educational training may be influenced by culturally determined conditions, with job opportunities being shaped by the social and economic environment of the country or region in which people live.

Despite underlying differences in approach, by the early 2000s, all member states made provision through the school system for vocational training, and they were progressively incorporating practical work experience and 'second chance' and 'alternance' schemes to help smooth the transition from school to work. Across the Union, entirely school-based initial vocational training remained the most common arrangement, accounting for more than 50 per cent of education at this level in Belgium, Italy and Sweden. Efforts to involve enterprises in the organization of vocational education and training programmes had resulted, however, in more than half of vocational training being delivered, at least partly, at the workplace, accounting for over 50 per cent of provision in Denmark and Germany. Nowhere was the workplace the main locus of vocational training [3.23, 2001, vol. 2, graph 2.1].

To ensure continued access to (re)training throughout working life, the employment guidelines for 2005–08 set an average EU participation rate in lifelong learning of 12.5 for working-age population (25–64) of at least 12.5 per cent by 2010. The average lifelong participation rate in training for EU25 stood at 10.8 per cent in 2005, due largely to the strong performance of the Nordic states, the Netherlands, Slovenia and the United Kingdom [1.18, 2005, p. 124].

Studies of continuing vocational training in enterprises confirmed that both provision and participation were much more common in northern than in southern Europe [2.5, 3/2002]. In the early 2000s in many of the central and east European member states, attempts to set up vocational training programmes were still being hampered by lack of resources and poor coordination between social partners, resulting in low levels of provision (Masson, 2003).

Labour force survey data for 2005 across the Union reflect the development of education and training provision for young people in relation to employment and activity rates for the 15 to 24 age group. Activity rates represent the proportion of the relevant age group either employed or unemployed. Since employment covers those working part and full time, it may include young people undergoing training schemes involving a combination of work experience and periods spent in training institutions, or students working part time to cover their cost of living. In 2005, the EU25 average activity rate for young people aged 15–24 was around 45 per cent, meaning that more than half of young people in this age group were not available for employment, and possibly in education or training. Again marked variations are found between member states, with rates ranging from 71 per cent in the Netherlands, 68 per cent in Denmark and 62 per cent in the United Kingdom, where part-time working was widespread across all ages, to less than 30 per cent in Bulgaria, Hungary, Lithuania and Luxembourg. Youth unemployment ratios, defined as a percentage of the population aged 15–24 seeking work, were highest in Poland at over 13 per cent, followed by Sweden, Slovakia and Finland, with over 10 per cent. Hungary recorded the lowest rate (4.3 per cent), with Cyprus, Ireland and Luxembourg also displaying levels below 5 per cent [4.14, 2006, pp. 258–86].

During the 1980s, the emphasis placed on vocational education and training, and qualifications implied that it would become increasingly difficult to find a job without a recognized qualification. By 2005, the high skilled (those having completed tertiary education) represented almost 20 per cent of working age population and the low skilled close to 34 per cent [4.14, 2006, p. 54]. Some countries have gone much further than others in improving provision of tertiary education. In 2003, the graduation rate from theoretical and practical programmes lasting at least two years, calculated as the total number of graduates per 1000 population in the 20–29 age group, had reached over 75 per 1000 population in France, Ireland, Poland and the United Kingdom, but it was below 30 per 1000 in Austria, the Czech Republic and Greece [2.5, 19/2005, figure 6]. Labour force survey data do not give a precise indication of the fit between qualifications and jobs, but they do suggest a close correlation between educational level and employment. Across the Union, employment rates were almost 36 percentage points lower for working age population with lower secondary-level qualifications than with tertiary-level education. Except for Slovenia, rates were consistently much lower for the low-skilled population in central and eastern Europe than in northern Europe. Despite the lower overall incidence of employment associated with low skills (46 per cent), it remains that the employment rate with medium skills fell below 70 per cent, suggesting that an adequate skill level may be a necessary but not a sufficient condition for meeting the changing requirements of labour markets [4.14, 2006, pp. 20–1].

In the early 1990s, the assumption that skill shortages were developing as a result of inadequate training was being called into question. In the Netherlands, where the output of qualifications appeared to have increased more rapidly than the skill requirements of jobs, concern was being expressed about the possible threat of over-qualification and 'educational crowding-out', giving the lie to exaggerated claims about the 'burgeoning job content of the economy as a whole and the need for educational levels to rise to keep pace with the increasing sophistication of the modern world of work' (Lindley, 1991, p. 193–4). The tendency was, increasingly, to overproduce graduates and underproduce technicians, resulting in the 'downward filtering' (Lindley, 1991, p. 203) of able people and the placing of graduates in what were previously non-graduate jobs. The phenomenon of diploma inflation and overeducation has since been identified in several member states (Büchel *et al.*, 2003).

Attempts to assess the precise relationship between investment in education and vocational training, research and development and economic performance are inconclusive, although the overall impact is believed to be positive and significant (Wilson and Briscoe, 2004, p. 3). Investment in education usually leads to higher productivity and earnings for the individual. An unintended effect of higher participation rates in education and training, and the demand for rising occupational skills levels is, however, that young people without academic and vocational qualifications are likely to be stigmatized and marginalized.

THE IMPACT OF EU POLICY ON NATIONAL SYSTEMS

Since the signing of the EEC Treaty in 1957, progressively the Community has broadened its social remit. In the area of education and training, policy objectives were extended to take account of the changing needs of the economy and of society at large. The demands of the labour market for more workers with a high level of knowledge and skills, and the ability to adapt to technological change stimulated action programmes designed to ensure that national education systems were equipped to respond not only to initial training requirements but also to the need for constant upgrading and updating of qualifications throughout working life. The growing emphasis on the importance of being able to operate across national and cultural boundaries gave a new impetus to the European dimension of education 'perceived as a practical economic necessity apart from its desirability on cultural and political grounds' [3.4, p. 40]. Within this context, the recognition of qualifications for academic and professional purposes can be interpreted as a necessary support for freedom of movement, which was a primary aim of the original treaty (see Chapter 9).

As in other areas of social policy at EU level, it is difficult to evaluate the success of policies for education and training or to assess their impact on national policy making. The Commission clearly defined its role in this area: it saw itself essentially as a 'catalyst and facilitator of cooperative and common action' [3.4, p. 41], working in accordance with the principle of subsidiarity and respecting diversity of provision. In the early 2000s, the Directorate-General for Education and Culture described the European Union as providing essentially 'a forum for the exchange of ideas and good practice' [3.21, home page, January 2006].

Although tangible results were achieved at regulatory level in terms of the mutual recognition of qualifications and the increase in the number of students and young people who had the opportunity to spend periods of study or gain work experience in other member states, and who might not otherwise have done so, the evidence is that the mobility of workers did not expand commensurably, suggesting that acceptance of qualifications may not be the key factor in relocation of labour as originally believed (see Chapter 9).

The impact of European policy on the harmonization of education and training systems may also have been much less than anticipated. It has been argued that, because the process of mutual recognition of qualifications involved close scrutiny of the structuring of occupations, it provoked a certain amount of convergence of concepts (Merle and Bertrand, 1993, p. 42). Some procedures were called into question, for example the *numerus clausus* imposed in higher education subjects such as medicine in different member states, the professional qualifications required for practice, length of studies, or the mix of qualifications and work experience. As in other areas of European social policy, the continued importance of the principle of subsidiarity and the reluctance of the Union to legislate encouraged a shift towards the idea of identifying common European standards through the exchange of information and good practice, which could serve as reference points, irrespective of differences in national educational systems.

Awareness of educational and training practices in other member states was undoubtedly enhanced, but here too it is not possible to demonstrate that greater cross-cultural knowledge and mutual recognition necessarily resulted in the convergence of education and training systems. The very different national training traditions, as exemplified by the corporatist German dual system, or the British neo-liberal on-the-job arrangement, would seem to reflect irreconcilable conceptions of training policy, demonstrating the extent to which national systems remained path dependent and 'highly societally specific' (Milner, 1998, p. 175).

The proportion of the population participating in post-compulsory secondary and higher education grew significantly throughout the Union, and educational opportunities for women, in particular, improved. However, little evidence can be found to show that these changes could be attributed to the Union's legislation and action programmes, or that they resulted in upwards convergence in terms of the quality of the labour force. Relatively high female participation rates in tertiary education were, for example, being recorded in the Baltic states before they joined the Union, and youth employment figures continued to show marked variations between countries within regions.

In the early 2000s, a strong consensus did seem to be emerging among member states over the need for better coordination between education and vocational training systems and for closer association of the social partners in the design and delivery of training. By bridging the gap between economic and social policy, investment in human resources through quality education and training was being projected as an important component of the European social model and of a European identity, where 'the three essential requirements of social integration, the enhancement of employability and personal fulfilment, are not incompatible' [3.9, p. 4]. The broad definition of lifelong learning developed by the Commission had been extended beyond labour market objectives to include active citizenship, personal fulfilment and social inclusion, emphasizing the centrality of the learner, the importance of equal opportunities and the quality and relevance of opportunities for learning throughout the life course.

Box 3   Secondary legislation and official publications relating to education, training and employability

3.1   Resolution of the Council and of the Ministers of Education, meeting within the Council of 9 February 1976, comprising an action programme in the field of education, *OJ* C 38/1 19.2.1976.

3.2   Council Directive 89/48/EEC of 21 December 1988 on a general system for the recognition of higher-education diplomas awarded on completion of professional education and training of at least three years' duration, *OJ* L19/16 24.1.1989.

3.3   Communication from the Commission to the Council, Education and training in the European Community. Guidelines for the medium term: 1989–92, COM(89) 236 final, 2.5.1989.

3.4   Memorandum from the Commission on higher education in the European Community, COM(91) 349 final, 5.11.1991.

3.5   Council Directive 92/51/EEC of 18 June 1992 on a second general system for the recognition of professional education and training to supplement Directive 89/48/EEC, *OJ* L 209/25 24.7.1992; supplemented by Council Directive 95/43/EC of 25 July 1995, *OJ* L 184/21 3.8.1995.

3.6   Conclusions of the Council and of the Ministers for Education, meeting within the Council of 11 June 1993, on furthering an open European space for cooperation within higher education, *OJ* C 186/1 8.7.1993.

3.7   Commission of the European Communities, The European dimension of education, Green paper, COM(93) 457 final, 29.9.1993.

3.8   European Commission, Growth, Competitiveness, Employment: the challenges and ways forward into the 21st century. White paper, OOPEC, 1994.

3.9   Commission of the European Communities, Education and Training. Teaching and learning: towards a learning society, White paper, COM(95) 590 final, 29 November 1995, OOPEC, 1994.

3.10 Commission of the European Communities, Education – training – research: the obstacles to transnational mobility, Green paper, COM(96) 462 final, 2.10.1996.

3.11 Communication from the Commission, Towards a Europe of knowledge, COM(97) 563 final, 12.11.1997.

3.12 The Bologna declaration of 19 June 1999, joint declaration of the European Ministers of Education.

3.13 Communication from the Commission, Towards a European research area, COM (2000) 6, 18.1.2000.

3.14 Report from the Commission, The concrete future objectives of education systems, COM(2001) 59 final, 31.1.2001; Detailed work programme on the follow-up of the objectives of education and training systems in Europe, *OJ* C 142/1 14.6.2002.

3.15 European Commission, A new impetus for European youth, White paper, COM(2001) 681 final, 21.11.2001.

3.16 Communication from the Commission, Making a European area of lifelong learning a reality, COM(2001) 678 final, 21.11.2001.

3.17 Council Resolution of 14 February 2002 on the promotion of linguistic diversity and language learning in the framework of the implementation of the objectives of the European Year of Languages 2001, *OJ* C 50/1 23.2.2002.

3.18 Decision No. 2241/2004/EC of the European Parliament and of the Council of 15 December 2004 on a single Community framework for the transparency of qualifications and competences (Europass), *OJ* L 390/6 31.12.2004.

3.19 Directive 2005/36/EC of the European Parliament and of the Council of 7 September 2005 on the recognition of professional qualifications, *OJ* L 255/22 30.09.2005.

3.20 Decision No. 1720/2006/EC of the European Parliament and of the Council of 15 November 2006 establishing an action programme in the field of lifelong learning, *OJ* L 327/45 24.11.2006.

3.21 Directorate-General for Education and Culture, home page: http://europa.eu.int/comm/education/index_en.html

3.22 Directorate-General for Research, home page: http://europa.eu.int/comm/research/index_en.html

3.23 Cedefop, *Key data on Vocational Training in the European Union* (occasional), available on-line: http://www.cedefop.eu.int/

3.24 Eurydice and Eurostat, *Key Data on Education in Europe*, OOPEC (periodic), available on-line: http://www.eurydice.org

3.25 Eurydice, *Key Data on Teaching Languages at School in Europe*, (occasional), available on-line: http://www.eurydice.org

4 Improving Living and Working Conditions

The emphasis in the Community's and Union's treaties and charter on workers' rights combined with the need to create conditions that would facilitate freedom of movement of labour between member states explains why issues concerning the equalization of living and working conditions have always been high on the policy agenda. As with social security and educational qualifications, disparities between member states in the treatment of workers could be seen not only as a factor inhibiting mobility but also as a source of unfair competition. The objective of simultaneously achieving harmonization and the improvement of living and working conditions, therefore, featured in the Treaty establishing the European Economic Community (EEC) [1.2]. It was retained in subsequent treaties and in the Community Charter of the Fundamental Social Rights of Workers of 1989 [1.12], albeit with the accent on working rather than living conditions.

In the EEC founder member states, industrial accidents and occupational diseases were among the first contingencies to be covered by national employment insurance. Since industrial health problems had long been a concern of the original member states, the Community's role in industrial welfare was primarily to try and stimulate interest in coordinating action to protect workers, thereby removing barriers to the freedom of movement of goods, services and labour. The rights of workers to a decent standard of living and a high level of protection at the workplace have continued to receive priority. Progressively, the areas encompassed under the general heading of living and working conditions have been clarified and widened to include health and safety at work, working hours, employment contracts, conditions governing collective redundancies and bankruptcies, information, consultation and participation of workers, the environment and public health.

As the Union's remit was extended (see Chapter 1), the improvement of living and working conditions remained firmly on the policy agenda. Although the approach has tended to remain cautious for reasons that will become more apparent in this chapter, living and working conditions provide another example of the way in which policy can be moved forward at EU level through the legislative process, action programmes and information campaigns.

The first part of the chapter looks at the development of Community policy, with particular reference to health and safety at work, working time arrangements and public health. Practices in individual member states are then compared, with a view to assessing the extent to which the Union's action may have encouraged member states to adopt common standards in line with the developing European social model.

COMMUNITY POLICY FOR IMPROVING LIVING AND WORKING CONDITIONS

The 1951 Treaty establishing the European Coal and Steel Community (ECSC) [1.1] set a number of precedents for the six original member states. Article 3(e) stated the aim of promoting improved working conditions and an improved standard of living for workers in the coal and steel industries while also seeking harmonization. The 1957 Treaty establishing the European Atomic Energy Community (EAEC) [1.3] devoted ten of its 225 articles to health and safety. Articles 30–9 set out the basic standards to be observed for the protection of the health of workers and the general public against the dangers of ionizing radiations, and laid down the legal procedures for ensuring they were harmonized and respected. This section examines how the themes of living and working conditions have developed in Community law, policy statements and action programmes since the 1950s.

Living and working conditions in the EEC Treaty

Several references were made in the EEC Treaty to the need to improve living and working conditions, although no clear guidance was given about how equalization between member states should be defined and achieved. Extending article 3(e) of the ECSC Treaty, article 117 affirmed 'the need to promote improved working conditions and an improved standard of living for workers, so as to make possible their harmonisation while the improvement is being maintained' [1.2]. Such improvements were expected to ensue automatically from the functioning of the common market, both through harmonization of social systems and from procedures for approximation of provisions as laid down by law, regulation or administrative action (see Chapter 2).

Among the tasks assigned to the Community, article 2 of the EEC Treaty referred to 'an accelerated raising of the standard of living'. Article 36 included an oblique reference to 'the protection of health and life of humans' in the context of the customs union. In addition, one of the objectives set for the European Social Fund was to improve employment opportunities for workers, thereby contributing to the raising of their standard of living (article 123).

The areas identified for close cooperation in article 118 of the treaty covered employment, labour law and working conditions, basic and advanced vocational training, social security, prevention of occupational accidents and diseases, occupational hygiene, the right of association and collective bargaining. Article 120 dealt with the equivalence of paid holiday schemes. The key aspects of working conditions were thus recognized as social policy issues, but the treaty did not specify the standards to be achieved, nor did it set a timetable for implementation.

Notwithstanding these limitations, in the field of industrial welfare, economic interests provided a powerful incentive for Community action in the early years of the EEC. Common standards of protection against industrial hazards were needed to prevent any one country from gaining a competitive edge and to avoid a situation where migrant workers might be treated differently from one member state to another. In the 1960s, studies were commissioned on topics such as occupational diseases, industrial safety, the influence of human factors in the prevention of accidents, and the health and protection of women and young people. Programmes were organized to enable senior managers to visit other member states with the intention of alerting them to practices elsewhere, and safety consciousness raising exercises were initiated. The Commission drafted a series of directives and recommendations in an attempt to standardize practices, to protect and compensate workers in the areas of industrial medical services and diseases, paying special attention to young workers and working mothers in industry. Substantial progress was made during the 1960s in reaching agreement over safety standards, thus creating a sound basis for future legislation.

Action programmes to improve living and working conditions

Industrial health and safety were already under consideration in 1974 when the Commission presented its social action programme (see Chapter 1). In the same year, the Council set up an Advisory Committee on Safety, Hygiene and Health Protection at Work. The Council's brief included issues such as training, research, data collection, groups of workers at risk, provision in sectors subject to special hazards, as well as the harmonization of regulations for products and processes. The Commission extended its interest to medical research and common action on emerging health problems, such as poor environmental conditions and stress. An environmental protection programme was prepared in response to growing public concern about pollution from noxious materials, and also in recognition of the fact that pollutants do not respect national borders.

In 1975, the Commission signalled its commitment to this rapidly developing policy area by establishing the European Foundation for the Improvement of Living and Working Conditions in Dublin. The foundation was set up to monitor progress, undertake analyses, studies and research. It was also made responsible for disseminating knowledge on a systematic and scientific basis concerning the consequences of economic development, diminishing natural resources and environmental quality, as well as persistent social and regional disparities in living and working conditions. Its brief included advising Community institutions and other policy-making bodies in member states on objectives and guidelines for action in areas of topical interest. By the early 2000s, the focus had shifted to job creation, mobility and work–life balance [4.17].

Living and working conditions in the Single European Act

The next landmark in policy for improving living and working conditions was the Single European Act (SEA) of 1986 [1.5]. A new article (118a) advised member states to 'pay particular attention to encouraging improvements, especially in the working environment, as regards the health and safety of workers'. It reiterated the aim of harmonizing conditions but introduced the important principle of qualified majority voting for decisions on legislative action in this area (see Chapter 1). Article 100a confirmed that health, safety, environmental and consumer protection were to be governed by qualified majority voting and added that 'a high level of protection' should be taken as a base. Article 118b referred to the need to develop the dialogue between management and labour at European level. Article 118a facilitated the legislative process, but it limited the scope for Community intervention to avoid imposing administrative, financial and legal constraints that might adversely affect small and medium-sized undertakings. Member states were left to maintain or introduce more stringent measures to protect workers.

The SEA coincided with a spate of action in the area of public health, even though the Community had no authority in this field. In

1987, the Commission launched its first public health initiative, 'Europe against Cancer', aimed at reducing mortality from cancer. The main thrust of policy was the promotion of cooperation in the area of research and dissemination of information about the most effective national practices. The programme contained actions for prevention, information, education and training, leading to proposals for a ban on smoking in public places, rules on the maximum tar content of cigarettes, and the labelling and advertising of tobacco products [4.6].

Living and working conditions in the 1989 Community charter

Despite the action programmes of the 1970s, the Community had been reluctant to intervene in the industrial bargaining process. Delors' attempt to launch the social dialogue was slow to gather momentum. By the late 1980s, however, worker participation and consultation over changes in working conditions and work organization were high on the collective bargaining agenda, as illustrated by the Community Charter of the Fundamental Social Rights of Workers [1.12]. Several articles in the charter focused on the improvement of living and working conditions, presented as an important element in policies for equalizing opportunities and promoting mobility. The charter provided a firm statement of the Community's objectives in this area, stating that:

> The completion of the internal market must lead to an improvement in the living and working conditions of workers in the European Community. This process must result from an approximation of these conditions while the improvement is being maintained, as regards in particular the duration and organisation of working time and forms of employment other than open-ended contracts, such as fixed term contracts, part-time working, temporary work and seasonal work. [1.12, §7]

In addition, the reference in the EEC Treaty (article 120) to maintaining 'the existing equivalence between paid holiday schemes' was made more specific. The charter laid down the right of workers to a weekly rest period and to annual paid leave, stipulating that the duration 'must be harmonised in accordance with national practices while the improvement is being maintained' [1.12, §8].

In line with the general aim of improving living and working conditions, Community policy on health protection and safety at the workplace was also set out in §19 of the charter, which stated that: 'Every worker must enjoy satisfactory health and safety conditions in his [*sic*] working environment. Appropriate measures must be taken in order to achieve further harmonisation of conditions in this area while maintaining the improvements made.' The same paragraph required that account should be taken of 'the need for the training, information, consultation and balanced participation of workers as regards the risks incurred and the steps taken to eliminate or reduce them'. The terms used to define levels of provision ('satisfactory' and 'appropriate') were unspecific, like those referring to social protection. As in §3, which covered freedom of movement and conditions of residence, and §8 on rest periods and annual leave, the objective of achieving harmonization was, however, made explicit (see Chapter 2).

Under a section on the protection of children and adolescents, the charter set out restrictions on working hours for young people and the prohibition of night work under the age of 18 [1.12, §22]. In recognition of the different practices adopted across the Community, and in accordance with the subsidiarity principle, exceptions could be made to conform to the stipulations in national legislation.

The Community charter thus confirmed and reinforced the general aims set out more than 30 years previously in the EEC Treaty. Work organization and the employment contract were presented as major components in the improvement of living and working conditions and as areas where the Community was, within limits, competent to act.

Implementation of the provisions of the 1989 Community charter

Although the charter did not have binding force, it did empower the Commission to submit proposals for initiatives under the terms of the treaties, with a view to adopting the legal instruments needed for effective implementation within the context of the completion of the Single European Market (SEM). The programme for implementing the charter [1.13] demonstrated the capacity of the Commission to work within the constraints of national and sectoral interests in taking forward action in this area. A number of specific proposals were made for binding instruments in fields where safety was a cause for concern.

Council Directive 89/391/EEC 'on the introduction of measures to encourage improvements in the safety and health of workers at work' [4.1], issued in 1989, laid down the main principles to be applied in other directives on the subject. It covered all sectors of activity and all workers except the self-employed and domestic servants. Employers were to take a much more proactive stance. Their obligations were clearly set out. Not only were they required to ensure health and safety of workers in every aspect of work, and to develop a health and safety policy, but they also had the duty of assessing and recording risks, informing and consulting workers, providing training and taking preventive measures. Workers were given the right to make proposals relating to health and safety and to appeal to stop work if in danger. In return, they had the duty to follow instructions from employers regarding health and safety and to report on potential dangers.

Following on from this framework directive, ten proposals were made to improve conditions for specific categories of workers. Council recommendations on occupational diseases were updated. A regulation was proposed on the establishment of a European Agency for Health and Safety at Work, which was set up in Bilbao in 1994. The agency was given the task of collecting and disseminating technical, scientific and economic information on health and safety at work, promoting the exchange of information and cooperation between member states, and contributing to the development of protective action programmes.

Despite the efforts made in this area and the problem of collecting reliable data, of approximately 120 million workers in the Community in the early 1990s about 10 million suffered an industrial accident or occupational injury every year [1.15, 1993, p. 65]. The aim was to alert member states to the importance of the social and economic aspects of problems concerning safety, hygiene and health at work and to make workers, employers and young people more aware of the risks at the workplace and the action needed to deal with them.

The Commission took advantage of the provisions of article 118a of the SEA to bring forward legislation that had made little progress during the 1980s, thereby demonstrating how qualified majority voting can be exploited within the context of health and safety at work to introduce contentious legislation. Despite continuing British opposition, a draft proposal was brought forward in 1990 covering the organization of working time. The aim was to protect workers against excessively long working hours and against an organization of working time that could be detrimental to their health and safety [4.2]. It raised the issue of the harmful effects of practices introduced under the banner of flexibility. Directive 93/104/EC 'concerning certain aspects of the organization of working time' [4.2], which was eventually adopted in November 1993, laid down a set of minimum provisions not only for daily and weekly rest periods, but also for conditions relating to shift work, night work, and health and safety protection for workers subject to changes of rhythm in their working hours. The minimum daily rest period was set at 11 consecutive hours for a 24-hour period, minimum paid holidays at four weeks, and the maximum working week at an average of 48 hours.

The definition of night work was extended to cover workers who occasionally worked at night, and provisions were made for health assessments. The Commission was concerned to avoid creating problems for individual firms or sectors of activity with special needs, for example because their activities are subject to seasonal fluctuations. A number of possibilities were, therefore, left open for derogation, and consultation procedures were strengthened. Employers and representatives of workers were not, however, to be prevented from concluding collective agreements on the organization of working time, provided equivalent compensatory rest periods were granted.

The Commission had also been trying since the early 1980s to have proposals adopted on a related topic, atypical work, in its efforts to resolve the problems created by the rapid growth in the number of workers not covered by a standard open-ended full-time employment contract. The interests of atypical workers were dealt with indirectly by two Council directives in 1991. In Directive 91/383/EEC [4.3], a proposal put forward as a measure for health and safety at work aimed to improve the conditions of workers with a fixed duration or temporary employment relationship. Directive 91/533/EEC [4.4] made provision for a form of proof of an employment relationship, as a means of improving the transparency of the labour market in a context where more flexible forms of employment – part-time, distance working, home or teleworking – had become widespread and were tending to marginalize large sectors of the labour force. The purpose of the directive was to clarify the essential conditions of the employment relationship.

A proposal for a directive concerning the protection at work of pregnant women, or women who have recently given birth, was also brought forward under article 118a within the meaning of the framework directive as a health and safety measure. Directive 92/85/EEC [4.7] covered not only exposure to agents liable to damage health but also the contentious issue of leave arrangements, duration of work and employment rights, which would most probably have prevented the passage of the proposal had it been subjected to unanimous voting.

Since the focus was on workers, the charter did not refer to public health. In 1991, however, the Commission had launched a programme for 'Europe against AIDS', aimed at containing and combating the spread of the disease throughout the Community [4.6]. A resolution of the Council and the Ministers for Health in the same year drew attention to the importance of health policy choices [4.5]. Member states were urged to work together to identify common problems of public health and, if appropriate, develop common solutions.

Living and working conditions in the amended treaties

The Agreement on Social Policy, signed in 1992 by all member states except the United Kingdom and annexed to the Treaty on European Union [1.6], set out further details of European policy in the area of living and working conditions. The provisions made were subsequently incorporated into the Treaty of Amsterdam [1.7] in 1997. The consolidated version of the EC Treaty [1.8, article 137] confirmed that measures could be taken by qualified majority voting to improve the working environment and working conditions, to protect workers' health and safety, to promote information and consultation, advance equality between men and women, and integrate persons excluded from the labour market. Unanimous voting was still required for matters concerning social security of workers, protection of employment contracts, representation, collective defence and codetermination, the employment conditions of third-country nationals and financial support for employment promotion. The right of association, to strike or impose lock-outs was explicitly excluded from the treaty provisions.

Council Directive 94/45/EC [4.9] on the establishment of works councils was the first directive adopted after the signing of the Agreement on Social Policy; its purpose was to improve the right of employees to information and consultation. The directive's stipulations applied to Community-scale undertakings with more than 1000 employees and at least two establishments in different member states, each employing at least 150 people. Due to the British government's opt-out, the directive did not apply to the United Kingdom.

During the 1980s, the British government had also blocked an attempt by the Commission to formulate a directive requiring the extension to part-time workers of the rules governing full-time workers. Council Directive 97/81/EC [4.10] on part-time work was finally concluded under a framework agreement between the social partners. The main objective was to eliminate discrimination against part-time workers by ensuring their rights on a *pro rata temporis* basis, while encouraging greater flexibility in the organization of working time in the interests of employees and management. The directive was binding as regards results, but it left national authorities free to choose the form and methods to be used, and to introduce more favourable provisions.

The revised treaties reinforced the Union's remit in the area of health and safety at work and working conditions. They also extended its powers into an area that had been only indirectly alluded to in the original treaty. The Union's activities listed in the consolidated EC

Treaty [1.8] included 'a contribution to the attainment of a high level of health protection' (article 3 §p). Article 152 of the new title XIII on public health set out the aim of ensuring a 'high level of human health protection...in the definition and implementation of all Community policies and activities', as exemplified by article 174 under title XIX on the environment. This aim was to be achieved by encouraging cooperation between member states and, if necessary, by lending support to their action (article 152 §2). As in other social areas, member states were to retain responsibility for coordinating their own policies and programmes and for delivering health and medical care, but the Commission was authorized to take initiatives to promote such coordination.

In the Maastricht Treaty, action at EU level was to take the form of research, health information and education, covering major health scourges such as drug dependence, an example subsequently removed by the Amsterdam Treaty, although a European Monitoring Centre for Drugs and Drug Addiction was established in Lisbon in 1994. Instead, an expanded and reinforced section of article 152 (§4 subsections a, b) in the consolidated EC Treaty laid down the measures the Council was empowered to take to achieve the objectives specified in the article. These changes reflected public concern in the 1990s about the spread of AIDS, the BSE crisis and the possible dangers to public health from genetically modified foods. A third subsection specified that incentive measures would be adopted to protect and improve human health. In this case, harmonization of national laws and regulations was explicitly ruled out. The final paragraph of the article (§5) stressed, once more, the importance of respecting the responsibilities of member states for the organization and delivery of health services and medical care.

In a communication 'on the framework for action in the field of public health' [4.5], published in the year following the signing of the Maastricht Treaty, the Commission reiterated the need for member states to identify common objectives and goals, and set out the legal bases for action at EU level. In 1996, the European Parliament and Council adopted a programme of Community action on health promotion, information, education and training within the framework for action in the field of public health for the period 1996–2000 [4.6]. The programme included actions on health promotion strategies and structures, specific prevention and health promotion measures, health information, health education and vocational training in public health and health promotion. At the same time, a third action plan to combat cancer (646/96/EC) and programmes of Community action on the prevention of AIDS (647/96/EC) and drug dependence (97/102/EC) were also adopted [4.6]. These actions were part of the Community's overall health promotion strategy. The aim was to encourage member states to cooperate in exchanging information, policies and programmes, and to coordinate their actions, thus foreshadowing the formal introduction of the open method of coordination (OMC) at the end of the decade.

With the completion of the SEM, the signing of the Community charter, the revisions to the EEC Treaty, the framework directive on health and safety at work, and the many action programmes proposed by the Commission, the Union's competence in the broad area of living and working conditions had become far reaching. The introduction of qualified majority voting in the SEA for issues concerning health and safety at work and the improvement of the working environment meant that member states would more easily be able to implement any measures thought necessary. It also implied that attempts could be made to use the revised voting and consultation procedures to push forward proposals in the social field that would most probably have been rejected if unanimous voting had been applied. The treaty revisions gave some impetus to Community action in the field of public health, moving it on from the focus on health and safety at work. By requiring that a high level of health protection should be ensured in the definition and implementation of Community policies and activities, article 152 highlighted the need for member states to cooperate in obviating all sources of danger to human health. The Commission sought to maintain the momentum by presenting a communication in 1998 'on the development of public health policy' [4.5], setting out the case for a fundamental revision to the Community's public health strategy in the face of new health threats, increasing pressures on health systems, the enlargement of the Union and the new treaty provisions.

Three main strands were identified for future Community policy: improving information for the development of public health; reacting rapidly to threats to health; and tackling health determinants through health promotion and disease prevention. In all three areas, the Commission clearly marked out the role it would play in collecting, analysing and disseminating information, in surveillance, and in promoting actions designed to improve public health, thus giving substance to the extension of its own remit.

Quality of life and work as fundamental rights

The objectives set by the European Council in Lisbon in March 2000 and in Nice in December 2000 [1.20] included the creation not only of more jobs but also of better quality work in a safe and healthy working environment. The Union's charter of fundamental rights [1.21] set the parameters for its sphere of action by affirming the freedom to choose an occupation and the right to engage in work (article II-15), to conduct a business, in accordance with Union law and national laws and practices (II-16), and the right to equality between men and women in all areas, including employment, work and pay (II-23). Under title IV on solidarity, workers' were assured of their right to information and consultation within the undertaking (II-27), to negotiate and conclude collective agreements, to take collective action to defend their interests, including strike action (II-28), to have access to a free placement service (II-29), to protection against unjustified dismissal (II-30), and to fair and just working conditions that respect their health, safety and dignity, limit maximum working hours, and allow rest periods and annual periods of leave (II-31). The charter made specific provision for the prohibition of child labour and protection of young people at work (II-32). In addition, it unambiguously confirmed the Union's commitment to improving standards of public health, stating that everyone has the right of access to preventive health care, medical treatment and a 'high level of human health protection...in the definition and implementation of all Union policies and activities' (II-35).

The Commission seized the opportunity in the run-up to enlargement to issue a series of communications [4.12], presenting a new strategy on health and safety at work for 2002–06 to improve quality in work. It advocated a comprehensive approach to make work pay, and develop high-quality, accessible and sustainable health and long-term care provision. Flexicurity, or the balance between 'flexibility in working time and security for workers', according to Directive 1999/70/EC [4.11], also moved onto the Union's agenda. In 2006, it was the subject of an extraordinary summit and a green paper [4.13], designed to provide an answer to the problem of how to combine flexible working conditions with social protection without endangering economic competitiveness in globalized markets [4.14, 2006, chapter 2; 4.16, 2006, chapter 7]. From a situation where employment had been of only indirect interest to the EEC founding members, progressively the Union had built up an arsenal of instruments for policy development, combining provisions in the formal treaties with binding legislation, the social dialogue and the OMC. By the early 2000s, together with public health, employment policy had thus become a major, if still contested, plank in the Union's commitment to economic growth and prosperity, and the improvement of living and working conditions.

WORKING CONDITIONS IN MEMBER STATES

The Union's treaty obligations, and the directives, recommendations and resolutions issued over the years established high target standards for living and working conditions, the provision of health and safety at work and for public health that member states are required to meet. With the notable exception of article 152 on public health in the consolidated EC Treaty and the relevant articles in the charter of fundamental rights, legal and policy documents have constantly emphasized the need to harmonize regulations and processes between member states. Yet, standards of health and safety at work, living and working conditions, public health and levels of compliance with Community legislation continue to show marked variations between countries.

The slow progress made by proposals from the Commission for reorganizing working time and resolving anomalies in working conditions may be explained, in part, by the problems involved in trying to reach agreement between countries with different collective bargaining arrangements. In some member states, for example France and other countries with a Latin tradition, decisions regulating employment contracts and working conditions are taken by central government and become an integral part of labour law. In countries with a stronger contractual tradition, such as Denmark and the United Kingdom, negotiations are generally decentralized, either at branch or enterprise level. Germany and the Benelux countries probably lie between the two extremes. Other national traditions, particularly those associated with differences in welfare systems, may also determine reactions to proposals aimed at avoiding distortion of competition by aligning working conditions. Member states may, for instance, be reluctant to support the institutionalization of new working time patterns in the cause of international solidarity when the impact would be to raise labour costs.

A major difficulty facing the Union in the early 2000s was how to ensure that member states with relatively poor provisions for health and safety at work can improve standards so that they approximate to those found in neighbouring countries, while avoiding any levelling down. Progressively, obstacles to harmonization have been recognized. Article 137 of the consolidated EC Treaty (§§2, 5) stipulates that national conditions and rules must be respected, that administrative and financial constraints should not be imposed on small and medium-sized enterprises (SME), and that individual member states should not be prevented from introducing or maintaining their own more stringent measures in these areas of social policy. The let-out clause for SMEs meant that countries, such as those in southern or central and eastern Europe, where commerce and industry continue to be largely dominated by small family firms and the informal sector, have been allowed to maintain lower levels of protection from industrial hazards. The Union thus formally admits, and accepts, the concept of a two-speed Europe and the distinction between core and periphery. In examining national policies for the improvement of working conditions, an attempt is made in this section to assess the extent to which they are compatible with the Union's requirements, while also providing an explanation for some of the problems that have arisen in trying to reach agreement at EU level.

Provision for health and safety at work

The momentum for policy on health and safety at work came largely from member states in northern Europe, where insurance schemes to protect workers against the consequences of industrial accidents were established before the end of the nineteenth century. A century later, the national constitutions of Belgium, Greece, Italy, Luxembourg, Portugal and Spain made provision for the control of health and safety at work. Basic occupational health and safety principles were set out in national legal codes and labour law in Finland, France, Germany and the Netherlands. In Denmark, Ireland and the United Kingdom, civil or common law established individual rights to agreed standards of health and safety at work [4.8, 1999, p. 121].

In several member states, in the late 1980s the scope of existing legislation already went beyond what was required by the 1989 directive [4.1]: Ireland and the United Kingdom, for example, covered self-employed workers, and legislation in Greece, the Netherlands and the United Kingdom offered protection for third parties. Most countries already had statutory provision for consultative procedures for health and safety at the workplace: elected works' councils in Germany, Italy, Luxembourg and the Netherlands; health and safety committees in Belgium, France and Portugal; elected safety representatives in Denmark and the United Kingdom. The requirements of the directive were expected to have most impact on Greece, Ireland and Spain [4.8, 4/92, p. 114]. The member states that joined the Union in the 1990s – Austria, Finland and Sweden – brought with them high health and safety standards and could readily comply with the 1989 directive. By the mid-1990s, all 15 EU member states had transposed the requirements of the directive into their national legislation, and their record on compliance in the area of health and safety at work was looking very strong

(European Commission, 1998). In the United Kingdom, questions were even being raised about the British government's tendency to over-implement Community directives and to be stricter in enforcing them than other member states (Burrows and Mair, 1996, p. 273).

As a prerequisite of EU membership, and to reduce the risk of social dumping and undue labour emigration, candidate countries are required to accept and transpose into national law the whole of the *acquis communautaire*, including social and employment measures. They are also expected to operate using the Union's policy instruments, notably the social dialogue and the OMC. Since the countries in central and eastern Europe that joined the Union in 2004 were already failing to implement their significant existing legislation for the protection of workers from industrial hazards, they had difficulty in conforming to the high standards set by the Union. Health and safety at work was considered to be an area where they would need considerable assistance to comply with the social *acquis* [8.12, vol. 2, p. 38]. Enterprises were not in a position to invest heavily in health and safety at work. In the late 1990s, fatal accidents at work were much more frequent in these countries than in EU15, but since most industrial accidents went unrecorded, official figures for the candidate countries underestimated the real extent of the problem (European Commission and Eurostat, 2004, table A.15). In collusion with workers and trade unions, employers often paid a risk premium for not implementing legislation (Vaughan-Whitehead, 2003, p. 62). Analysis of Eurobarometer survey data shows that workers in the 13 accession and candidate countries were twice (24 per cent) as likely to report negative dangerous or unhealthy working conditions as workers in EU15 member states (Alber and Fahey, 2004, p. 31).

Working arrangements and flexibility

Agreement among member states has more easily been reached over technical standards than over the deployment of human resources. The growing problem of unemployment since the mid-1970s, the diversification of forms of work as a result of technological change, the declining number of workers in manufacturing and agriculture, and growth in the service sector, combined with the increasing proportion of women in the workforce, gave a new impetus to policies designed to deal with the impact of flexible practices on working conditions. European legislation on employment contracts, the organization of working time, atypical and part-time work affords some interesting examples of the shifting emphasis in policy and the resistance to change associated with disparities in existing practices between member states. National legislation and statistics on various aspects of working arrangements provide an indication of the reasons why some member states supported, or opposed, any harmonization designed to reduce competitive advantage.

In the early 1990s when Directive 91/533/EEC [4.4] was under discussion, flexibility in the form of fixed-term contracts was most widely used in Spain, accounting for over 30 per cent of employment, and was least common in Luxembourg (3–4 per cent), Austria, Belgium and the United Kingdom (5–6 per cent). Women were, everywhere, more likely than men to be employed on fixed-term contracts [4.14, 2003, pp. 212–16]. All member states, except the United Kingdom, had transposed the directive by the deadline in 1993 (European Commission, 1998, pp. 14–17), but the use of fixed-term contracts was still not regulated in Denmark, Ireland and the United Kingdom by the late 1990s (European Commission, 1997, p. 45). Despite EU legislation, the proportion of workers reported to be on fixed-term contracts in EU25 countries rose between the mid-1990s and early 2000s. In Spain, the level remained at over 30 per cent, and it was close to 20 per cent in Portugal. Poland saw a particularly marked increase during the period, reaching 25.7 per cent in 2005 [4.14, 2006, table 6, pp. 260–86].

By the early 2000s, the primary reason given by workers in Belgium, Finland, Greece, Portugal and Spain for being employed on fixed-term contracts was that they had not been able to find a permanent job. Among younger people, the main reason given in Austria, Germany, Italy and Luxembourg was that a temporary work contract was being combined with a training arrangement [4.15, 2003, table 32].

High levels of informal, or undeclared, work were a major source of concern for governments because of the effect they could have not only on working conditions and state revenues but also on competitiveness by lowering labour costs. During the 1990s, the number of undeclared workers was thought to be growing, with estimates ranging from 2 per cent of gross domestic product (GDP) in the United Kingdom to 16–17 per cent in Italy and over 20 per cent in Greece. By the end of the decade, three patterns could be identified in the candidate countries: a low level and decreasing share of GDP (8–13 per cent) in the Czech Republic, Estonia and Slovakia; a medium level and decreasing share (14–23 per cent) in Poland, Slovenia, Hungary, Latvia and Lithuania; and a high level and increasing share (21–30 per cent) in Bulgaria and Romania (Renoy *et al.*, 2004, tables 1, 2). A contributing factor to high levels of undeclared work was that employees were frequently required to change their status to self-employed, thereby enabling employers to reduce taxes and social contributions and avoid labour legislation governing working conditions. Self-employed workers then declared the minimal legal activity, thereby limiting their tax liability, but also their social protection rights (Vaughan-Whitehead, 2003, pp. 68–80).

Another aspect of working arrangements subject to marked national variations in practices is working hours. Not only the United Kingdom, which had opposed legislation on working time in the name of flexibility, but also France, Greece, Italy, Luxembourg and Portugal, failed to meet the deadline for transposing Directive 93/104/EC [4.2] on the organization of working time into national law by 1996 (European Commission, 1998, pp. 165–70). Such was the opposition of the Conservative government in the United Kingdom to the directive that it instituted proceedings before the European Court of Justice challenging the validity of the directive on the grounds that the wrong legal base had been used. It argued that the directive went beyond the concept of the working environment and constituted a misuse of the Council's powers (Burrows and Mair, 1996, pp. 279–83). The change of government to Labour in 1997 brought the ideological shift needed for the directive to be implemented, and the directive was transposed into British law in 1998 [4.2]. It was then amended in 2000 by Directive 2000/34/EC [4.2], for transposition by 2004, to extend the scope to transport industries and doctors in training.

A review of the workings of the amended directive in 2003 was the occasion to re-examine the operation of the original directive. The United Kingdom, where a large proportion of workers agreed to sign the opt-out clause, was found to be the only member state where working hours had increased over the decade [4.2, 2003, p. 10]. With the notable exception of the United Kingdom, no clear relationship emerges between length of working hours and legislation on the duration of working time. In 2004, 14 member states had set a statutory limit of 48 hours a week. Only Belgium had fixed the maximum at under 40 hours [4.18, 2004, table 1]. Collectively agreed average weekly working hours were generally lower. They were set at 40 hours in ten member states, and 35 in France, where the reduction in working hours in the early 2000s had been designed to resolve the problem of high unemployment [4.18, 2004, figure 1].

During the 1990s, average weekly working hours fell across the Union, although hours usually worked remained above collectively agreed hours except in Lithuania. In 2005, France and the Netherlands were recording the lowest full-time weekly hours usually worked with 39 or less, whereas Austria, Latvia and the United Kingdom reported the highest figures with over 42. Seven of the 12 countries above the EU 25 average were fifth-wave member states. Everywhere men worked more hours than women. In the United Kingdom, the gender differential reached 4 hours [2.5, 9/2005, table 6; 4.14, 2006, table 7].

In comparison with western Europe, the member states from central and eastern Europe were lagging behind in terms of the regulation of working hours. When they joined the Union in 2004, they were recording average weekly working hours, particularly in agriculture, well above the EU15 average, with very little difference between men and women. Again, official statistics underestimate real working hours, both because of the unregulated hours worked in the informal economy and by self-employed workers, and due to under-reporting of the total number of hours in the construction and manufacturing sectors (Vaughan-Whitehead, 2003, pp. 56–61).

Night work was another area covered by the working time directive. When it was adopted in 1990, two patterns could be identified. In Belgium and the Netherlands, night work was generally forbidden but with derogations for a number of activities. Elsewhere, night work was generally permitted, unless expressly prohibited [4.8, 4/92, p. 40]. In several cases, namely Belgium, France, Germany and Greece, restrictions on night work applied to women. In others, Italy, Luxembourg, the Netherlands and Portugal, the prohibition applied only to pregnant women. Elsewhere, the ban on night work had progressively been lifted for all adults. In 2005, between 10 and 20 per cent of the workforce in EU25 reported sometimes carrying out night work. The highest rates for regular night work were recorded in Slovakia, Malta and the United Kingdom and the lowest in Cyprus [4.14, 2006, p.51].

The 1993 directive included provisions for weekly rest periods and annual paid leave. Practices again varied cross-nationally. In all member states except the United Kingdom, weekly rest periods had been introduced into legislation or collective agreements by the date for implementation of the directive. In most cases, employees who worked on a Sunday had the right to take a compensatory day of rest in the following week or could receive financial compensation [4.8, 4/92, pp. 45–6]. Denmark and the United Kingdom had no legal statutes governing public holidays; elsewhere the number of days ranged from six in the Netherlands to 14 in Spain. Paid annual leave was governed by legislation except in the United Kingdom. The number of days ranged from 15 in Ireland to 30 in Spain [4.8, 4/92, p. 49]. By 2004, all member states made statutory provision for at least 20 days paid leave. In countries operating collective agreements for annual leave, the number

‚ranted generally exceeded the statutory minimum: by eight or ₁ys in the Denmark, Germany, Italy, the Netherlands and Sweden. ₁he law was thus providing at least a safety net. When public holidays were added to annual leave, EU27 average collectively agreed annual leave reached 34 days. Sweden recorded the largest total number of days with 44, followed by France with 41 and Germany with 40. The average for the fifth-wave member states, at 30.5, was below the EU15 figure, with Estonia, Lithuania, Poland and Slovenia providing the smallest number [4.18, 2004, figures 7, 8, table 7].

Part-time work affords another means of adapting the total volume of working time and raising labour productivity. Although Directive 97/81/EC [4.10] on part-time work was not adopted until 1997, the proportion of women employed on a part-time basis had increased during the 1990s across the Union. As with temporary contracts, the regulation of part-time work afforded a means of removing obstacles to competitiveness. When the directive was introduced, the overall distribution of part-time work showed important variations from one member state to another, ranging from under 5 per cent of total employment in Greece to almost 38 per cent in the Netherlands. Rates of over 20 per cent were also recorded in Denmark and the United Kingdom. Part-time work was predominantly a female working pattern, affecting about 33 per cent of women but only 12 per cent of men in the workforce. In the enlarged Union, in 2005 the lowest level of all for men and women was recorded in Bulgaria with 2.1 per cent, followed by Slovakia, Hungary, the Czech Republic and Greece, with 5 per cent or less. By contrast, in the Netherlands, the overall rate had risen to more than 46 per cent. Austria, Belgium, Denmark, Germany, Sweden and the United Kingdom were all reporting rates over 20 per cent [4.14, 2006, pp. 260–86].

The term 'part-time' may be something of a misnomer in that part-time hours can be close to full-time hours. In 2004, women part-timers usually worked nearly 26 hours a week in Romania, and between 23 and 25 hours in the Czech Republic, France, Hungary and Sweden, compared with over 18 hours in Germany and Spain. The relationship between full and part-time hours is ambivalent: in the Czech Republic and Romania both arrangements involve long hours, whereas in Slovenia and the United Kingdom long full-time hours are matched with short part-time hours, and in Belgium and France short full-time hours correspond to long part-time hours [2.5, 9/2005, table 6].

During the 1990s, progressively member states sought to align the rights of part-time and full-time workers, usually by providing *pro rata* entitlements. As for other aspects of working conditions, in Denmark arrangements were a matter for individual and collective agreements. In the United Kingdom, employers and employees were left to make their own contractual arrangements, although part-time workers were entitled to the same statutory rights as full-timers. In several countries, reductions or exemptions were granted from social security contributions to make part-time work attractive for employers. Where part-time arrangements existed in the new member states, they were mainly found in agriculture, often providing a supplementary income, but frequently without social protection cover (Vaughan-Whitehead, 2003, pp. 77–80).

Issues involving working arrangements have continued to be a concern of the Union for two main reasons. Firstly, working time is a factor in production capacity that can be used to create competitive advantage or disadvantage, as exemplified by the use of undeclared or temporary labour. Secondly, by adapting working time and making arrangements more flexible, governments have been seeking a solution to the unemployment problem. EU data on the relationship between hours worked and GDP show that, when they joined the Union in 2004, compared with EU15 member states, the central and east European countries, were recording much higher growth in GDP per hour worked together with longer average weekly working hours when part- and full-time rates are combined [4.14, 2006, tables 4, 7]. Linkages between flexible working arrangements and unemployment are more difficult to demonstrate due to the many socio-economic and ideological factors shaping national practices (Bredgaard and Larsen, 2005).

LIVING CONDITIONS IN MEMBER STATES

Directives aimed at improving living and working conditions have focused primarily on issues regarding the workplace and, more generally, the working environment. Industrial health and disease, and health and safety at work were areas where the Union was able to move relatively quickly to adopt common policies, whereas public health and wider environmental concerns were less legitimate targets for intervention at EU level. Public health has been a wholly legitimate component of policies for improving living conditions only since the 1990s.

Access to health care and quality of life

Whereas the EEC Treaty advocated harmonization of social security systems (see Chapter 2), but progressively abandoned the concept in favour of cooperation, the alignment of public health provision was an area of little interest for the Community's founder members, compared with health and safety at work. Given the very marked differences in healthcare systems between member states, it is not difficult to understand why, when reference is made to public health, as in the revised treaties, the principle of subsidiarity has been strongly upheld.

Except for Italy, which, despite having introduced a national health service in 1978, had a mixed system, all the healthcare schemes of the EEC founding members were based on employment-insurance contributions, which gave workers entitlement to income-related sickness benefits in cases where they were prevented by ill health or disability from pursuing their economic activity. Both workers and their dependants had the right to medical treatment, and provision was extended to pensioners, unemployed people and other categories without a regular income from employment. The countries that joined the Community in the 1970s – Denmark, Ireland and the United Kingdom – had state-run national health services, financed from taxation, to which all residents had access on the basis of need. Of the countries that became EC members in the 1980s, Greece and Spain operated a mixed system closer to that of the continental model but strongly subsidized by the state and heavily reliant on private medicine. Portugal provided health care through a national health service on the basis of residence. Spain introduced such a service in 1986. Of the 1990s member states, Austria operated a social insurance scheme, whereas Finland and Sweden provided health care on the basis of residence, funded mainly from taxation but organized at local or regional level. During the 1990s, healthcare provision in central and eastern Europe underwent the transition from a centralized publicly-funded universal system to a predominantly social insurance employment-related variant of the Bismarckian model, with Cyprus and Latvia retaining a mainly tax-based system (see Chapter 2).

By the early 2000s, virtually the whole population in the EU25 member states was covered for health care, be it through a nationwide health service in return for insurance contributions, through private insurance, taxation, social assistance schemes or, increasingly, through a combination of arrangements. Economic, political, social and demographic pressures for reform were, however, being exerted on healthcare systems across the Union and beyond, provoking greater diversification in funding and delivery mechanisms. Population ageing, rising expectations for healthcare standards, combined with the need to contain public spending to meet the criteria for Economic and Monetary Union (EMU), triggered a wave of reforms in member states. Most countries adopted strategies aimed at establishing 'a viable balance between various market-oriented mechanisms in allocating resources and managing institutions, on the one hand, and a complicated mix of public sector decentralization, sharpened state vigilance, and greater citizen empowerment, on the other' (Figueras *et al.*, 1998, p. 4). Countries with national health services introduced quasi-market incentives, involving contracting for services and competition between providers. In the continental healthcare systems, governments increased their powers of control and regulation to protect equity and solidarity. Cost-sharing arrangements and global budgets were being applied everywhere to contain demand for services. More effective delivery mechanisms, in terms of both processes and outcomes, were being sought, often resulting in decentralized services and a reduction in the amount of in-patient hospital care [2.2; 2.3; 2.4, 2006, II].

Equality of access to health care within the Union has served as a major justification for state intervention, not only in systems where services are provided on a universal basis but also, increasingly, in those with insurance-based systems. Access to health care continues to vary both within and between countries, depending on the conditions governing entitlements. By 2006, very few countries imposed a qualifying period before giving access to health treatment. Patients usually had a free choice of medical practitioner, albeit within certain limitations. Public sector hospital treatment was usually free of charge, but several countries levied a *per diem* maintenance charge on hospital beds. Charges were generally made for medicines, often on a variable scale according to the financial circumstances of the patient and/or the nature of the illness. General practitioners were either salaried employees or paid on a capitation basis, often combined with a fee for service, borne partly by the patient, or payment for treatment was made in full by the patient and was then partially reimbursed [2.4, 2006, II].

Patterns of provision can affect access to services. In all member states, the total number of hospital beds has been falling since the 1980s, particularly in the central and east European countries. In 2002, the number per 100,000 population ranged from under 400 in Denmark, Ireland, Portugal, Spain and the United Kingdom to over 800 in Austria, the Czech Republic and Lithuania. The number of physicians per 100,000 population was also changing, extending from under 230 in Poland, Romania, Slovenia and the United Kingdom to over 600 in Italy (World Health for All Database, 2006). During the 1990s, admission rates and the average length of stay were higher on average in central and eastern Europe than in EU member states, explained to a large extent by norm-based planning and the heavier reliance in these countries on hospital care (Edwards *et al.*, 1998, pp. 237–40).

Whatever the administrative arrangements and the sources of funding, all member states have in common the growing cost of healthcare provision and their efforts to contain spending in this area. In the early 2000s, after expenditure on old age, health represented the second largest budget head for social benefits across the Union. Ireland and the Czech Republic were devoting more than a third of their social protection expenditure to health care, although only Ireland spent more on social benefits for health than for old age, due to its relatively youthful population [2.5, 14/2006, table 4]. In relation to GDP, total healthcare expenditure ranged from nearly 7 per cent in Luxembourg to almost 11 per cent in Germany among EU15 member states, and from 5.5 per cent in Estonia to almost 10 per cent in Malta among the new member states (World Health for All Database, 2006).

The relationship between expenditure on medical care and standards of health is not, however, straightforward, since other social, environmental and cultural factors determine quality of health and care. Cost containment and efficiency drives may not necessarily affect health outcomes as much as was expected by their critics. Marketization can, for example, result in a rapid rise in transaction costs and greater inequality in access, without bringing a significant improvement in the general standard of health care, as demonstrated in the 1990s by the Czech case (Kokko *et al.*, 1998, p. 305). Differences persist between member states in the incidence of certain diseases. In the early 2000s, life expectancy was generally lower in the new member states than in EU15 countries, due to higher death rates from cardiovascular and circulatory diseases associated with tobacco, alcohol and diet. The incidence of trachea, bronchus and lung cancer was over 66 per 100,000 population in Hungary, compared with 20 to 25 per cent in Cyprus, Portugal and Sweden. Regular daily smoking rates reached almost 38 per cent among the population aged over 15 in Greece but fell to 16 per cent in Sweden (World Health for All Database, 2006).

Nor does satisfaction with health care appear to be closely related to the level of spending on health and social protection. Indicators of satisfaction with different life domains place health at the top of the list in Cyprus and in second position in Greece, Ireland and Poland, whereas health is low on the list for Portugal. Common to almost all the fifth-wave member states is the low level of satisfaction with their standard of living, but this is a perception that they share with Germany and Portugal [4.17, 2004, table 5].

FROM WORKING TO LIVING CONDITIONS

One of the pessimistic conclusions drawn from analyses of the pressures working for and against social Europe in the early 1990s was that the social dimension of the Union would become 'a fragmentary arrangement, with the Community presence confined to specific segments of the labour market' (Teague and McClelland, 1991, p. 21). Matters relating to health and safety at work or the working environment provide a good example of what readily came to be regarded as legitimate areas for European intervention, on the grounds that action was needed to provide a satisfactory level of social protection for migrant workers and to avoid distortion of competition. At that time, health and safety at work were described as the 'most active aspect of EC social policy in the employment field' (James, 1993, p. 135). The quantity of legislation on the subject confirmed that the Commission had been more active in this area of social policy than in most others and had taken the initiative in setting standards across the Union.

If the terms 'approximation' and 'harmonization' were used in the 1989 Community charter with reference to living and working conditions, and health and safety at the workplace, whereas they were absent from the paragraphs on social protection, it may be, at least in part, because the principle of standardizing procedures for protecting workers proved to be much less contentious, and possibly more attainable, than the setting of targets for other aspects of working conditions and public health. The Union was able to build on national precedents for health and safety at work and, when the SEA came into force in 1987, to play a central coordinating role, progressively bringing national legislation into line with Council directives and recommendations. The 1989 framework directive was particularly noteworthy in that it probably went further than national legislation in its requirement that employers should adapt working conditions to meet individual needs.

The restructuring of working hours and arrangements for the social protection of part-time workers, or the harmonization of national health systems, were much more contentious areas of policy than health and safety at work in terms of supranational competence. They had to await the introduction of qualified majority voting and the British opt-out from the social chapter, which prepared the way for an extension of Union intervention in the 1990s. Article 3 of the consolidated EC Treaty [1.8] made the attainment of a high level of health protection into one of the Union's objectives, enabling the use of instruments such as action programmes, legislation and research. Even though it explicitly excluded any harmonization of national laws and regulations, the new title on public health confirmed the further extension of the Union's remit, aimed at encouraging greater cooperation between member states. A spate of communications from the Commission in the late 1990s and early 2000s built on the treaty commitment, clearly setting out plans for developing public health policy in a context of European enlargement and with reference to the wider range of policy instruments at its disposal [4.12].

Many reasons help to explain the shift in emphasis from health and safety at work to the quality of working and living conditions, and health protection for the whole population. Pressures to control public spending in the run-up to EMU encouraged governments to look for efficiency gains, and to seek an optimal and equitable distribution of resources. These pressures for change coincided with population ageing and growing care needs, as well as the decline in the working age population, creating problems for the funding of healthcare systems. At the same time, rising public expectations, advances in medical science and new threats to public health had implications for the demand and provision of services in an increasingly open and borderless market. As in other areas of social policy, member states responded by showing their support for a common commitment to achieving high standards. An important challenge for the twentieth-first century was to find ways not only of attaining but also of maintaining equally high standards across an increasingly diversified Union, particularly in countries where the social *acquis* had yet to be fully implemented.

Box 4   Secondary legislation and official publications relating to the improvement of living and working conditions

4.1   Council Directive 89/391/EEC of 12 June 1989 on the introduction of measures to encourage improvements in the safety and health of workers at work, *OJ* L 183/1 29.6.1989.

4.2   Commission proposal for a Council Directive concerning certain aspects of the organization of working time, COM(90) 317 final, 3 August 1990, *OJ* C 254/4 9.10.1990; Council Directive 93/104/EC of 23 November 1993 concerning certain aspects of the organization of working time, *OJ* L 307/18 13.12.1993, amended by Directive 2000/34/EC of 22 June 2000 to cover sectors and activities not covered by Directive 93/104/EC, *OJ* L 105/41 1.8.2000; Communication from the Commission concerning the re-exam of Directive 93/104/EC concerning certain aspects of the organization of working time, COM(2003) 843, 30.12.2003.

4.3   Council Directive 91/383/EEC of 25 June 1991 supplementing the measures to encourage improvements in the safety and health at work of workers with a fixed-duration employment relationship or a temporary employment relationship, *OJ* L 206/19 29.7.1991.

4.4   Council Directive 91/533/EEC of 14 October 1991 on an employer's obligation to inform employees of the conditions applicable to the contract or employment relationship, *OJ* L 288/32 18.10.1991.

4.5   Resolution of the Council and the Ministers for Health, meeting within the Council of 11 November 1991, concerning fundamental health-policy choices, *OJ* C 304/5 23.11.1991; Commission communication on the framework for action in the field of public health, COM(93) 559 final, 24.11.1993; Communication from the Commission on the development of public health policy in the European Community, COM(98) 230 final, 15.4.1998.

4.6   Decision No. 645/96/EC of the European Parliament and of the Council of 29 March 1996 adopting a programme of Community action on health promotion, information, education and training within the framework for action in the field of public health (1996 to 2000), *OJ* L 95/1 16.4.1996; Decision No. 646/96/EC of 29 March 1996 adopting an action plan to combat cancer within the framework for action in the field of public health (1996 to 2000), *OJ* L 95/9 16.4.1996; Decision No. 647/96/EC of 29 March 1996 adopting a programme of Community action on the prevention of AIDS and certain other communicable diseases within the framework for action in the field of public health (1996 to 2000), *OJ* L 95/16 16.4.1996; Decision No.. 102/97/EC of 16 December 1996 adopting a programme of Community action on the prevention of drug dependence within the framework for action in the field of public health (1996–2000), *OJ* L 19/25 22.1.1997.

4.7   Council Directive 92/85/EEC of 19 October 1992 on the introduction of measures to encourage improvements in the safety and health at work of pregnant workers and workers who have recently given birth or are breastfeeding, *OJ* L 348/1 28.11.1992.

4.8   Commission of the European Communities, The regulation of working conditions in the Member States of the European Community, vol. 1, *Social Europe Supplement*, 4/92; OOPEC, 1999.

4.9   Council Directive 94/45/EC of 22 September 1994 on the establishment of a European Works Councils procedure in Community-scale undertakings for the purposes of informing and consulting employees, *OJ* L254/64 30.9.1994.

4.10 Council Directive 97/81/EC of 15 December 1997 concerning the Framework Agreement on part-time work concluded by UNICE, CEEP and the ETUC, *OJ* L 14/9 20.1.1998.
4.11 Council Directive 1999/70/EC of 28 June 1999 concerning the framework agreement on fixed-term work concluded by ETUC, UNICE and CEEP, *OJ* L175/43 10.7.1999.
4.12 Communication from the Commission, Adapting to change in work and society: a new Community strategy on health and safety at work 2002–2006, COM(2002) 118 final, 11.3.2002; Communication from the Commission, Improving quality in work: a review of recent progress, COM(2003) 728 final, 26.11.2003; Communication from the Commission, Modernising social protection for more and better jobs: a comprehensive approach contributing to making work pay, COM(2003) 842, 30.12.2003.
4.13 Commission of the European Communities, Modernising labour law to meet the challenges of the 21st century, Green paper, COM(2006) 708 final, 22.11.2006.
4.14 European Commission, *Employment in Europe*, OOPEC (annual).
4.15 Eurostat, *Labour Force Survey*, OOPEC (replaced from 2004 by quarterly and annual reports), available at: http://ec.europa.eu/eurostat
4.16 European Commission, *Industrial Relations in Europe*, OOPEC (biennial).
4.17 European Foundation for the Improvement of Living and Working Conditions, European quality of life surveys (periodic), available at: http://www.eurofound.eu.int
4.18 European Industrial Relations Observatory, Working time developments (periodic), available at: http://www.eiro.eurofound.eu.int

5 Family Policy on the European Agenda

An underlying principle of European social policy, progressively adopted by the institutions of the European Union (EU), is that national governments should be left to determine how their social protection systems are framed, financed and organized. The Commission has been particularly reluctant to intervene in family welfare, the more so because social policy, as laid down in the founding Treaty of the European Economic Community (EEC) [1.2], centred on workers' rather than individual citizenship rights. The Community had no formal competence to act in the area of family affairs. In addition, and perhaps to a greater extent than in the case of policy for young and older people or ethnic minority groups, views on the objectives and instruments of family policy are divided along ideological lines, both within and between countries. In some member states, family life is considered to belong to the private domain and is, therefore, forbidden territory for explicit state intervention. The resulting diversity of practices is such that the Commission would have been faced with an intractable task if it had sought to extend its social policy remit to the coordination of policies targeting family life.

Under the EEC Treaty [1.2, articles 51 and 122], the obligations of EU member states with regard to family units were confined to promoting freedom of movement of workers and their dependants, and to reporting on the social situation, which, from 1969, included a chapter on matters relating to the family. Nor did subsequent amended versions of the treaties [1.6; 1.7; 1.8] introduce any direct references to family policies. By contrast, the Council of Europe's social charter of 1961 was much less inhibited in its approach to family welfare. For the Council, action in support of families was not contingent on the employment relationship or on freedom of movement. Rather, the social importance of families was openly recognized: 'The family as a fundamental unit of society has the right to appropriate social, legal and economic protection to ensure its full development.' The duties of the state towards individual family members, whether or not the family unit was legally constituted, were stipulated in the social charter (part I §§16–17). Forty years later, following the precedent set by in the Council of Europe's charter, the Charter of Fundamental Rights of the European Union [1.21], signed in Nice in 2000, went some way towards lending legitimacy to family matters in the Union.

Since so little attention is paid to family affairs in the Community's and Union's treaties, this chapter begins by reviewing the direct and indirect references to the family dimension of social policy in official documents, and locates them within the context of freedom of movement and socio-demographic change, the two routes used to justify EU interest in this policy area. Consideration is then given to the different ways in which family life is conceptualized and constructed in member states and to an analysis of the family policy-making process at national level. The conclusion examines the possible implications of EU social policy for families and for the rights of children.

EUROPEAN FAMILY POLICY IN EMBRYO

The social protection systems of most of the EEC founder members were strongly influenced by the Bismarckian statist corporatist model of welfare, with its guiding principle that workers should be guaranteed benefits and a substitute income calculated from their previous earnings in return for the payment of employment-related insurance contributions (see Chapter 2). Since the main objective of the EEC Treaty was to promote economic growth and facilitate free movement of workers, goods and services, the only reference to family members was in article 51 [1.2], which extended social security rights to intra-European migrant workers and their dependants on the same basis as for nationals in the host country. Ten years later, Council Regulation (EEC) No. 1612/68 [9.2] set out provisions for family members to gain access to derived rights as dependants of a migrant worker (see Chapter 9). The preamble to the regulation explicitly stated that 'obstacles to the mobility of workers shall be eliminated, in particular as regards the worker's right to be joined by his [*sic*] family and the conditions for the integration of that family into the host country'. Article 10 defined the family members who fell within the terms of the regulation: '(a) his spouse and their descendants who are under the age of 21 or are dependants; (b) dependent relatives in the ascending line of the worker and his spouse'. Moreover, the provisions for the admission of migrant workers applied to all family members 'dependent on the worker referred to above or living under his roof in the country whence he comes'. The regulation specified, however, that intra-European migrants should be treated in the same way as workers and their families in the host country, so as to avoid any discrimination with regard to social protection, education and other forms of social support (see Chapter 9).

Moving family policy onto the Community's agenda

Despite an early reference in the 1974 social action programme to the objective of ensuring 'that family responsibilities of all concerned may be reconciled with their job aspirations' [1.11, p. 2], no family-related measures were developed in the 1970s. In 1983, however, the European Parliament formulated a resolution 'on family policy in the European Community' [5.2], designed to ensure that family policy should become 'an integral part of all Community policies' (§1c). Such intervention was justified by reference to article 2 of the EEC Treaty [1.2], which gave the Community the broad task of raising living standards, and to article 235, which empowered the Council to act unanimously on a proposal from the Commission, after consulting the European Parliament. The resolution expressed concern about the implications of the changing structure of the family, the different role being played by women in society and within the family, the growing number of lone-parent families, and '*de facto* families'. The Commission was called upon to draw up an action programme, to introduce a comprehensive family policy and, where appropriate, to harmonize national policies at Community level [5.2, §B, 6, 7].

The Council did not respond immediately with any formal action. Then, prompted by a series of worrying reports on demographic trends, in 1989 the Commission drafted a communication 'on family policies', in which it reviewed the changes occurring in society and pointed to the essential role assumed by the family 'in the cohesion and the future of society' [5.3, p. 12]. Four areas of common interest were identified: the means of reconciling work and family life and sharing family responsibilities; measures to assist certain categories of families; consideration of the most deprived families; and the impact of Community policies on the family, in particular the protection of children during childhood [5.3, p. 3]. The Commission justified action at Community level not on the basis of ideology but on the grounds that the family played an important economic role, serving as a 'touchstone for solidarity between generations' and a means of achieving equality between men and women. It noted that action would have to be pragmatic to 'respect the special features of different national policies already created and the varying socio-economic contexts in which such policies play a role' [5.3, p. 15]. Almost immediately the Council responded formally by reiterating most of the proposals made in the communication. Signally, it decided to substitute the theme of equal opportunities for the reconciliation of professional and family life [5.4] (see Chapter 6).

The issues raised by the Commission were not pursued in the Community Charter of the Fundamental Social Rights of Workers adopted in the same year [1.12]. Like the 1974 social action programme [1.11], the charter was primarily concerned with the employment-related rights of workers (see Chapter 1). It did take some account of the status of women as working mothers by recognizing that men and women needed support to enable them 'to reconcile their occupational and family obligations', but again on the understanding that employment status was paramount (§16).

Although the Community had legitimized its interest in family policy by the late 1980s, little progress had been made towards defining a 'comprehensive' European family policy as requested by the European Parliament in 1983. A concrete outcome of the Council's conclusions was, however, the establishment in 1989 of a network of 12 independent national experts (expanded to 15 when the Community was enlarged during the 1990s), known as the European Observatory on National Family Policies. Its brief was to monitor demographic trends, collect information on the situation of families, analyse measures relating to families taken by member states, and report back annually to the Commission, thereby contributing to the Community's knowledge base on social conditions in member states.

Keeping family policy on the European agenda

The Agreement on Social Policy, annexed to the Treaty on European Union in 1992 [1.6], did not directly address family matters. As in article 122 of the EEC Treaty, it conferred on the Commission the task of producing an annual report on social developments. Article 7 specified, however, that the report should indicate the progress made in achieving the objectives set out in article 1, and explicitly referred to the demographic situation in the Community. The same article empowered the European Parliament to invite the Commission to draw up reports on problems concerning the social situation. These provisions were incorporated into the consolidated version of the EC Treaty [1.8, article 143], thereby confirming the Commission's mandate for monitoring family structures as a component of socio-demographic change, and reporting on related social problems. At the same time, the European Parliament was given an opportunity to contribute to the social policy agenda.

The 1992 Council Recommendation 'on the convergence of social protection objectives and policies' [2.1], adopted shortly after the signing of the Treaty on European Union, was much more explicit than the Agreement on Social Policy about the place of family matters on the European agenda. Not only did it set out the aims of removing 'obstacles to occupational activity by parents through measures to reconcile family and professional responsibilities' (§6c), and of integrating individuals who wished to enter the labour market after bringing up children (§6b); it also advocated developing targeted benefits for categories of families in need (§6a). While the 1994 white paper on European social policy did not make any proposals for establishing an EU family policy, it stressed that the Union needed a broadly based social policy that took account of family life [1.15, p. 7].

The United Nations had proclaimed 1994 the International Year of the Family, with the theme of family resources and responsibilities in a changing world, and the motto: 'Building the smallest democracy at the heart of society'. The Commission used the occasion to take a number of initiatives on behalf of the Union, including a Eurobarometer survey of how Europeans perceive the family and the policies implemented by their governments. Like subsequent surveys, it demonstrated convincingly that the family remained an essential value for the vast majority of Europeans. The Commission organized a major conference in conjunction with the German presidency on the future of families, and the European Observatory on National Family Policies produced a report on changing family policies in the member states (Dumon, 1994).

In the preface to an issue of *Social Europe* devoted to 'The European Union and the Family' [5.6], which summarized European and national trends, the Commissioner for social affairs, Pádraig Flynn, stressed the role played by the Commission in identifying similarities and differences in the reactions of member states to changing family patterns, and in stimulating debate through the exchange of information and pooling of experience. Three areas were highlighted for special attention: analysis of the impact Community policies can have on the family; the development of equal opportunities policies, particularly with reference to labour markets; and measures to support families, especially those at risk [5.6, p. 10].

The European Parliament marked the close of the International Year of the Family with a resolution 'on protection of families and family units' [5.5], which argued for a comprehensive approach to family policy at EU level, thereby integrating the interests of families into all Community measures. Families were to be protected, irrespective of type and structure. Special attention was to be given to the needs of children, particularly in lone-parent families and underprivileged households, and measures were advocated to promote equal opportunities for women and men and to deal with domestic violence and child abuse.

The Confederation of Family Organizations in the European Communities (Coface), which had begun its work as a European action committee soon after the signing of the EEC Treaty, contributed to the drafting of the resolution. By the 1990s, Coface embraced more than 70 family organizations across the Union and had consolidated its role as the 'voice' of families in Europe, addressing issues such as the impact of the extension of the Union's powers under the Maastricht Treaty, the risk of a levelling-down of social standards and the need for measures to protect the interests of children and disabled people [5.6, pp. 42–6].

Despite the high profile give to family affairs in 1994, the only reference to the family in the medium-term social action programme for 1995–97 [1.16, p. 21] was in the context of equal opportunities, where the reconciliation theme was pursued. The 1998–2000 social action programme referred to the implications of changing patterns of family life for employment and social protection systems as one of the social challenges facing the Union that the programme was designed to meet [1.19, p. 7]. The communication from the Commission on the modernization and improvement of social protection in the European Union pursued the same theme with the aim of making tax and benefit systems, especially family benefits, more employment friendly [1.17, p. 6].

When the question of family life was addressed formally in the 1990s, the primary justification was not the promotion of family wellbeing. Rather, the main purpose was to protect the health and safety of pregnant workers [4.7], maximize labour market flexibility [4.10], enhance competitiveness by enabling parents to reconcile employment and family responsibilities [6.12], facilitate freedom of movement of workers [9.2] or encourage greater equality of opportunity [6.4]. By the late 1990s, little, if any, progress had been made through hard law towards achieving the aims set in the 1980s by the European Parliament, Commission and Council. The Commission's demographic and social protection reports continued to reiterate the concerns expressed in the 1980s, albeit with greater emphasis on the effects changing household structures were having on the composition of the labour force and on intergenerational relationships [2.2, 1997, pp. 32–6; 5.7, 1997, p. 18].

The launching of Economic and Monetary Union (EMU) provided a new incentive for the Commission to address family matters on the grounds that the efficacy of economic and social policy would be improved if more account was taken of its impact on families. The Commission argued that the failure to adapt social policies in response to socio-demographic change would entail economic and social costs; that family-sensitive social policies can make a contribution to economic performance; and that social policies can serve as a productive factor [1.17; 1.19]. Although the promotion of family policy and the protection of the family unit had not been legitimized as formal treaty commitments, by the late 1990s the Commission had thus found ways of bringing family affairs within its social remit.

In the early twenty-first century, demographic issues were high on the agenda: the postwar baby-boom generations were reaching retirement age, bringing sharply into focus the impact of population ageing on the work force, the sustainability of pensions and public provision of health and social care services (see Chapter 7). Despite shorter life expectancy in the central and east European member states, the steep fall in fertility rates during transition provided a further impetus for policy responses. The main theme of a conference, held during the Irish Presidency, to mark the tenth anniversary of the United Nations Year of the Family was the modernization and development of social policy to meet the challenges posed by the impact of change on families. The Commission went on to publish a green paper in 2005, entitled 'Confronting demographic change', followed by a communication in 2006 on the demographic future of Europe [1.25], in which it emphasized the central role of families in society and called for public policies to support families and extend their life choices by facilitating the reconciliation of employment with family commitments, assisting families in their caring tasks and removing obstacles to choice.

Whereas the Commission's policy initiatives in the area of family affairs were long restrained by its limited competence, the Union's legitimacy to intervene was extended after 2000 due to both the treaty obligation to monitor demographic trends and the inclusion in the Charter of Fundamental Human Rights [1.21] of several articles concerned with respect for private and family life (II-7), the right to marry and found a family, albeit in accordance with national laws (II-9), the rights of the child (II-24) and the right of access to measures designed to facilitate the reconciliation of family and professional life (II-33). After 50 years of EU social policy, incrementally but firmly, the family life of EU citizens had become an explicit topic on the policy agenda.

CHANGING FAMILIES AND FAMILY POLICIES

The focus on employment-related rights and benefits and the Council's and Commission's reluctance to intervene to harmonize national welfare systems meant that member states largely continued to develop their own policy agendas in areas such as family life that were not directly controlled by European legislation. Due to the lack of consensus over the role governments should play and over the objectives and instruments of family policy, no wholly satisfactory and generally accepted operational definition of family life, or of family policy, has been formulated at EU level. The family concept, as defined for statistical purposes in studies of changing family structure over time, emphasizes relationships within households. By contrast, the institutional definitions used to assess the legal status of family members and entitlements to social protection are more interested in relationships within families (Hantrais, 2004, chapter 2). Nonetheless, the 1989 communication from the Commission [5.3] and the 1992 Council Recommendation 'on the convergence of social protection objectives and policies' [2.1, p. 49] identified changing family situations as one of the comparable trends across member states that may lead to common problems, thereby justifying the formulation of common objectives. Changes in family structure were, it argued, likely to affect the ability of families to provide support for their members. The premises on which welfare states were based in most countries were being undermined as the intergenerational balance was upset, and the stability of marriage and family unity were increasingly disrupted [2.2, 1993, pp. 119–21].

In line with the Union's concern about demographic trends and the possible impact of social protection measures on families, the focus in this section is on changing family structures in EU member states and their implications for institutional definitions of the family and for family policy. Change in family structure is analysed as an indicator of the extent to which common trends can be discerned and of the way that traditional assumptions about the family as a unit for social protection have been called into question.

Defining and measuring family change

Since 1973, when the Council of Ministers adopted Directive 73/403/EEC [5.1] on the harmonization of census dates and the standardization of information, data have been collected by Eurostat on the number of marriages, age at marriage, its duration, the number of births to women belonging to different generations, total period fertility rates (the total number of births to all women of childbearing age in a given year) and cohort or completed fertility rates (the number of births to women during the reproductive phase of their lives), age at childbirth, household size and structure [5.8].

Attempts have been made to standardize data so that they can be used to quantify patterns of family building and structure, to record changes over time and compare trends between countries. In recognition of changing family patterns and the growing interest in demographic trends across the Union, progressively data collection has been extended to take account of factors that are more difficult to record, either because of social taboos or because reliable information is not readily available. For example, Eurostat collates national data on the number of extramarital births, lone parenthood and cohabitation. The definitions for these indicators often diverge between member states (Hantrais, 2004). The European Community Household Panel (ECHP) survey, launched in 1993 under the auspices of Eurostat, and subsequently replaced in 2003 by EU Statistics on Income and Living Conditions (EU–SILC), was designed to provide comparable microdata over time on income, employment and the general living conditions of households in EU member states. These surveys cover health, education, housing, income, transitions between different life stages, and living and working arrangements. For census purposes, Eurostat has adopted the United Nations' definition of the family unit, based on the 'conjugal family concept', which defines the family nucleus as two or more persons within a private or institutional household who are related as husband and wife, as cohabiting partners, or as parent and child. Thus a family comprises a couple without children, or a couple with one or more children, or a lone parent with one or more children.' (United Nations Statistical Commission/Economic Commission for Europe, 1998, §191)

Data collected in national censuses generally concern private households rather than families. The United Nations Statistical Commission defines households either as a person living alone, or as a group of persons living together, whether or not they are related, providing themselves 'with food and possibly other essentials for living', and who 'may pool their income to a greater or lesser extent' (§182). In recognition of changing family living arrangements, in 1998, the UN recommendations removed the reference in the 1987 version to 'a married couple', and provision was made for reconstituted families, where 'at least one child is a non-common child' (§195).

Changing family structure

During the period since the EEC was established in 1957, the size and structure of families in member states have been transformed. Far-reaching changes have occurred in patterns of family formation and dissolution, with the result that alternative family forms and non-family households have become widespread. Family size has decreased due to the decline in birth rates and in the number of generations living together. From the mid-1960s, as effective means of contraception became more widely available, and legislation was enacted in most member states to enable the whole population, at least in theory, to have access to birth control, the average total period fertility rates for EU25 countries declined steeply from an estimated 2.66 in the early 1960s to around 1.49 40 years later. The EU rate had fallen well below that level in the United States; it was among the lowest in the world, but above Japan and the Russian Federation. The ten countries that became EU members in 2004 increased the EU population by 28 per cent, but they brought with them some of the lowest low total fertility rates (1.22 and 1.23 in the Czech Republic and Poland) [5.8, 2006, tables A-3, D-4].

Although the trends observed in fertility rates have generally been in the same direction across the Union over the past half century, and the gap between the most and the least prolific nations has been narrowing, important variations remain both between and within member states in the timing, pace, sequencing and degree of change. Across the Union, women have been postponing the age of childbearing. The mean age of EU25 women at first birth had risen from 24.6 in 1965 to 28.3 years in 2004, but all the central and east European countries were recording age at first birth below the EU25 mean [5.8, 2006, table D-9].

Completed fertility rates confirm the overall fall in the long term: Ireland, Portugal and the Netherlands had experienced the most marked decline for the 1930–60 cohorts of women, and Sweden the smallest. For women born in 1960, Cyprus, France, Ireland, Poland, Romania and Slovakia reported completed fertility rates above replacement level, estimated at 2.1 children for every woman of childbearing age. Data for the Nordic countries suggested that some catching up was occurring after a period of delayed childbirth [5.8, 2006, table D-6].

Voluntary and involuntary childlessness is a growing phenomenon in several EU member states (Sardon, 2006, table 7). In the early 2000s, Austria, West Germany and Italy were recording a high proportion of childlessness for women born in 1966 associated with very low fertility rates. France and Sweden displayed high fertility combined with low childlessness. England and Wales were distinguished by high rates of childlessness and of teenage births: almost 10 per cent of pregnancies resulting in births in 2004 were to women aged under 20 (National Statistics, 2006, p. 54). Rates in Estonia and Lithuania, which also recorded high levels, peaked in the early 1990s before falling sharply (Council of Europe, 2003, country tables).

As a consequence of lower fertility rates and greater life expectancy, the proportion of the population aged 0–19 in EU25 decreased from around 32.6 per cent in 1960 to 22.3 per cent by 2005. Italy reported the lowest proportion with 19.2 per cent and Ireland the highest with 27.9 per cent. The decline in the size of this age group was expected to continue during the twenty-first century. Over the same period, the proportion of the population aged over 60 had increased from 14.8 to 21.9 per cent across EU25, ranging from 25 per cent in Italy to 15.3 per cent in Ireland. Although the total dependency ratio (population aged 0–19 and above 60 as a proportion of population aged 20–59) had fallen from 90.1 to 79.2 between 1960 and 2005, attention was focused in the early 2000s on the predicted and irreversible increase in the old age dependency ratio over the next half century. Natural growth in population size was already negative in almost all the new central and east European member states in 2004, often without a compensatory effect from net migration [5.8, 2006, tables B-3, B-4, C-3, C-5, C-6].

Falling birth rates combined with more diverse family living arrangements meant that household size and structure were also changing. Household size varies considerably within and across member states. The proportion of one-person households had reached 15 per cent or more of all households by the early 2000s in the Nordic states, but was closer to 5 per cent in southern Europe and Slovenia. By contrast, households with three or more adults were more common in southern Europe and rare in the Nordic states [5.7, 2003, pp. 179, 199].

While births were being delayed and family size was declining, first marriages were being postponed to a later age, from 23.8 in 1960 to 28 in 2004, and marriage rates were falling, representing 4.8 per 1000 population in the early 2000s, compared with 8 per 1000 in 1960 across EU25. Apart from Slovenia, which was also displaying the lowest marriage rate at 3.3, age at marriage in the central and east European countries was lower than in EU15 member states. In Sweden, it reached 31.1 [5.8, 2006, tables G-3, G-6]. The rejection or postponement of marriage does not mean that couples are no longer forming partnerships. Comparisons of unmarried cohabitation rates across the Union are unreliable, because the phenomenon is conceptualized and measured using different criteria from one society to another, and because cohabitees form an unstable and heterogeneous category. The limited data available suggest that unmarried cohabitation had become a widespread living arrangement in Finland and Sweden by the early 2000s, affecting over 20 per cent of all couples [5.7, 2002, p. 118]. It was especially prevalent among the younger age groups, and was increasingly associated with extramarital births, which accounted for more than 31 per cent of all live births in 2004 in EU25 member states, compared with 5 per cent in 1960. Here, the highest rates were being recorded in Estonia and Sweden at over 56 per cent. Bulgaria, Denmark, Finland, France, Latvia, Slovenia and the United Kingdom recorded over 40 per cent, compared with under 5 per cent in Greece [5.8, 2006, table D-8].

During the same period, marriage as an institution became increasingly fragile. The proportion of marriages dissolved by divorce had reached 35 per cent across EU25 in 2003, compared with 12 per cent in 1970. Rates of over 50 per cent were being reported in Belgium, Finland and Sweden. Rates were much lower in the southern member states, Ireland and Poland [5.8, 2006, table G-11].

Whereas half a century earlier, unmarried motherhood was a condition that went unrecorded in censuses, and lone parenthood was most likely to be the result of bereavement, by the early 2000s, lone parenthood was much more often the outcome of extramarital relationships, divorce or separation. The available data suggest that, except in the southern European countries, almost 10 per cent of families with children aged below 15 in EU15 were living in lone-parent families. The United Kingdom recorded the highest rate with 19.8 per cent, and Spain and Slovakia the lowest at less than 2 per cent [5.7, 2003, pp. 117, 137].

While indicators of postponement of family formation and reduction in family size would appear to be converging, those for family de-institutionalization would seem to be diverging. The Nordic states have tended to lead the field in adopting less conventional patterns of family formation, while maintaining fertility rates above the EU mean. This pattern has been followed by France and, to a lesser extent, by the Netherlands and the United Kingdom. Whereas, prior to unification, East Germany was closer to the Nordic pattern, West Germany retained a more conventional approach to institutional forms of marriage and family building, as did Austria and Belgium, Ireland and the southern European countries. The effect of transition in central and eastern Europe was equally varied, with Poland and Slovakia remaining closer to traditional family patterns, and the Baltic states moving furthest towards de-institutionalized family life (Hantrais, 2004, figure 3.1).

The picture of family structure that emerges from the data examined in this section is not unequivocal, making it difficult to identify a single European family model that could be targeted by a common family policy. Subject to individual variations in degree, the trends identified raise a number of policy issues that member states were addressing in the early 2000s, albeit in accordance with their own approaches to the organization and delivery of social protection. In some countries, the de-institutionalization and destabilization of the family unit were seen as posing a threat to a social order founded on a commitment to marriage and family as a basic social institution, placing the most vulnerable groups (dependent women and children) at risk. Policy makers had to decide whether or not to recognize alternative family forms in fiscal and social policy, whether to seek to promote family building, whether to try and prevent family breakdown, and whether to support families through periods of transition (Hantrais, 2004, pp. 67–72).

Changing legal rights of family members

Statistical representations of family structure are determined to a large extent by the institutional frameworks that set the legal parameters of the family at national level. The definitions used for demographic and institutional purposes are not, however, identical, and these differences do matter for family policy. For example, policy makers may take account of marital status or the legal recognition of paternity in determining eligibility for tax relief and social security entitlements, whereas statistical records are based on different criteria.

Many changes in family structure have gradually been given official recognition, even if they are not always written into codes of law (Hantrais, 2004, pp. 112–16). From the 1960s, national legal frameworks were, for example, being adapted to reflect the fact that the husband was no longer the undisputed head of the family and its sole or main breadwinner. Increasingly, parental responsibility for children came to be shared between married partners, and the breakdown of marriage was legally endorsed. The situation was less clear-cut in the case of unmarried cohabiting couples. The Nordic states, France and the Netherlands went furthest in recognizing the legal rights of unmarried couples, including same-sex couples. Germany, Spain, the Baltic states and Czech Republic moved in the same direction. By the early 2000s, in several countries, cohabiting couples could officially register their partnership. By contrast, in Ireland their rights were restricted, and in Greece the issue had not yet reached the political agenda.

Practices regarding the attribution of paternity and the sharing of parental responsibility in unmarried couples continued to differ markedly from one member state to another, despite the guidelines laid down by the Council of Europe in 1975 in its European Convention on the Legal Status of Children Born out of Wedlock. As it became technically easier to establish paternity, children acquired the right to know the identity of their biological parents. The responsibilities of parents towards one another and towards their children were formalized, including the legal pursuit of absent fathers. Efforts were made to ensure that parents shared responsibility for their children equitably, taking account of the child's best interest, as laid down in the Charter of Fundamental Rights of the European Union [1.21], which stipulated that 'Every child shall have the right to maintain on a regular basis a personal relationship and direct contact with both his or her parents, unless that is contrary to his or her interests' (article II-24, §§2, 3). Children acquired the right to express their views on matters concerning their well-being, and these views had to be taken into account (article II-24, §1).

Family relationships have been recognized to varying degrees in national taxation systems. Despite the shift during the 1990s from the family or couple to the individual as the basic unit for taxation, France retained the family as the income tax unit, and Germany continued to operate a system that favoured married couples with one high and one low-income earner. Progressively, the distinction was removed between married and unmarried households with regard to taxation by bringing the situation of married couples into line with that of unmarried cohabitees, rather than the reverse. In France, the Netherlands and Sweden, the same tax rate applied as for married couples. However, in most other EU member states in the early 2000s, unmarried childless cohabitees continued to pay more tax than married couples.

These examples show how public policy progressively responded to pressures to adapt and modernize legal frameworks to take account of the spread of alternative family forms. As with demographic trends, EU member states moved in the same direction, but the pace and momentum for change varied. As a result, the rights of family members continued to differ from one country to another.

Defining family policies and identifying policy objectives

Variations between countries in the way the family is defined and taken into account in legal statutes, as outlined in the previous section, reflect persisting differences not only in the principles underlying national family policies, but also in the socio-economic and political contexts in which they are formulated and implemented. A distinction is often made between countries with explicit and implicit family policies. In the 1970s, Czechoslovakia, France, Hungary and Sweden were presented as exemplars of explicit family policies, whereas Austria, Denmark, Finland, Germany and Poland were described as having a tradition of explicit but more narrowly focused family policy (Kamerman and Kahn, 1978). Explicit family policies can be characterized as being far-reaching, coherent and legitimate. The United Kingdom has often served as an example of an EU member state with an implicit, or even negative, family policy, in the sense that governments went so far as to reject the idea of such a policy area. Nonetheless, they did implement measures that were likely to have an impact on families and were considered elsewhere to belong to family policy.

In an early report, the European Observatory on National Family Policies broadly defined family policy as 'measures geared at influencing families', but excluded the unintended outcomes for families of measures implemented in other policy areas (Dumon, 1991, p. 9). The 1994 report on changing family policies conferred on the observatory a much broader remit. It identified three types of family policy: policy targeting families as groups rather than individuals; the family dimension in social and fiscal law, extending to private sector provision and non-governmental organizations; and the family impact of all policies (Dumon, 1994, pp. 325–6). Successive coordinators of the observatory were thereby allowed considerable latitude in interpreting their brief.

One of the reasons evoked at the beginning of this chapter to explain why the Union did not develop its own family policy was the problem of reaching a consensus over objectives. As in other policy areas, the aims and consequences of family policy can be manifest or latent, direct or indirect, mutually consistent or inconsistent. Over the postwar period, governments in member states formulated their own policy objectives in line with their political ideology, their approach to policy making, and as a response to their interpretation of the needs of families in the context of the changing socio-economic and cultural climate.

Few countries, if any, can be said to have pursued wholly coherent family policy objectives. Inconsistency may be explained to a large extent by the potential conflict of needs with which policy makers have to contend. Policies formulated in other areas, such as health, education or employment, are likely to have an impact on families and may also lead to conflicts over objectives. For example, policies that are intended to preserve traditional family structures may be in conflict with others aimed at the pursuit of equality of opportunity. Given that resources are never infinite, choices have to be made that often involve moral judgements. These conflicts of interest raise a number of questions. Should policy concentrate support on families that conform to traditional family types – married couples and their legitimate offspring – or should they recognize and institutionalize new family forms, such as cohabitation and lone parenthood? In other words, should they try to stem change, keep pace with it or even promote it? Within this same framework, should policy makers seek to influence family size or the timing of childbirth? Should family policy be universally applied to all families, or should it operate as a form of social solidarity and, by being selective, help only families most in need? Should attention be focused on individuals rather than on the family unit? Should women be encouraged to stay at home to look after young children, or should the state provide facilities that enable women to combine employment outside the home with childrearing? How effective are family policies?

In their attempts to deal with these questions since the signing of the EEC Treaty [1.2], EU member states pursued three main policy objectives, reflecting the different rationales underlying their welfare regimes: income (re)distribution, pronatalism and equal opportunities. Some member states pursued all three objectives simultaneously, albeit with different emphases depending, among other things, on the political ideology of the governments in power. Most countries sought to use family policy as a means of redistributing income, either horizontally from individuals or couples without children to those with children, or vertically from high to low income earners, often targeting families most in need. In many cases, both horizontal and vertical redistribution was pursued, increasingly with emphasis on helping children at risk, in line with the child-centred approach confirmed by the charter. Policy was also adapted to take account of the fact that young people were remaining dependent on their parents until a later age.

In the early 2000s, the Commission exploited the widespread concern about population decline to prompt national governments to provide incentives designed to encourage couples to have more children. Over the postwar period, and even before, Belgium and France had been pursuing this objective in their family policies, making their pronatalist aims explicit. Several of the central and east European countries openly espoused the same objective when they joined the Union. By contrast, the Federal Republic of Germany, until the late 1980s, and the United Kingdom, until the late 1990s, deliberately avoided formulating policies that might be interpreted as promoting population growth due to its expansionist connotations. The equal opportunities objective progressively moved up national agendas as EU-level policies were developed to take account of the need for support measures to help parents, both men and women, reconcile employment with family life, and as gender mainstreaming was brought into operation across policy areas (see Chapter 6).

Formulating and implementing family policies

Some governments went further than others in formalizing the responsibilities of the state towards families. Among EU25 member states, the Nordic countries and the United Kingdom were unusual in not expressing their support for families in national constitutions. In gathering information about the composition of households and family living arrangements, in establishing the responsibilities of the state towards families, and in determining eligibility for benefits, the state inevitably encroaches on the personal lives of individuals and infringes their privacy. Public policy might, therefore, be thought to contravene article II-7 of the Union's charter of fundamental rights [1.21], which states that 'Everyone has the right to respect of his or her private and family life, home and communications'. Article II-9 goes on to guarantee the right to marry and found a family 'in accordance with the national laws governing the exercise of these rights'.

Government intervention in family affairs can take several forms; it may involve prohibitive, permissive or proactive policies. Despite strong opposition in countries with a powerful Catholic lobby, most governments moved away from prohibitive legislation, for instance for divorce or abortion, although in the early 2000s Ireland and Poland still operated restrictive laws on abortion. In most cases, permissive legislation was extended to take account of alternative family forms, as illustrated in the previous section. Since the founding of the EEC, all member states have pursued proactive family policies. Family allowances (the term used in French-speaking and southern European countries) and child benefit (the term used in northern Europe) are examined here as the most visible and explicit measures illustrating national differences in the formulation and implementation of proactive family policy.

In most member states with insurance-based social security systems (see Chapter 2), family allowances were conceived as part of the wage package, and employment-related contributions were the main or sole source of funding. In the early 2000s, only employers paid earmarked contributions in Austria, France, Italy and Luxembourg. In Greece,

Malta and Portugal, both employers and employees contributed. Elsewhere, the direct link with employment was broken, and funding was sourced from taxation [2.4, 2006, table I].

As in statistical data, the definition of a dependent child applied in assessing entitlement for benefit changes from one country to another, reflecting differences in policy orientations. The level of benefit varies according to factors such as family size, the birth rank of the child, age or the length of education, to the extent that children cannot be said to be of 'equal value'. In the early 2000s, the amount of benefit per child increased with the number of children in most member states, and supplements were paid for large families in Austria, Slovenia and Sweden. In the United Kingdom, the amount paid was higher for the first than for subsequent children, whereas in France, no benefit was paid for the first child. The Czech Republic based the level of benefit on a national 'child's needs' rate. Adjustments were made according to children's ages in a third of the member states; generally they were upwards, but Denmark and Lithuania paid lower rates for older children. Benefit was targeted at low-income families in the southern European countries and several of the fifth-wave member states, in some case with an income ceiling on eligibility. In a few instances, benefit was conditional upon social insurance contributions, but with provision for unemployed parents to draw child benefit [2.4, 2006, table IX].

The age limit for benefit varied between member states. The minimum was set at age 15 in the Czech Republic and Latvia, although Lithuania operated a system where only families with three of more children could receive child benefit after the age of seven. With the exception of the Nordic countries, Italy and Spain, benefit continued to be paid for older children who remained in education and training. Germany and Luxembourg applied the highest age limit at 27 for receipt of benefit, and Cyprus set a different age limit for men and women. Austria, France and Germany observed an earnings threshold. The limit was raised or removed for disabled dependent children in half the member states, and benefit was paid for unemployed children up to the age of 21 in Austria, Germany and Malta [2.4, 2006, table IX].

Before statistics began recording a steep rise in the incidence of extramarital births, cohabitation and lone parenthood, most countries already made some form of provision for lone parents as a result of divorce or bereavement. Never-married mothers were also catered for, primarily to ensure that their children would not suffer financially from having only one parent. By taking lone parents, and particularly lone mothers, into account as both statistical and benefit categories, the *de facto* situation of a growing number of lone parents was thus given legitimacy. Lone parents have also been identified as a target group for social work and special benefits, usually because of their low incomes. In the early 2000s, lone parents either received supplements to family allowances or they were eligible for social assistance. In Greece, the supplement was paid only to widowed parents, invalids or soldiers. Advances on maintenance payments were made in more than half the member states, usually with provision for recovery from the defaulting parent [2.4, 2006, tables IX, XI].

Differences in eligibility rules and benefit rates mean that the treatment accorded to families with children can vary considerably between member states. For example, lone parents in workless households were entitled to receive benefit and housing allowance at the poverty threshold in Denmark, Germany, the Netherlands, Poland and the United Kingdom (see Chapter 8). Only in Poland, however, did couples in jobless households with two children relying on social assistance receive benefit at a sufficient level to provide them with a disposable income above the poverty threshold. Both types of household were exposed to a particularly high risk of poverty in Hungary and Spain. For children aged 0–14, the reduction in the poverty risk due to social transfers, excluding pensions, was estimated to be 65 per cent or more in the Nordic states in 2003. It was much lower in southern Europe, and less than 10 per cent in Greece [8.15, 2006, figures 2.8, 3.2].

These figures do not take account of transfers in kind, tax credits or tax allowances. Nor do they mean that individuals and families escape poverty in the longer term by improving their self-sufficiency. Scrutiny of the distribution of family benefit in cash in the early 2000s indicated that their value in purchasing power standards (PPS) per person aged 0–19 was most generous in Luxembourg, followed by Austria, Germany, Belgium and France. The southern European countries and Slovakia (one of the two fifth-wave countries in the study) were low spenders. The high spenders usually gave greater weight to benefits in cash than in kind and in the form of income replacement during maternity leave. Family/child tax allowances were also an important component of family benefit for most of the high spenders [2.5, 19/2003, figure 1].

THE FAMILY DIMENSION OF EUROPEAN SOCIAL POLICY

Just as the social dimension had long been subordinated to the economic interests of the European Community and Union, the welfare of the family unit was excluded from the original social policy remit of the EEC. In accordance with the subsidiarity principle, family matters remained outside the competence of European institutions, except if they concerned the dependants of migrant workers, or were subsumed under measures to ensure health and safety at work, equality of opportunity between women and men, and the general improvement of living standards. Although the consolidated version of the EC Treaty [1.8] did not introduce any direct reference to family policy, 50 years later, through these indirect routes, the topic had been integrated into the Union's policy remit. In the same way that gender was eventually mainstreamed (see Chapter 6), the case could have been made for formalizing the analysis of the family impact of all EU policies as an explicit treaty commitment. Instead, it was left to the Commission to initiate action in support of families by other means, prompted by the sustained efforts of Coface and, from the 1980s, of the European Parliament.

During the 1990s, the Commission used its mandate for reporting on the demographic situation and on social problems to draw attention to family values as a stabilizing force in society, to identify the contribution that family-sensitive policies could make to economic performance and to alert governments to the costs of neglecting family factors [1.17; 5.6]. The priority given at the turn of the century to policies encouraging more women with children to enter and remain in employment justified refocusing attention on women as working mothers and on policies for reconciling paid work with family life (see Chapter 6).

The Commission was assisted in its efforts to record and analyse changing family forms and family policies in EU member states by Eurostat through its data collection function, and by the European Observatory on National Family Policies through its monitoring activities. During the 1990s, the observatory carried out its task with a specific commitment to improving the quality of life for all families. Its national experts pooled information and ideas, advised the Commission and helped to identify and disseminate good practice. Although many of the other social policy networks and observatories created in the 1970s and 1980s were disbanded, the family policy observatory operated throughout the 1990s, indicating the symbolic importance attributed to family matters, and a measure of agreement between member states over its continued funding. The observatory, however, closed when the Union expanded its membership in 2004, and the Directorate General for Employment, Social Affairs and Equal Opportunities replaced the networks of national experts with networks for monitoring the social situation, one of which was responsible for demographic issues.

Demographers, political scientists, economists and sociologists, particularly in France, long debated whether public policy influenced demographic trends and, more especially, family structures, but without reaching a definitive conclusion (Hantrais, 2004, chapter 7). In the absence of evidence-based policy capable of demonstrating what works and why across the Union, it is difficult to assess whether the activity of EU institutions and organizations, and the exchange of information and ideas at EU level have had an impact on national family policies and, the more so, on behaviour, or to know whether a more formal Union competence would result in greater convergence of policy objectives and outcomes. In the 1990s, despite some similarity in policy developments, analysis of the child benefit package was unable to discern much evidence of convergence across EU15 member states in their approach to meeting the cost of child raising (Ditch *et al.*, 1998, p. 68).

In this chapter, it has been argued that significant shifts in national policy were a response to changes in family structure rather than the reverse, at least insofar as permissive legislation was concerned. It seems unlikely, for example, that legislation on the rights of the dependants of migrant workers substantially increased intra-European mobility (see Chapter 9), but changing family structures may have made it necessary to revise existing legislation. For example, the definition of dependency used in Council Regulation (EEC) No. 1612/68 [9.2], although broader than in many EU member states, was restricted to the heterosexual institution of marriage, thereby excluding unmarried and same-sex cohabiting couples. The definition of 'member of the family' in article 1(i) §§i–ii of Regulation No. 883/2004 [9.1] omitted all reference to the form of union between parents, deferring to national eligibility criteria. Since intra-European migrant workers are, by law, entitled to the same treatment as nationals in the host country, the rights of migrants with non-conventional living arrangements could, therefore, still differ as they moved from one member state to another as a result of persisting differences in national legislation.

The Union's unswerving commitment to respect the diversity of national systems in the area of family policy and its rejection of the notion of harmonization or unification can also have the perverse effect that national provisions for families may contravene article 13 of the amended EC Treaty [1.8] outlawing discrimination on grounds of sexual orientation. Articles II-7, II-9 and II-24 in the Charter of Fundamental Rights of the European Union [1.21] made available new avenues for individuals to have recourse to European jurisdiction. Family policy was thus likely to continue to provide a persuasive example not only of the complexities of the policy-making process but also of the ways in which changes in the living arrangements of families can have an impact on national and EU legislation.

Box 5   Secondary legislation and official publications relating to family policy and the European agenda

5.1 Council Directive 73/403/EEC of 22 November 1973 on the synchronization of general population censuses, *OJ* L 347/50 17.12.1973.

5.2 Resolution of the European Parliament on family policy in the European Community, 9 June 1983, *OJ* C 184/116 11.7.1983.

5.3 Communication from the Commission on family policies, COM(89) 363 final, 8.8.1989.

5.4 Conclusions of the Council and the Ministers Responsible for Family Affairs, meeting within the Council of 29 September 1989, regarding family policies, *OJ* C 277/2 31.10.1989.

5.5 Resolution from the European Parliament on protection of families and family units at the close of the International Year of the Family, 14 December 1994, *OJ* C 18/96 23.1.1995.

5.6 European Commission, The European Union and the family, *Social Europe*, 1/94.

5.7 European Commission, *The Demographic Situation in the European Union*, OOPEC (annual 1993–97); *The Social Situation in the European Union* (annual 2000–2005).

5.8 Eurostat, *Demographic Statistics*, replaced by *Population Statistics* in 2004, OOPEC (biennial), available at:
http://ec.europa.eu/eurostat

---

6 The Gender Dimension of Social Policy

Whereas family life is an area in which the Commission and some national governments have been reluctant to intervene directly, women's rights have long been on the European policy agenda; not, it can be argued, from a desire to achieve equality between the sexes, but as a means of ensuring fair competition between member states. The initial motivation for Community intervention in gender issues was to avoid any one member state gaining a competitive edge by paying women at lower rates than men. The pressure for legislation was said to come mainly from the French, who had enshrined the principle of equal pay in their 1946 constitution and wanted other member states to follow suit so that France would not be at a competitive disadvantage due to higher labour costs (Quintin, 1988, p. 71; Hoskyns, 1996, pp. 45–5).

In the early years of the European Economic Community (EEC), interest in equality between the sexes coincided with both second-wave feminism and the development of socio-economic conditions conducive to women's emancipation (Buckley and Anderson, 1988, p. 5). Economic reconstruction, expanding educational opportunities and changes in family structure all contributed to producing an environment in which national governments were receptive to proposals for promoting greater gender equality.

Progressively, Community institutions extended their remit to cover many aspects of women's economic activity. Already in the 1960s, the Commission was organizing studies and conferences, and formulating recommendations on the workings of article 119 of the EEC Treaty [1.2], which dealt with equal pay. In the Community's social action programme of 1974 [1.11], implementation of the equal pay principle was one of the priority actions. During the 1970s, the focus of attention broadened to encompass equal treatment in access to employment, training, working conditions and social security. From 1977, the European Social Fund was used to support training for women over the age of 25. Exchange of information and experience was promoted through international activities, underpinned by a series of action programmes in the 1980s. The Commission monitored the situation, initiated research, and took action against individual governments through the European Court of Justice (ECJ), thereby building up a strong body of case law. Although, as exemplified by equal pay, national law and practice clearly influenced the Union, the impetus provided by Council directives and rulings from the ECJ served as a powerful incentive for legislative change in individual member states (Hantrais, 2000).

By the 1980s, European women were developing a strong constituency, and women's pressure groups played an active role in taking forward gender policy, both informally and through more formal channels instituted at Community level. The 1990s were marked by two important developments for gender policy: the adoption of measures at Community level to help parents reconcile occupational and family life, and gender mainstreaming. Opinion has, however, been divided over the extent to which they constituted real progress for equal opportunities. Views also diverge over the impact that policy formulated at EU level can have on the everyday lives of women as workers and mothers within member states. As in other policy areas, the extent and pace of change in behaviour and attitudes towards women's roles in society vary according to factors such as the wider policy environment, labour market prospects, and national trends in family building and structure.

To enable a better understanding of the developing policy process at EU level, this chapter begins by examining in more detail the Union's policy framework for promoting gender issues. The impact of the implementation of EU action on national policy formation and practice is then considered, with particular reference to the characteristics of employment patterns and the relationship between paid work and family life. In conclusion, an attempt is made to assess the interaction between EU and national gender policy, and the progress made towards greater equality of opportunity.

EUROPEAN LEGISLATION AND WOMEN'S SOCIAL RIGHTS

In accordance with the overall objectives of the EEC Treaty, the attention paid to gender in EU legislation has been primarily to women as workers (see Chapter 1). This section examines the many legal and other instruments used at EU level to promote women's labour market rights and equal opportunities at work. It analyses the gradual shift in focus towards the reconciliation of employment and family life, and the introduction and consolidation of mainstreaming and work–life balance.

Equality in the Community's and Union's treaties and charters

In the 1957 EEC Treaty under the chapter on social provisions, article 119 referred explicitly and unambiguously to the right of women to equal pay with men. Originally, the article had been included in a section of the treaty on the distortion of competition but, in the final stages of the negotiations, it was moved to the title on social policy, most probably with a view to strengthening the social dimension (Hoskyns, 1996, p. 57). The ground had been prepared for the equal pay principle by the adoption in 1951 of Convention 100 of the General Conference of the International Labour Organization. By the time the EEC Treaty was signed, the convention had been ratified by Belgium, France, Germany and Italy. Convention 100 concerned 'equal remuneration for men and women workers for work of equal value', whereas article 119 laid down the principle that 'men and women should receive equal pay [rendered by the broader term *rémunération* in the French version] for equal work'. The controversial phrase 'equal value' was omitted. Instead, to appease the French, pay and equal pay were defined in terms that were more specific than for any other aspect of social policy. Pay meant 'the ordinary basic or minimum wage or salary and any other consideration, whether in cash or in kind, which the worker receives, directly or indirectly, in respect of his [*sic*] employment from his employer'. Equal pay implied that 'pay for the same work at piece rates shall be calculated on the basis of the same unit of measurement' and 'that pay for work at time rates shall be the same for the same job'.

Despite its insistence on the status of women as paid workers, article 119 provided a useful basis for developing equal opportunities legislation at European level. Articles 100 and 235 of the treaty enabled the Commission to prepare directives not only on equal pay but also on equal treatment. Article 100 made it possible to issue directives to approximate provisions across member states, and article 235 conferred the power to legislate by unanimous voting when action was necessary to achieve EEC objectives, and provision was not made under other articles. The treaty thus established a framework for promoting the harmonization of national legislation for women in paid work.

At the same time as the Commission was bringing forward proposals relating to the organization of life outside the workplace, the main focus of policy adopted at Council level was clearly the rights and opportunities of women as paid workers. The 1989 Community Charter of the Fundamental Social Rights of Workers [1.12, §16] gave confirmation that: 'Equal treatment for men and women must be assured. Equal opportunities for men and women must be developed.' Further action was called for to ensure implementation of the equality principle, particularly in access to employment, remuneration, working conditions, social protection, education, vocational training and career development. A reference was also introduced in §16 to the need for measures 'enabling men and women to reconcile their occupational and family obligations' with a view to achieving greater equality of opportunity.

The Agreement on Social Policy appended to the Maastricht Treaty [1.6] confirmed the orientation towards workers' rights by reiterating *verbatim* the terms of article 119 of the EEC Treaty. A paragraph in circuitous wording was added, however, advising member states that they should not be prevented 'from maintaining or adopting measures providing for specific advantages in order to make it easier for women to pursue a vocational activity or to prevent or compensate for disadvantages in their professional careers' (article 6 §3). This statement has been construed to mean national governments can take positive action to counter discrimination, an issue disputed since the 1970s.

Not only did the 1997 Treaty of Amsterdam [1.7] reinstate the social chapter in the main body of the treaty, following the British opt-in, it also confirmed the Union's strong commitment to gender equality and gave it a legal base. A new paragraph was introduced referring to work of 'equal value', and §3 of article 6 in the Agreement on Social Policy was strengthened by substituting the 'under-represented sex' for 'women'. The two new paragraphs of (renumbered) article 141 in the consolidated version of the EC Treaty thus read as follows:

> 3. The Council, acting in accordance with the procedure referred to in article 251, and after consulting the Economic and Social Committee, shall adopt measures to ensure the application of the principle of equal opportunities and equal treatment of men and women in matters of employment and occupation, including the principle of equal pay for equal work or work of equal value.

> 4. With a view to ensuring full equality in practice between men and women in working life, the principle of equal treatment shall not prevent any Member State from maintaining or adopting measures providing for specific advantages in order to make it easier for the under-represented sex to pursue a vocational activity or to prevent or compensate for disadvantages in professional careers. [1.8, article 141, §§3–4]

In line with the objective of mainstreaming gender, a reference was added in article 2 of the revised EC Treaty to 'equality between men and women', and a catch-all paragraph was included at the end of the revised article 3 §2, stating that 'In all the activities referred to in this Article, the Community shall aim to eliminate inequalities, and to promote equality, between women and men.' A new article inserted in the Treaty of Amsterdam (article 13 in the EC treaty) gave the Council authority to take action to combat discrimination, including that based on sex. EEC Treaty article 118 was expanded to incorporate supporting measures to integrate 'persons excluded from the labour market' and 'equality between men and women with regard to labour market opportunities and treatment at work' (amended article 137 §1).

The new title VIII on employment in the consolidated version of the EC Treaty required the Council to draw up annual employment guidelines [1.18]. One of the four pillars in the 1998 and 1999 employment guidelines was the strengthening of equal opportunities policies. It pointed to the need to tackle gender gaps by reducing unemployment among women and the under- or over-representation of women in certain sectors and occupations. It went on to highlight the need for measures to enable women and men to reconcile work and family life, referring to parental leave, part-time work, flexible working arrangements and childcare services, as well as policies to facilitate the return to work. By the late 1990s, the Union's treaty obligation to provide for equal opportunities had thus been confirmed and extended, although the primary, if not sole, justification for action remained paid work.

Under title III on equality, article II-23 in the Charter of Fundamental Rights of the European Union [1.21], which was incorporated into the Union's draft Constitution in 2003 [1.10], extended the right to equality beyond the workplace, making provision for positive action:

Equality between men and women must be ensured in all areas, including employment, work and pay.

The principle of equality shall not prevent the maintenance or adoption of measures providing for specific advantages in favour of the under-represented sex. [1.21, article II-23]

Article II-21 outlawed discrimination on grounds of sex under the same terms as race, colour, ethnic or social origin, genetic features, language, religion or belief, political or any other opinion, membership of a national minority, property, birth, disability, age or sexual orientation.

Secondary legislation on women's rights

The Union has used a variety of instruments to promote greater equality of treatment and opportunity for women, ranging from commitments in treaties (described in the previous section), through Council directives, Council and Commission recommendations and resolutions, conclusions and communications, to action programmes proposed and implemented by the Commission. This section examines the secondary legislation and soft law drawn up to ensure the application of the treaties in national law and practice.

In 1975, the Commission issued its first directive in the area of equal opportunities. Council Directive 75/117/EEC 'on the approximation of the laws of the Member States relating to the application of the principle of equal pay for men and women' [6.1] enlarged on the provisions of article 119. In particular, it clarified and extended the meaning of the principle of equal pay to work of equal value, as assessed by job evaluation schemes. The directive explicitly outlawed discrimination on grounds of sex, not only where an employee feels s/he is being directly discriminated against because s/he is paid less than an employee of the opposite sex, but also where conditions are imposed which exclude or impede the progress of members of one sex, and which are not essential for the job. While the directive gave employees who felt they had grounds for complaint the right to legal redress, the concepts of work of equal value and indirect discrimination remained difficult to operationalize. Over the years, a series of landmark judgements on cases brought before the ECJ helped to clarify the position for national legislators (Byre, 1988; Burrows and Mair, 1996, pp. 21–32; Shaw, 2000).

Subsequent directives built onto the framework provided by article 119 and the 1975 directive. The following year, Directive 76/207/EEC extended the equality principle to 'equal treatment for men and women as regards access to employment, vocational training and promotion, and working conditions' [6.2]. Directive 79/7/EEC, which was adopted in 1978 and finally came into force in 1984, addressed the principle of 'equal treatment for men and women in matters of social security' [6.3]. Member states were given six years to implement the directive because of its complexities and the costs involved. Directive 79/7/EEC was supplemented in 1986 by Directives 86/378/EEC [6.6] and 86/613/EEC [6.8], which extended the principle of equality of treatment to occupational schemes and self-employed men and women. Direct or indirect discrimination on grounds of sex was prohibited in the scope of social security schemes, conditions of access and calculation of benefits, where, for example, a married woman's employment did not entitle her husband to benefits, or occupational schemes were only open to men.

Although the three directives removed the automatic exclusion of women from benefit entitlements earned as full-time workers, they did not cover survivors' and family benefits, and they left open the possibility of excluding the determination of pensionable age, advantages for persons who have brought up children and the granting of increases for long-term invalidity, old age, industrial accident and occupational disease benefits for a dependent wife. Another important omission was that they did not directly address the issue of part-time or unpaid work. A draft directive on voluntary part-time work, first proposed in 1981, was not adopted until 1997 (see Chapter 4), although cases brought before the ECJ resulted in some recognition of women's rights as part-time workers. While the ECJ was, subsequently, more liberal in acknowledging women's needs as part-time workers, its judgements signalled the intention not to interfere with this aspect of the organization of family life and the division of household labour.

A proposal for a directive, issued in 1983 and amended in 1984, addressed the question of parental leave and leave for family reasons, but was similarly not adopted for more than a decade [6.4]. However, the less binding Council recommendation 'on child care', adopted in 1992 [6.12], included special leave for parents to look after their own children, as well as measures to encourage men and women to share family responsibilities for childcare and the education of children. The recommendation was the outcome of a long process of negotiation over childcare provision within the framework of policy on equal opportunities and the reconciliation of family obligations with employment. The ground had been prepared by the European Commission's Childcare Network, which began operating in 1986. The network took as its basic premise that the inequality in the conditions under which men and women supply their labour is socially determined, and that childcare affects both women's opportunities for participation in the labour market and their general well-being, whether or not they are in paid employment. Equality is thus as much an issue for men as for women (European Commission Childcare Network, 1990, p. 2).

Council Directive 92/85/EEC 'on the introduction of measures to encourage improvements in the safety and health at work of pregnant workers and workers who have recently given birth or are breastfeeding' [4.7] affords another example of how the Commission handled a contentious issue by bringing forward a proposal under the framework directive as a health and safety measure. As with Directive 93/104/EC 'concerning certain aspects of the organization of working time' [4.2], it was adopted by qualified majority voting (see Chapter 4). Essentially, the health and safety directive sought to provide a minimum level of protection by proposing that women who are working at the time when they become pregnant, or who are registered as unemployed, are automatically entitled to 14 weeks' maternity leave with pay and without loss of employment-related rights. Another aspect of women's working conditions was tackled in a Council recommendation 'on the protection of the dignity of women and men at work' [6.11], which outlawed sexual harassment at the workplace.

In the 1994 white paper on European social policy, the Commission announced its intention to keep all these items on the agenda for the remainder of the decade. Legislation was to be pursued on part-time work. On the question of parental leave and career breaks, the possibility of a framework directive was to be examined as a measure aimed at reconciling professional and family life, with a view to establishing minimum standards. The implementation of the recommendation on childcare was to be monitored, baseline data were to be established on childcare infrastructures and services, and the issue of gender stereotyping was also to be addressed [1.15, pp. 41–5].

Under the terms of the Agreement on Social Policy appended to the Treaty on European Union [1.6, articles 3–4], procedures were put in place to enable management and labour to initiate the contractual process. Council Directive 96/34/EC 'on the framework agreement on parental leave concluded by UNICE, CEEP and the ETUC' [6.4] was the first example of recourse to the new procedure. The directive made provision for leave of at least three months to be taken up to the time when the child reached the age of eight. It stipulated that the right should be granted to each parent on a non-transferable basis. No reference was made to a payment being required during the leave period; member states were given discretion to decide under what conditions to grant leave. Although the directive was binding with regard to the results to be achieved, it thus left member states to choose the forms and methods of implementation. The British opt-out had meant that the United Kingdom was not bound by the directive. Following the change of government and the incorporation of the Agreement on Social Policy into the Treaty of Amsterdam, an amended version of the directive, 97/75/EC [6.4], was therefore adopted in 1997, extending its provisions to the United Kingdom. While the earlier draft of the directive was written in the context of equal treatment for men and women, the 1996 version has to be situated in relation to growing pressures to increase labour market flexibility as a component of the Union's employment strategy. The 1990s directives marked a shift in emphasis towards non-labour market factors in the guise of reconciliation of employment with family life, but they did not signal a break with the employment-based origins of equality policy. They can therefore be interpreted as introducing work-friendly rather than women-friendly measures.

The link with employment was reinforced by the inclusion of childcare in the employment guidelines. The Barcelona European Council in March 2002 went on to conclude that factors preventing women from participating in the labour market should be removed, among other means by ensuring the provision of 'infant welfare' for 33 per cent of children under the age of three and for 90 per cent of children aged three to six by 2010 [1.20]. To facilitate the monitoring process, in conjunction with Eurostat, the Commission initiated the development of a methodology for the collection of harmonized statistics on childcare (European Commission, 2004). Also in 2002, the Council and Parliament agreed an amendment to Directive 76/207/EC on equal treatment in employment, defining sexual harassment and establishing it as a form of sex discrimination. Directive 2002/73/EC [6.2] made provision for enforcement, compensation and sanctions, requiring employers to introduce preventive measures against sexual harassment and to report regularly to employees on equality in the enterprise. Directive 2004/113/EC 'on equal treatment for women and men in the access to and supply of goods and services' [6.19], based on article 13 of the EC Treaty, extended legislation to goods and services that fell outside the areas of employment, private and family life.

Community action programmes on equal opportunities for women

Directives represent one of the most concrete and binding outcomes of the Union's activities in the area of women's rights. While legislation provides a framework for action, the Commission was aware that the law alone cannot ensure equality of opportunity. Throughout the 1960s, the Commission regularly reported on the difficulties of putting the equal pay principle into practice. One of the objectives of the 1974 social action programme was to achieve greater equality between men and women not only with regard to pay but also in access to employment, vocational training and improvements in working conditions. The programme made reference for the first time to the existence of the political will to adopt measures to ensure that family responsibilities could be reconciled with job aspirations [1.11, p. 2]. Subsequently, the Commission registered its intention to act as a prime mover in the area of equal opportunities by establishing a Women's Bureau in 1976 (renamed as the Equal Opportunities Unit in 1994), and by initiating a series of action programmes promoting equal opportunities for women.

The programmes aimed to raise awareness, disseminate information and mobilize what were described as 'equality partners', including the two sides of industry and non-governmental organizations.

The first equal opportunities action programme for the period 1982–85 [6.5] stressed the need to put equal opportunities into practice, by means of positive action programmes designed to enable women to overcome their disadvantage in relation to men, extending to a more equal sharing of family responsibilities. The second action programme, covering 1986–90 [6.5], addressed the consolidation of the legal rights of individuals and sought to promote positive action to overcome the non-legal barriers to the achievement of equal opportunities. A section was devoted to the sharing of family and occupational responsibilities, proposing action to promote parental leave, childcare services and the reorganization of working time.

The Council responded to the provision made in the Community charter in its resolution 'on the third medium-term Community action programme on equal opportunities for women and men', covering the period 1991–95 [6.10]. The programme was presented against the background of the conditions and opportunities created by the completion of the internal market and the need to develop new policies and measures taking into account the social and economic changes of the 1990s and beyond. The Council recommended that 'better use should be made of women's abilities and gifts so as to permit their full participation in the process of European development'. Women's participation was, moreover, described as 'an essential factor in European economic and social cohesion' [6.10, p. 1]. Pursuing this line of argument, the Council stressed the need for measures to reconcile professional and family life. As argued in the previous chapter, the justification for extending Community policy to family affairs consistently focused on the status of individuals and their effectiveness as workers. The resolution stressed the need not only to improve the position of women in society, but also to promote the participation of women in the decision-making process in public, economic and social life.

In accordance with the principles of complementarity and subsidiarity, the third action programme identified separately measures that fell under the Commission's responsibility and those that individual member states were expected to implement. It also provided for the integration of equality issues into general mainstream policy at EU and national level. These two principles were exemplified in the New Opportunities for Women (Now) initiative for the promotion of equal opportunities in the field of employment and vocational training. The initiative was established within the framework of the structural funds and involved a partnership between the Union and national governments, as well as between regional and local administrations, vocational training agents, socio-economic partners, research and information centres on women. To help women create small businesses and cooperatives or return to employment, Community support could extend to guidance and advice, technical assistance, such as awareness-raising actions, and the collection and dissemination of information on good practice and vocational training. As an enabling device, the Commission undertook to support the provision of childcare facilities, including the operating costs of facilities linked to vocational training centres and the training of childcare workers. It thereby extended its remit beyond the workplace into areas where previously – like some national governments – it had been reluctant to intervene, although the interest in childcare was, as stated in the white paper on social policy, to a large extent motivated by its job creation potential [1.15, p. 43].

The fourth medium-term Community action programme on equal opportunities for men and women for the period 1996–2000 [6.13] was adopted by a Council decision in 1995. Subsequently, it was extended through to 2008, with annual progress reports being issued by the Commission. Article 2 of the programme defined and gave substance to the principle of mainstreaming, which had been floated in the third action programme. The intention was 'to promote the integration of equal opportunities for men and women in the process of preparing, implementing and monitoring all policies and activities of the European Union and the Member States having regard to their respective powers'. Mainstreaming implied an integrated approach and more streamlined management to ensure a higher profile for equal opportunities. The programme advocated partnership – within the Commission, with competent national and regional authorities, between social partners, between women and men, and with non-governmental organizations – as the key to changing attitudes and breaking down the rigidity of sex roles in all aspects of economic and social life.

The Commission further developed its approach to mainstreaming in a communication issued in 1996 [6.15], affirming the political will to act, and explaining that all policies should be scrutinized from the planning stage and evaluated from a gender perspective to take account of their possible effects on the situation of women and men. The text said very little about the strategies and instruments to be used to implement mainstreaming; no timetable or budget was set. Reference was made to the Commission's remit for producing an annual report on the policies implemented and action taken. The reports were intended to give visibility to Community policy on equal opportunities, to contribute to the development of its strategy, and serve as a reference point for the Commission and for present and future member states. In 1999, a follow-up report on the communication pointed out that the progress made had been piecemeal, and identified the risk that mainstreaming might result in the abandonment of policies specifically targeting women, as exemplified by the disappearance of a designated budget line in the Socrates programme for equality-oriented projects [6.15, p. 9]. The report therefore advocated retaining the dual approach by combining mainstreaming with specific measures for positive action. It also recommended devoting resources to gender impact assessments of policies, the collection of comparative sex-disaggregated statistics, the setting up of gender proofing procedures within the directorates-general, and the organization of training in gender analysis and assessment for officials.

By the late 1990s, through treaty commitments, secondary legislation and the Commission's action programmes, equality issues had thus achieved a prominent position on the European social policy agenda. The Treaty of Amsterdam had recognized equality between women and men as a primary political objective, a strong body of legislation had been built up on equal pay and equal treatment, and the action programmes, reports and guidelines provided a firm basis from which to move forward. However, as with other areas of social policy, it was not difficult to find an economic motivation for the equality policies that had been given such a high profile in the official rhetoric. The action initiated was confined to a single dimension of women's lives, and the information collected indicated that, despite the measures taken, equality of opportunity was far from being an everyday reality for most women and men in the Union.

A Council resolution in 2000 'on the balanced participation of women and men in family and working life' [6.17] extended the reach of EU policy. It presented the advantages to both sexes of achieving more equal sharing between men and women of care for children and other dependants. More balanced participation was portrayed as 'an essential aspect of the development of society', and maternity, paternity and the rights of children as 'eminent social values to be protected by society' [6.17, p. 5 §4]. Measures for reconciling working and family life were needed not only to serve the interests of employers and employees, but also to promote changes in structures and attitudes [6.17, p. 6 §1c]. The resolution called upon national governments and enterprises to grant individual and non-transferable rights to paternity leave as an incentive for take up of leave by men, improve childcare structures, protect lone-parent families, harmonize school and working hours, and promote information and awareness campaigns. The Union was invited to put its own institutions in order with regard to equal treatment and representation, and to increase the Commission's monitoring activities.

In 2001, the Commission began implementing its Community framework strategy on gender equality [6.18], accompanied by annual work programmes. The strategy was based on forward planning, the setting of specific objectives and monitoring of activities and results. The work programmes defined horizontal priorities aimed at all the directorates general (DGs) and services, as well as specific objectives and actions for each DG in its respective policy area. The programmes were designed to scrutinize the impact of various policies on gender equality and to promote the breakdown and analysis of statistical data by sex. Recurring priority themes included the gender pay gap for 2001, the reconciliation of work and family life for 2002, the gender balance in decision-making for 2003 and gender stereotyping for 2004.

Following EU enlargement in 2004, the title of the Directorate General for Employment and Social Affairs was extended to include Equal Opportunities. As confirmation of the commitment to the principle of mainstreaming gender, plans were launched for the establishment of a European Gender Institute in 2007 as a clearing house for information and exchange of good practice. The framework strategy had prepared the ground by identifying the Commission's areas of action, spanning economic life, equal participation and representation, social rights, civil life, gender roles and stereotypes. All public and private bodies and institutions with an interest in establishing gender equality were urged to become involved through awareness raising activities, analysis and evaluation, and strengthening of capacity. To mark International Women's Day in 2006, the Commission launched a roadmap for equality between women and men, containing concrete actions to help bridge the gender gap and a series of indicators for monitoring progress [6.20].

FROM EU LAW TO NATIONAL POLICY AND PRACTICE

Whereas in the previous chapter no clear picture emerged of what might be considered as a European family policy, in the area of equality between men and women at work, the Union can be credited with having formulated and actively promoted a more coherent body of policy, and with having played a more prominent role in shaping national legislation. Incentives have been introduced to ensure enactment, procedures have been established for monitoring the effectiveness of policy, and penalties can be incurred for infringements. This section begins with a review of the transposition of European equality legislation into national regulatory frameworks. Transposition does not, however, guarantee compliance or changes in attitudes and practices. Attention is therefore also given to identifying distinctive developments in the patterning of gender relations in EU member states.

Transposing European legislation into national law

In the areas of equal pay and equal treatment, some member states have been at the forefront of change, others have kept pace with European legislation, yet others have only gradually implemented directives, generally in response to infringement proceedings [6.21, 1997, chart 3]. Cases brought before the ECJ have also helped to resolve problems arising over implementation. The much-quoted Kalanke and Marschall cases [6.16], for example, made clear that positive action in favour of women is compatible with European law, except in the specific case of unconditional preferential quotas.

Even the founder member states had to adapt national legislation to comply with European law. Although national equal pay legislation predated European law in France, where the 1946 constitution affirmed the equality principle, work of equal value was not formally defined in law until 1983. The French authorities had not, in fact, foreseen how the ECJ would interpret article 119. Nor had lawyers and policy makers been able to predict how European directives would be used to enforce the equality principle (Lanquetin *et al.*, 2000, pp. 70–6). The Italian constitution of 1947 provided for the same pay for equal work, while also offering protection to women workers to enable them to fulfil their family functions. The implementation of the equal pay principle in the 1960s was, however, an extremely conflictual process (Bimbi, 1993, pp. 147–8; Del Re, 2000, pp. 111–13). Although Germany had a basic law on equal rights dating back to 1949, infringement proceedings were avoided by belatedly adopting legislation on equal pay in 1980 [6.7, p. 16]. Several of the other founder member states were introducing legislation on equal pay for work of equal value in the early 1970s when the European directives were being drafted. In Belgium the principle of equal pay for work of the same or equal value in the Collective Labour Agreement of 1975 was given binding force in the private sector. The

Grand-Ducal regulation of 1974 in Luxembourg included an equal value clause. The Netherlands followed suit in 1975. The member states that joined the Community in the 1970s had also been developing their own national legislation. The United Kingdom passed an Equal Pay Act in 1970. Ireland's Anti-Discrimination Act of 1974 included an equal pay clause. The Danish equal pay law dates from 1976, but infringement proceedings were initiated against Denmark for not including the term 'equal value' [6.7, pp. 9–34].

Most member states extended their legislation to cover illegal dismissal on the basis of sex and to make provision for legal redress, with the burden of proof resting on employers. Some established monitoring procedures through organizations such as the Equal Opportunities Commission, which was set up in 1975 in the United Kingdom, or the Equality Status Council established in 1978 in Denmark.

The countries that joined the Community in later years were required to bring their national legislation into line with European law that they had had no hand in drafting. In the case of equal rights and equal opportunities directives, this did not seem to present any major problems for the new member states in the 1980s and 1990s, since national legislation had been moving in the same direction. On joining the Community, the Spanish government was quick to draw up the necessary legislation in adapting its own provisions to take account of European directives. Quite radical changes had been occurring in women's legal status since the mid-1970s. The Civil Code was amended in 1975 to recognize women's full legal capacity. The Spanish constitution of 1978 enshrined equality as an essential constituent element of a legally established social and democratic state. Reference was made specifically to non-discrimination based on sex in relation to work, and this principle was embodied in the Workers' Statute and the Basic Law on Employment. Similarly, Portugal had made profound changes to its constitution in 1976 and 1982 to grant new legal status to women. The constitution laid down the principles of equality and non-discrimination not only at work and in education but also between spouses. Greece had already included an article in its 1975 constitution establishing equal rights between the sexes, and this principle was extended by transposing the detail of Directive 75/117/EEC into national law, which came into force in 1984 [6.7, p. 103].

In most countries, implementation of Directive 76/207/EEC on equal treatment in access to employment, promotion, vocational training and working conditions was a longer process than for equal pay, and infringement proceedings were initiated against all the nine earlier member states over some aspect of their national legislation [6.7, pp. 69–72]. Despite the long period allowed for implementation of Directive 79/7/EEC on equal treatment in social security, not all member states had complied by the target date of 1984 [6.7, pp. 76–83]. The relevant law was adopted in Germany in 1985 and in Belgium and Luxembourg in 1986. By 1997, Directives 86/378/EEC and 96/97/EC on equal treatment in occupational social security schemes had still not been transposed into national legislation in Belgium, Denmark, Luxembourg and the Netherlands (European Commission, 1998, pp. 36–8).

Austria and the two Nordic states that joined the Union in the 1990s had all enacted laws governing equal pay and equal treatment. Sweden had some of the earliest equality legislation dating back to the 1940s in the public sector. Austria's equal pay act was adopted in 1978, and Finland passed a law on equality between women and men in 1986. Finland and Sweden instituted Gender Equality Ombudsmen. Despite Sweden's distinguished record on equality, EU membership brought much closer scrutiny of Swedish equality law. The Gender Equality Ombudsman tested the conformity of Swedish equal opportunities law with EU legislation. As a result, the scope of the Swedish act against discrimination in employment, adopted in 1980, was extended in 1992 in a new equal opportunities act, subsequently revised in 1994. The amended law tightened up regulations on wage discrimination, made the meaning of the concept of equal work more precise and introduced regulations concerning indirect discrimination and sexual harassment (Bergqvist and Jungar, 2000, pp. 171–6).

When Directive 92/85/EEC, which provided for paid maternity leave, was adopted, all except Ireland and the United Kingdom already made some form of statutory provision. However, the Commission initiated infringement procedures against France, Ireland, Italy, Luxembourg and Sweden in 1999 for not fully or correctly complying with the stipulations laid down in the directive. By the deadline of June 1998, few member states had met the formal requirement for transposition of Directive 96/34/EC on parental leave, although all but Greece, Ireland, Luxembourg and the United Kingdom offered statutory parental leave at the end of 1997. Sweden was well advanced, having instituted parental insurance as early as 1974 (European Commission, 1998, pp. 47–9).

The ten countries that joined the Union in 2004 were required to transpose nine directives in the field of equal opportunities as a basic condition of membership. Institutional and administrative structures to facilitate the implementation and enforcement of equality rights were underdeveloped in most of the new member states. When the European

Council met in Göteborg in 2001 [1.20], the Czech Republic, Estonia, Hungary, Latvia, Lithuania, Poland and Slovakia were deemed to have made excellent progress in transposing the directives, whereas much of the *acquis* remained to be transposed in Cyprus, Malta and Slovenia. Progress was slow in Bulgaria and Romania, and their accession was postponed until 2007 [6.21, 2001, p. 17].

These examples suggest that European law was less effective as a force for initiating reform at national level than as an instrument for accompanying or accelerating change. This was to be expected since directives are the outcome of a compromise reached between member states. However, instances of resistance can be identified when individual member states felt that their own legislation was already adequate to cover the contingencies provided for in directives, or when they claimed that the social and economic cost of implementation would be unreasonable. Legislation affecting working time, maternity and parental leave, and childcare was opposed, and in some cases blocked, for these reasons. The United Kingdom, in particular, developed a reputation in the 1980s for its almost systematic opposition to European equality legislation, on the grounds that the measures proposed would entail additional labour costs for employers or endanger their flexibility to respond to market demands. Although the United Kingdom established a good record for transposing directives in the areas of employment and social policy [1.15, 1994, table 1], in 1997 it was, with Germany whose transposition record was average, the member state that had been issued with the largest number of rulings from the ECJ on EEC article 119 and the 1970s equality directives [6.21, 1997, chart 3]. As a result of ECJ rulings, on several occasions the United Kingdom was forced to change its own legislation to comply with European law (Burrows and Mair, 1996). By contrast, Italy, which had a very poor record for transposition, had received only one ruling from the ECJ. This may say more about the effectiveness of the British Equal Opportunities Commission in bringing cases before the courts than about the status of equal opportunities in the two countries. In any event, transposition does not necessarily imply that legislation is translated into good practice at national level.

Women's access to rights as workers and mothers

Analysis of European law as it affects women shows clearly how attention was paid almost exclusively to their rights as workers. Gradually, EU directives recognized that women may need special treatment in their capacity as working mothers, thereby juxtaposing the potentially competing aims of equality and difference, which, for example, led to conflicts in France (Lanquetin *et al.*, 2000) and to paradoxes in Italy (Del Re, 2000). As argued in previous sections, the inclusion of women's rights on the European agenda was justified by economic reasons: the flexibility required to enable parents to reconcile paid work with family life was 'employment friendly' before being 'women friendly'. This section looks at the way that some of the measures designed to extend women's rights as workers and as working mothers impacted on gender relations in EU member states.

Individualized rights

A consequence of the directives on equal treatment for men and women in social security schemes was the shift towards the individualization of rights in employment-insurance schemes. Accordingly, individuals are more often assessed independently of their family situation with regard to social security and income tax. Individualization means that women and men are required to pay the same earnings-related contributions and taxes. In return, they gain access to the same rights to sick pay, pensions, unemployment and other benefits arising from employment. Individualization was promoted in the white paper on social policy [1.15, p. 42] and in the Commission's communication on modernizing and improving social protection [1.17, section 2.4] as a means of removing discrimination in social protection and fiscal policy and reducing women's dependency on male breadwinners. The communication recognized, however, that direct social security rights could disadvantage women because of their lower pay, more interrupted and less secure patterns of employment, and that derived rights, such as survivors' pensions, could provide more generous entitlements for women whose former spouse earned a high income (see Chapters 7, 8).

Yet, in the early 2000s, no EU member state operated a completely individualized system of social protection. As indicated in Chapter 5, child benefit, for example, varied according to family income in several of the southern, central and east European countries. The most widely documented, and arguably most important, area of concern for equality policy is pension rights, where individualization highlighted the need for compensatory measures to take account of the shortfall in the contributions paid by women into occupational pension schemes. Most countries gave some form of recognition in pension calculations to women who spend time out of the labour market performing caring duties, either by crediting them with additional years of social insurance contribution or by reducing the number of years needed for entitlement to a full pension. In Greece, for example, women who raised children were credited with up to 4.5 years for time spent out of the labour market. In Austria, such time was considered as a working period calculated at the rate of four years per child. In the Czech Republic, women who have brought up five or more children could retire four years earlier than those who have not raised any children. In calculating pension entitlement, both Ireland and the United Kingdom took account of up to 20 years spent out of the labour market caring for relatives [2.4, 2006, table VI].

Arrangements for maternity leave

When the Commission drafted a proposal for the provision of 14 weeks' statutory maternity leave on full pay in 1990, the United Kingdom reacted by claiming that the directive would cause 'a dramatic change in entitlement to paid leave from work in the UK' [6.9, p. 1]. Under national law, a working woman had no automatic right to maternity leave. Under the Employment Protection Consolidation Act of 1978, she had the right to return to work only if she fulfilled certain qualifying conditions. Entitlement to maternity pay, which was separate from maternity leave and governed by the Social Security Act of 1986, was also subject to a qualifying period. The Commission's proposal was therefore expected to have important repercussions for the amount women would receive during maternity leave and to impact on labour costs for employers. Countries that already had more generous schemes for paid maternity leave were, by the same token, keen to see these measures extended across the Union to avoid being at a competitive disadvantage. In the event, Directive 92/85/EEC [4.7] stipulated that member states could make maternity pay conditional on a period of not more than 12 months employment and set it at a level 'at least equivalent to' the sick pay to which the woman would have been entitled (article 11 §3). Almost all EU25 countries opted to assimilate maternity to sick pay and administered them together [2.4, 2006, table IV].

In 1992, most governments did not need to make major changes to their arrangements to bring their practices into line with the directive. By the time it was due to take effect, all the then member states made provision for at least 14 weeks' leave, and Italy offered up to five months. Portugal extended the period of maternity leave from 90 days to 14 weeks in 1995 to comply with the directive. Across the Union, mothers were protected against unlawful dismissal and given a guarantee of reinstatement after maternity leave (European Commission Network on Childcare, 1994, pp. 49–52).

With the exception of Malta, the member states that joined the Union in 2004 all operated generous arrangements for maternity leave, exceeding 14 weeks. The Czech Republic and Slovakia provided for 28 weeks, rising to 37 in the case of lone mothers or multiple births. Practices varied regarding payment. Although several EU25 member states offered 100 per cent of previous earning over a set period for at least part of the leave, a cap was often applied, and Malta made a flat-rate payment. Slovakia paid the lowest proportion of previous salary at 55 per cent. In 15 member states, however, unlike child benefit, maternity benefit, like paid work, was taxable [2.4, 2006, table IV].

Arrangements for parental leave

The proposal to harmonize provisions for parental leave across EU member states raised similar issues to maternity leave for the United Kingdom, which had no statutory provision, although a number of firms had introduced career break schemes. Leave was provided in Ireland only under certain collective agreements. Belgium offered leave of absence in the form of a career break to look after children (European Commission Network on Childcare, 1996, table 5). By the time the parental leave directive was due to be implemented in 1998, all but four EU15 member states had put in place formal statutory leave arrangements. In some cases, however, it was difficult to distinguish parental leave and childcare benefit from maternity leave. Ireland had not introduced general legislation. The United Kingdom had undertaken to comply and was given until the end of 1999 to do so. [2.4, table IV].

By 2004, all member states in the enlarged Union operated arrangements for statutory parental leave, varying from three months in the United Kingdom to three or more years in the Czech Republic, Germany, Finland, France, Latvia, Lithuania, Poland, Slovakia and Spain. According to the directive, entitlement to parental leave was to be non-transferable. In effect, half the member states attributed leave jointly to both parents. Where entitlement was on an individual basis, the total period of leave was reduced if one parent did not take up his/her allowance. Nine member states made no payments during parental leave, whereas the others provided fixed-rate flat payments, or a percentage of a national minimum wage or of former earnings, sometimes on a sliding scale. When calculated on the basis of effective leave weighted by level of payment, it was estimated that Lithuania made the most generous provision, followed by Sweden and Hungary. Provision was least generous in Cyprus, Ireland, Malta and the Netherlands (European Commission, 2005, table A.6).

Not only coverage but also take-up of parental leave varied across member states, as well as within countries where arrangements were decided under collective agreements. Despite incentives to encourage both parents to take leave when their children are young, take up did not necessarily correspond closely to the generosity of provision. In the Czech Republic, Estonia and Germany, for example, take up by mothers was almost universal, whereas low rates were reported in Ireland, Italy and the United Kingdom. The persistently marked difference observed in take up between women and men may be explained to a great extent by the pay gap, the parent with the lower income being more likely to take leave. Cultural norms continued to provoke negative reactions at the workplace and in society at large towards men who took leave to care for young children. Efforts to maximize flexibility, as proposed in the directive, by making it possible for leave to be taken on a part-time basis, appear to have reinforced the incentive for women to take the available leave, since they were more accustomed to part-time working patterns than men. In most countries, the public sector, where women made up the majority of employees, operated the most generous arrangements for leave and for reinstatement after periods away from the labour market. The net effect of these factors was that only in Luxembourg, the Netherlands and Sweden did more than 10 per cent of eligible men take leave. Even in these cases, men usually took shorter periods of leave. They, therefore, preferred to take paternity, rather than parental, leave, because it involved a smaller number of days (European Commission, 2005, pp. 48–54).

The directive specified that member states could continue to apply, or introduce, more favourable provisions than those set out in the agreement. As illustrated by the examples quoted above, the various forms of parental leave continued to be conceptualized differently from one member state to another. Paid parental insurance in Sweden was regarded as one of the pillars of equality policy, aimed at making it easier for both women and men to combine parenthood and employment (Bergqvist and Jungar, 2000, p. 161). In France, the allowance paid to parents raising their own children was seen as a means of enabling mothers to take an extended break from employment, without losing employment rights, whereas in Germany paid leave was considered rather as a benefit, or maternal wage, for mothers who 'chose' to stay at home to look after their children (Fagnani, 1996, p. 135). In the United Kingdom, parental leave, the guarantee of reinstatement and childcare had to be 'sold' to employers as strategies enabling them to make direct savings on training and recruitment by retaining well-qualified female workers (Home Office, 1998, p. 26).

Provision of childcare

When the Council recommendation 'on child care' was adopted in 1992 [6.12], the *Länder* of former East Germany and Denmark had by far the most extensive public provision of childcare for children aged under three, followed by Belgium, France and Finland. At the other end of the scale, West Germany, Greece, Ireland, Spain and the United Kingdom stood out as being particularly poor providers of publicly funded care (European Commission Network on Childcare, 1996, table 6). Ireland and the United Kingdom were also distinguished by the fact that childcare services did not give priority to the children of parents in paid employment but rather to children at risk.

Childcare provision confirmed the situation regarding maternity and parental leave, and benefits. Clearly, some member states already went much further than others in supporting parents and in helping to reconcile employment with family life, albeit for different reasons and with differing outcomes as far as strategies are concerned for combining labour market activity and sharing family responsibilities (Hantrais, 2000, pp. 184–90). The justification for promoting public childcare arrangements had evolved at EU level. When the European Childcare Network began operating in 1986, the primary objective was to respond to the need for good quality childcare as a means of assisting working mothers, supporting the development of young children, and promoting the role of men in caring for children. By 1996, the network had been discontinued, and the climate had changed. The Commissioner responsible for Employment and Social Affairs, Pádraig Flynn, was stressing the importance of removing obstacles to full participation in the labour market, and of enabling parents, and especially women, to make 'their proper contribution to economic and social life' [6.14, p. 5]. This approach was pursued at the Barcelona European Council meeting in 2002, which confirmed that the aim of the childcare targets was to eliminate 'counterincentives for women participating in labour' [1.20].

Despite the lack of strictly comparable data, it was estimated that, by 2005, Belgium, Denmark, France, the Netherlands and Sweden had already reached the Barcelona target for 2010 of childcare places for 33 per cent of children under the age of three. Nine countries were recording levels below 10 per cent, although the figures did not take account of pre-school provision, which was available from an earlier age in several of the central and east European member states. When part-time arrangements were included, eight member states had already met the Barcelona target of 90 per cent childcare coverage for children aged between three and six. However, these figures conceal important differences in access, affordability and attitudes towards institutionalized care (European Commission, 2004, 2005, pp. 33–46). Findings from European Values Surveys about the perceived impact on young children of mothers' work outside the home and surveys of attitudes towards public childcare indicate how public opinion varied (European Commission, 2005, box 3), reinforcing concern that a possible side-effect of policy for working mothers was the devaluing of motherhood.

Gender equality at work

An underlying reason for individualizing rights in the 1990s was to encourage the participation of women in the labour force, partly on the grounds that derived rights could have a negative effect on the labour supply. The progressive shift towards the reconciliation of employment and family life in equality policy also signalled the primary concern with labour market flexibility. Scrutiny of trends in employment patterns for women and men during the 1990s and into the early 2000s, in conjunction with data on the ageing of the labour force reinforced concern about the future European labour supply. Further support for a more egalitarian sharing of employment opportunities was, therefore, being justified as a means of ensuring both the quantity and quality of the labour force [6.20, p. 10]. Women, it has been argued, were not being utilized to their full capacity, either because many of them spent lengthy periods out of the labour force, or because they did not work full time (Rubery and Smith, 1999, p. 7).

Although women's economic activity rates increased steadily across EU15 from the mid-1970s, while those of men were falling, everywhere in EU27, rates for women remained lower than for men [4.14, 2006, pp. 258–86]. Even in the younger age groups, where availability is less subject to family constraints, rates for women were consistently below those for men, indicating that, despite equality legislation, women still experienced more difficulty than men in finding initial employment and in remaining economically active. The available evidence suggests that legislation to ensure equal pay for work of equal value and improve women's opportunities in access to training and employment had not enabled them to enter the labour market or to advance their employment careers on equal terms with men [6.21, 2005, pp. 9–10]. Analysis of the situation in the member states in central and eastern Europe calls into question some of the assumptions underlying EU15 gender equality policy. During the Soviet era, women had no choice but to work full time. Gender employment and pay gaps were much smaller than in most EU15 member states. Through the enterprise, women were guaranteed maternity and parental leave, childcare, health services, education and leisure facilities. Gender equality was not the driver of policy (Pascall and Manning, 2000). The retrenchment of public services combined with labour market restructuring during the 1990s led to a steep fall in employment rates for both men and women.

In the early 2000s, across EU27, women were more likely to be in lower paid, less secure employment than men, to work part-time or to be employed on fixed-term contracts. In 2005, female part-time rates were near or above 40 per cent in Austria, Belgium, Germany, Sweden and the United Kingdom. They reached 75 per cent in the Netherlands. The Czech Republic, Greece, Hungary and Lithuania recorded under 10 per cent, and in Bulgaria and Slovakia, rates fell below 5 per cent. Except in Estonia, Ireland, Sweden and the United Kingdom, women were also more likely than men to be unemployed [4.14, 2006, pp. 260–86].

Female employment rates varied according to the age and number of children but to differing degrees from one country to another. In 2003, rates for women with two children aged under 12 were highest in Denmark, Lithuania and Slovenia, and lowest in the Czech Republic, Hungary, Italy and Malta. The difference between women with one and three children was most marked in the Czech Republic, Hungary and Slovakia. Whereas children's age appeared to have little effect on female employment rates in Austria, Italy, Luxembourg, Malta, the Netherlands, Portugal, Slovenia and Spain, age was a significant factor determining rates in the Czech Republic, Estonia, Hungary and Slovakia, which are the countries with the lowest employment rate for women with very young children. This finding seem to suggest that women in these countries who took parental leave to raise young children were being recorded as economically inactive [2.6, 4/2005, charts 2, 3].

Nowhere had occupational segregation disappeared, as measured by the division of paid work between what were commonly seen as men's and women's jobs [6.21, 2005, p. 10]. Not only did women continue to be concentrated in the least secure and least well-paid sectors of employment, but also the growing proportion of women in lower skilled service jobs made such low-paid work even more female dominated. Although more women were entering and remaining in paid employment for longer periods, they tended to be concentrated in the caring professions and public sector employment, where working conditions were more flexible and 'women friendly', but where pay was often lower than in the private sector. Analysis of occupational segregation shows that, whereas legislation was implemented on equal pay for the same work, it was difficult to prove discrimination on the basis of equal value for different work, or avoid the gendering of jobs and the potential incompatibility of flexibility and equality (Rubery *et al.*, 1999).

For so long as equal pay, equal treatment and access to social security provisions depended on full-time continuous working patterns, it was clear that large proportions of women in many member states would be excluded from welfare rights or entitled to lower rates due to their interrupted employment patterns, precarious or part-time status. As a result, large numbers of women had to rely on a male breadwinner for derived rights or resort to means-tested benefits (see Chapter 8).

THE GENDER IMPACT OF EQUALITY POLICY

Although European legislation extended the equal treatment principle to social security entitlements, it has been demonstrated throughout this chapter that the continuing focus on paid employment was a significant factor in preventing the Union from adequately addressing 'the combined sources of inequality between the sexes' (Meehan, 1993, p. 194). Since women were more often than men marginalized as workers, they were over-represented among the population groups most likely to suffer in individualized, employment-based systems of social protection, thus exacerbating not only gender inequalities but also differences between groups of women and between families according to whether they contained single, dual or no-earners.

European legislation deferred to the subsidiarity principle in setting minimum standards that member states were invited to overstep. Although, in reports and guidelines, attention was drawn to examples of good practice, and governments were obliged to introduce legislative change to comply with directives, as amply demonstrated by the examples quoted in this chapter, the result was not convergence in the level and standard of provision. Women would still seem to have fared better in member states where entitlements to benefits were provided on a universal basis of citizenship than in those where employment-insurance contributions formed the basis for welfare entitlements. This observation applies, however, only for so long as the benefit system was dependent solely on taxation and provided flat-rate payments and a high standard of care for everyone. Most countries either already had, or were moving towards, a mixed economy of welfare, enabling some groups to obtain benefits over and above a guaranteed minimum rate, generally on the basis of occupational and private schemes (see Chapter 2). In such systems women, who customarily had interrupted employment patterns and worked in low-paid insecure jobs, were likely to continue to suffer disadvantages in access to welfare.

Moreover, many of the gains on the equality front could work against the interests of women, illustrating the dangers inherent in equality policies if they do not take full account of possible side-effects. The gradual erosion of wage differentials due to equal pay legislation could, for example, reduce the advantage to employers of recruiting women, contributing to higher rates of female unemployment and lower job security for women. The individualization of welfare and tax benefits could also work to the disadvantage of women on low incomes, as argued above. When a high standard of employment rights was targeted specifically at women, it could result in them being crowded out of the job market because of the heavy demands they were expected to make on employers. Equal rights for part-timers could mean, for example, that the low income from short part-time hours, after social insurance deductions, made part-time work unattractive for employees, while the additional labour costs discouraged employers from recruiting part-time workers. Arrangements for extended maternity and parental leave could also discourage employers from taking on women of childbearing age.

Although attempts were made to guard against such negative discrimination at EU and national level, it proved difficult to strike a balance between the twin goals of equality and difference. By the early 2000s, EU institutions had built up a strong regulatory framework, supported by soft law and an active women's lobby. Membership of countries such as Sweden had pushed forward the concept of mainstreaming. However, like the equal treatment directives of the 1970s, mainstreaming focused more on equality of process than of outcomes. Like the positive action programmes of the 1980s, it acknowledged differences between the sexes and concentrated on improving opportunities for women, but it did so by seeking to change systems and structures. Unlike the legislative approach, mainstreaming gave the initiative to the Commission and extended its competence, as demonstrated by the equal opportunities report for 2005, which set out to address men as well as women in an effort to promote greater gender equality in both paid work and private life. However, as in the past, the aim was to ensure that gender policies contributed to employment and growth and tap into the 'productive potential of women' [6.21, 2006, p. 3].

The implementation of paid parental leave, shared between both parents, and the recognition in pension entitlements of periods spent out of the labour market undertaking unpaid caring work at home went some way towards promoting what has been described as the worker-carer model of the citizen, applied to both men and women (Lister, 1997, p. 168). Whether European legislation and its translation into national law and practice can be credited with having brought about changes in attitudes and behaviour, and whether the Union can and should go any further in attempting to influence national policies regarding the division of labour in public and private life are set to remain controversial issues well into the twenty-first century.

Box 6   Secondary legislation and official publications relating to the gender dimension of social policy

6.1   Council Directive 75/117/EEC of 10 February 1975 on the approximation of the laws of the Member States relating to the application of the principle of equal pay for men and women, *OJ* L 45/19 19.2.1975.

6.2   Council Directive 76/207/EEC of 9 February 1976 on the implementation of the principle of equal treatment for men and women as regards access to employment, vocational training and promotion, and working conditions, *OJ* L 39/40 14.2.1976; Council Directive 2002/73/EC of 23 September 2002 amending Council Directive 76/207/EEC on the principle of equal treatment for men and women as regards access to employment, vocational training and promotion, and working conditions, *OJ* L 269/15 05.10.2002.

6.3   Council Directive 79/7/EEC of 19 December 1978 on the progressive implementation of the principle of equal treatment for men and women in matters of social security, *OJ* L 6/24 10.1.1979.

6.4   Commission proposal for a Council Directive on parental leave and leave for family reasons, COM(83) 686 final, 22.11.1983, *OJ* C 333/6 9.12.1983; amended proposal, COM(84) 631 final, 9.11.1984, *OJ* C 316/7 27.11.1984; Council Directive 96/34/EC of 3 June 1996 on the framework agreement on parental leave concluded by UNICE, CEEP and the ETUC, *OJ* L 145/4 19.6.1996; Council Directive 97/75/EC of 15 December 1997, amending and extending, to the United Kingdom of Great Britain and Northern Ireland, Directive 96/34/EC on the framework agreement on parental leave concluded by UNICE, CEEP and the ETUC, *OJ* L 10/24 16.1.1998.

6.5   Commission of the European Communities, Equal opportunities. action programme 1982–1985, *Women of Europe Supplement*, No. 9, 1982; Commission of the European Communities, Equal opportunities, 2nd action programme 1986–1990, *Women of Europe Supplement*, No. 23, 1986.

6.6   Council Directive 86/378/EEC of 24 July 1986 on the implementation of the principle of equal treatment for men and women in occupational social security schemes, *OJ* L 225/40 12.8.1986; Council Directive 96/97/EC of 20 December 1996 amending Directive 86/378/EEC on the implementation of the principle of equal treatment for men and women in occupational social security schemes, *OJ* L 46/20 17.2.1997.

6.7   Commission of the European Communities, Community law and women, *Women of Europe Supplement*, No. 25, 1987.

6.8   Council Directive 86/613/EEC of 11 December 1986 on the application of the principle of equal treatment between men and women engaged in an activity, including agriculture, in a self-employed capacity, and on the protection of self-employed women during pregnancy and motherhood, *OJ* L 359/56 19.12.1986.

6.9   Commission of the European Communities, Background report: protection at work for pregnant women or women who have recently given birth, ISEC/B25/90, 5.10.1990, London.

6.10 Council Resolution of 21 May 1991 on the third medium-term Community action programme on equal opportunities for women and men (1991 to 1995), *OJ* C 142/1 31.5.1991.

6.11 Commission Recommendation of 27 November 1991 on the protection of the dignity of women and men at work, 92/131/EEC, *OJ* L 49/1 24.2.1992.

6.12 Council Recommendation of 31 March 1992 on child care, 92/241/EEC, *OJ* L 123/16 8.5.1992.

6.13 Council Decision of 22 December 1995 on a medium-term Community action programme on equal opportunities for men and women (1996 to 2000), 95/593/EC, *OJ* L 335/37 30.12.1995.

6.14 European Commission, Work and childcare: implementing the Council recommendation on childcare. A guide to good practice, *Social Europe Supplement*, 5/96.

6.15 Commission Communication, Incorporating equal opportunities for women and men into all Community policies and activities, COM(96) 67 final, 21.2.1996; Progress report from the Commission on the follow-up of the Communication: Incorporating equal opportunities for women and men into all Community policies and activities, COM(1998) 122 final, 4.3.1998.

6.16 Case C–450/93 Eckhard Kalanke v Freie Hansestadt Bremen [1995] ECR I–3051, on positive discrimination in the appointment and promotion of men and women; Case C–409/95 Hellmut Marschall v Land Nordrhein-Westfalen [1997] ECR I–6363, on priority for women in promotion.

6.17 Resolution of the Council and of the Ministers for Employment and Social Policy, meeting within the Council, on the balanced participation of women and men in family and working life, *OJ* C 218/2, 31.7.2000.

6.18 Communication from the Commission, Towards a Community framework strategy on gender equality (2001–05), COM(2000) 335 final, 7 June 2000, accompanied by annual work programmes.

6.19 Council Directive 2004/113/EC of 13 December 2004 implementing the principle of equal treatment between men and women in the access to and supply of goods and services, *OJ* L 373/37 21.12.2004.

6.20 Communication from the Commission, A roadmap for equality between men and women – 2006–2010, COM(2006) 92 final, 1.3.2006.

6.21 European Commission, *Equal Opportunities for Women and Men in the European* Union; Equality *between Men and Women*, OOPEC (annual), available on-line from 2005 at:
http://europa.eu.int/comm/employment_social/equ_opp/index_en.htm

7 Policy for Older and Disabled People

The emphasis placed on workers' rights in the Community's and Union's treaties and charter signalled that European social policy was only indirectly concerned with categories of the population who did not gain entitlements to social protection as active members of the labour force. The Treaty establishing the European Economic Community (EEC) [1.2], and later the Single European Act (SEA) [1.5] and the Treaty on European Union [1.6], made no reference to older or disabled people. A statement on European policy for these two potentially disadvantaged categories of former or would-be workers was, however, introduced into the Community Charter of the Fundamental Social Rights of Workers [1.12], and a new article on non-discrimination in the Treaty of Amsterdam [1.7] identified disability and age among the areas where discrimination was to be eliminated. As with family policy (see Chapter 5), demographic factors explain why older people have moved onto the social policy agenda. Throughout the 1990s, one of the major challenges facing the Union was how to prepare for the demographic imbalance predicted for the twenty-first century, and how to tackle associated issues, such as intergenerational equity and the social and economic integration of older and disabled people. Policy makers were faced with the problems of ensuring the sustainability of pensions and the provision of adequate and effective social and health care in a context of financial stringency, and where many of the premises on which welfare states had been founded were being called into question.

This chapter focuses primarily on the policy implications of the ageing of the Union's population, and the related needs of elderly and infirm people. Firstly, it considers the development of European social policy for older and disabled people, with reference to the Union's legal framework, the Commission's action programmes and other policy instruments applied in these areas. The social and economic problems associated with demographic ageing are then examined across member states. National social protection provisions for older and disabled people are analysed to determine how policy makers in member states have responded to changing needs, particularly with regard to pensions and informal caring. Finally, an attempt is made to assess the impact of actions taken at European level on national policy making and on inter-generational relations within member states.

DEVELOPING POLICY FOR OLDER AND DISABLED PEOPLE

Changing demographic structures have given rise to a number of policy issues that have been addressed at EU level on the basis that their implications go beyond the realm of action by individual nations. Greater life expectancy, combined with falling birth rates, means that the proportion of the population aged 80 or over has grown at an unprecedented rate. Concern about the possible impact of such changes on the funding and provision of benefits and pension schemes, and thus on workers' mobility, public expenditure and international competition, helps to explain why the Union's institutions identified ageing as an area for concerted action by member states. The social and economic integration of disabled people was of interest on humanitarian grounds, and because their participation in a regular working environment was seen as an asset for the Union. Their exclusion from work and social life was said to constitute an underutilization of experience and talent, and a waste of resources [7.15, pp. 6, 21]. This section examines the different forms of action taken at EU level with reference to the objectives and policy measures that have been proposed and implemented.

Provision for older and disabled people in EU treaties and charters

Concern that differences in the treatment of older or disabled people might prevent the effective operation of the common market was implicit in the EEC Treaty. Articles 51 and 121 made provision for migrant workers to aggregate entitlements to benefits during periods spent in other member states, and for common measures to be implemented to ensure their rights to social protection, which could take the form of an adequate pension in old age. Articles 117 and 118 on social policy referred to the expectation that member states would work closely together to achieve these objectives by harmonizing their social systems.

In addition to the need to ensure that differences in social protection systems would not impede freedom of movement, another reason why older and disabled people were of indirect interest to the EEC founder members was that differences in the method of funding pensions and health care might affect the competitiveness of goods, services and manpower in countries with social insurance schemes that relied heavily on employer and employee contributions. Some member states feared they might be at a competitive disadvantage because of their relatively high labour costs and more generous provision. The danger of welfare tourism, whereby nationals from one member state can be attracted by more generous social provision elsewhere in the Community, was also relevant for older and disabled people. Similarly, according to the concept of social dumping, governments might find it financially attractive to subcontract caring to other member states with higher productive efficiency or lower labour costs (see also Chapters 1, 2, 9).

More than 30 years after the signing of the EEC Treaty, although the original reasons for European intervention remained, the Community charter of 1989 [1.12] formally recognized the aspirations of older and disabled people for independent living. While affirming its intention to respect national systems and leave member states to make their own arrangements, the charter made clear the obligation to ensure minimum rights for older and disabled people to help them overcome their financial and other handicaps. It recommended that, on retirement, every worker should be able 'to enjoy resources affording him or her a decent standard of living' (§24) and should be entitled 'to sufficient resources and to medical and social assistance specifically suited to his [*sic*] needs' (§25). The section on disabled persons (§26) stipulated that provision should be made for 'additional concrete measures aimed at improving their social and professional integration', namely vocational training, ergonomics, accessibility, mobility, transport and housing.

The Agreement on Social Policy appended to the Treaty on European Union [1.6] did not refer specifically to age or disability, but a new article outlawing discrimination on these grounds was introduced into the Treaty of Amsterdam [1.7], becoming article 13 in the EC Treaty [1.8] and a central theme in Council Directive 2000/78/EC [7.17, articles 5, 6]. Article 13 gave the Council the authority to act unanimously, after consulting with the European Parliament, to 'take appropriate action to combat all forms of discrimination'. Article 129 enabled the Council to adopt incentive measures for developing the exchange of information and best practice in the field of employment, and article 137 (§1) bestowed the power to act to promote the integration of persons excluded from the labour market.

The Charter of Fundamental Rights of the European Union [1.21], agreed in Nice in 2000, prohibited discrimination on grounds of disability and age (article II-21). Article II-25 explicitly identified the right of older people 'to lead a life of dignity and independence and to participate in social and cultural life', while article II-26 recognized the right of people with disabilities 'to benefit from measures designed to ensure their independence, social and occupational integration and participation in the life of the community'. Article II-35 laid down the right of everyone to health care, in accordance with national laws and practices, and to health protection, based on implementation of Union policies and activities. By the early 2000s, provisions were thus in place for action in support of older and disabled people, an issue recognized as a legitimate concern for EU member states on a number of counts.

Secondary legislation for older and disabled people

During the 1980s before the Community charter was adopted, the European Parliament had addressed the situation of older and disabled people in several resolutions. Broad themes relevant to their interests had been placed on the agenda. Resolutions on the social integration of handicapped people [7.1] in 1981 and the situation and problems of older people [7.2] in 1982 were followed in 1986 by resolutions on services for older people [7.4] and measures to improve their situation in member states [7.5].

Although no binding legislation was implemented specifically for older or disabled people, directives adopted under the aegis of equal treatment for men and women (article 119 of the EEC Treaty) covered pension rights. Directive 79/7/EEC on equal treatment in matters of social security [6.3], which was extended to occupational social security schemes and to self-employed workers [6.8] in 1986, aimed to tackle an important source of inequality by giving women greater access to social security entitlements in their own right (see Chapter 6). Women, or specifically married women, had previously been excluded from some state and occupational pension schemes. In 1982, a Council recommendation set out the principles of Community policy with regard to retirement age [7.3]. The document was not concerned with gender differences, but a report from the Commission in 1992 on the application of the recommendation [7.3] raised the issue, and noted that it was under examination in most member states where retirement age was different for men and women. Flexible arrangements for retirement were considered further in a Council resolution in 1993 [7.11].

The programme for the application of the 1989 Community charter [1.13] made provision for action in all the areas identified. Although binding legislation was still not considered appropriate, and none was adopted during the 1990s, a proposal was issued in 1991 for a Council directive 'on minimum requirements to improve the mobility and the safe transport to work of workers with reduced mobility' [7.8]. A name change for the unit responsible for disabled people from 'Measures for the Disabled' to 'Integration of the Disabled' in 1993 confirmed the shift of emphasis in policy announced in the charter.

    The 1992 Council Recommendation 'on the convergence of social protection objectives and policies' [2.1] treated disability as 'incapacity for work', an approach pursued in the employment strategy [1.18]. The aim was to ensure minimum means of subsistence and social and economic integration through benefits so that disabled people could maintain 'their standard of living in a reasonable manner in accordance with their participation in appropriate social security schemes' [2.1, p. 51]. The recommendation also provided a clear statement of the principles governing social protection for older people [2.1, p. 52]. Building on §§24–5 of the 1989 Community charter, it placed the onus on member states to guarantee a minimum level of subsistence to all older people in accordance with national and European provisions. Strong guidance was offered to national governments on the measures needed to combat the social exclusion of older people. The Council recommended that workers should have the right to carry on working after minimum pensionable age and to maintain a replacement income throughout retirement. Entitlements were to be extended to workers with incomplete careers, and schemes were to be adapted in response to demographic change. The stated aim was again to prevent any disparities between member states in spending on care for older and disabled people that might impede workers' mobility within the Union. The justification for Council Directive 98/49/EC 'on safeguarding the supplementary pension rights of employed and self-employed people moving within the European Union' [9.17] was that it would eliminate one of the remaining obstacles to free movement of workers (see Chapter 9).

Soft law as a policy option for older and disabled people

Despite the absence of specific references in the Community's and Union's treaties and the relative lack of binding legislation, action programmes for older and disabled people predate the Community charter. The 1974 social action programme [1.11, p. 2] advocated measures to promote the vocational and social rehabilitation of handicapped people. Within the general context of improving quality of life for all European citizens, the Commission drew up and implemented a series of action programmes to support older people and ensure the economic and social integration of the 10 per cent or so of the Community's population affected by a physical, sensorial or mental handicap.

The first action programme specifically aimed at disabled people was adopted in 1981, providing support for national efforts through technical exchanges of experience in the areas of education, training, employment, social security and care systems, communications, mobility and housing [7.1]. In 1988, the Council adopted a second Community action programme for the period 1988–91 under the title 'Handicapped People in the European Community Living Independently in an Open Society' (Helios) [7.6], designed to promote social integration and an independent lifestyle for people with disabilities. Within the programme, a computerized information system and network for disabled people in Europe were set up, under the name of Handynet, containing information about technical aids and the addresses of specialist companies and organizations. A further three-year programme was established in 1993, with the focus on the integration of young people with disabilities into ordinary systems of education and the promotion of independent living for disabled people. Particular reference was made to older people with the aim of contributing to the economic and social cohesion of the Union [7.10].

The European structural funds have served as a financial instrument at Community level to support initiatives such as Employment-Horizon for the integration of disabled people into the world of work. A European Disability Forum was launched in 1993, designed to ensure the flow of information between EU institutions, national authorities and non-governmental organizations. In a communication issued in 1996 'on equality of opportunity for people with disabilities' [7.13], the Commission stressed the importance of integration as the key to inclusion in mainstream society. Member states were to achieve greater equality of opportunity by empowering people with disabilities, removing access barriers to participation, opening up all spheres of activity and making public opinion receptive to equality issues for people with disabilities. The priority to be given to enhancing employability of disabled people was signalled in the 1999 employment guidelines when the topic moved into the first pillar of the employment strategy [1.18].

Meanwhile, separate actions had been adopted for older people with disabilities. A Council decision in 1991 established a programme of concerted Community actions, following a communication from the Commission on the subject [7.7]. The aim was to monitor and exchange information on demographic trends and their impact on health and social protection systems, while also looking at measures for improving the mobility of older people and helping them to lead independent lives. Another more nebulous objective was to promote solidarity between generations. The positive contribution of older people to economic and social life was recognized, and the Commission undertook to ensure that their income would be protected.

Under the programme, an Observatory on Ageing and Older People was set up with responsibility for providing the Commission with authoritative reports about the situation of older people in all member states and the policies being pursued. The observatory had a monitoring role similar to that of the European Observatory on National Family Policies (see Chapter 5). Its efforts were to be concentrated on four areas: living standards and way of life, employment and the labour market, health and social care, and the social integration of older people in both formal and informal settings (Walker, 1993, p. 2; Walker and Maltby, 1997, pp. 4–5). The working definition of social policy for older people was couched in broad terms to include the impact of social and economic policies on older people, regardless of whether they originated from the public, private or voluntary sectors. In particular, member states were to address 'the challenges resulting from present and future demographic developments and the consequences of an ageing population for all Community policies' (Walker, 1993, p. 2), implying the mainstreaming of ageing, as was later the case for gender.

The year 1993 was proclaimed as the European Year of Older People and Solidarity between Generations. The intention was to heighten society's awareness of issues concerning older people, to promote intergenerational solidarity and involve older people in the process of Community integration [7.9]. The 1994 white paper on European social policy [1.15] also focused on the theme of integration. The Commission proposed to draw up a code of good practice for employers and to introduce measures to eliminate discrimination against disabled people. With older people, they were identified as categories not to be excluded from the benefits of a more integrated Europe, since they were capable of making an active contribution to society [1.15, p. 49].

The Commission adopted a responsive stance, acting to promote and facilitate the exchange of knowledge and experience through support for initiatives at EU, regional and local level. Progressively, during the 1990s, reference was made to the problems associated with population decline and ageing to justify interest in the well being of older people. In a proposal for a Council decision 'on Community support for actions in favour of older people' [7.12], covering the period 1995–99, the

Commission identified four key areas for close attention: improving the situation of older women; management of an ageing workforce; the transition from work to retirement; and care and access to care for dependent older people. The proposal did not achieve unanimity at the Council, but one of the strands – the retention, reintegration and retraining of older workers – became the focus of a guide to good practice produced in 1998, building on the findings from a project coordinated by the European Foundation for the Improvement of Living and Working Conditions on combating age barriers (Walker, 1998).

A key issue throughout the 1990s and since has been how to sustain pension arrangements after the year 2000. A report to the Commission in 1996 from the EU network of experts on supplementary pension provision analysed the case for greater involvement of the private sector in the funding and delivery of pensions [7.14, p. 5]. Supplementary schemes were no longer seen as a marginal phenomenon, but rather an 'indispensable "pillar" of the social protection structure' in the context of demographic, economic and social change. Supplementary pension schemes were of legitimate interest for the Union as an instrument for promoting freedom of movement for workers and capital. A strong argument in favour of supplementary pensions was the negative impact on labour costs of the heavy reliance on earnings-related contributions and thus on employment. They also afforded a possible solution to the problem of how to provide retirement pensions in the longer term. Another argument used was the need to move away from the pay-as-you-go principle, on which most of the employment-insurance schemes were based, towards alternatives such as funded arrangements involving (private) institutional investors, which are less sensitive to changes in the size and composition of the labour force. The cost of introducing full funding for first-tier pensions was not, however, considered to be viable. The report expressed doubts about the willingness of employers to substitute compulsory insurance contributions for voluntary employer-sponsored supplementary provision. It was anticipated that, if such arrangements were mandatory, pension levels might be lowered, as had happened in France, Greece and the Netherlands when entitlements to employment-insurance based pensions had been curtailed.

In a contribution to the United Nations' International Year of Older People in 1999, the Commission issued a communication entitled 'Towards a Europe for all ages', setting out its policy strategy for dealing with the implications of population ageing in the twenty-first century [7.15, p. 6]. It recommended developing measures in four areas. Firstly, concerted action was needed to maintain the capacity of workers and to promote lifelong learning and flexible working arrangements. Secondly, attention was to be paid to reversing the trend towards early retirement, exploring new forms of gradual retirement and making pension schemes more sustainable and flexible. Thirdly, in the area of health and old age care, research and studies were to be initiated to develop adequate responses to healthcare needs. Finally, the Commission was fulfilling its treaty obligations by promoting action to combat discrimination, unemployment and social exclusion among older people. These themes were reiterated in proposals to apply the open method of coordination (OMC) to pensions, health and long-term care.

The Lisbon European Council in 2000 had addressed the issue of the sustainability of pensions as a central component in the modernization of social protection. The Stockholm European Council in 2001 recommended using the OMC in the field of pensions [1.20]. The OMC was seen as the most effective instrument for responding to the common problems associated with population ageing. The Council advocated a three-pronged strategy to tackle the financial implications of population ageing: avoid rising levels of public debt by ensuring that the long-term commitments of pension systems can be met; implement comprehensive labour market reforms, including tax and benefit systems, to encourage higher employment rates and protect pension entitlements; and reform pension systems to contain pressures on public finances, maintain a sound financial basis and ensure a fair intergenerational balance.

In the same year, the Laeken European Council and Commission pursued the issue of pension reform [1.20; 7.16]. The Council endorsed the common objectives of achieving adequacy, financial sustainability and adaptability of pensions. Its recommendations included adopting a working method based on the OMC to enhance dialogue and cooperation between member states. The Commission's 2003 and 2006 reports on pensions [7.20] stressed the need to continue the reform process, in particular by increasing effective average retirement age, which was still below the level of the late 1960s. Subsequently, the Council moved to implement an integrated life-cycle approach to pension and healthcare systems in support of participation in employment and longer working lives, including appropriate incentives to encourage work and disincentives to discourage early retirement [1.18, 2005 guideline 18].

A communication from the Commission in 2004 defined a detailed common framework for high-quality, accessible and sustainable health care and long-term care, with particular reference to older people, based on the OMC [7.18]. The Commission drew attention to the need to deal with the implications of revisions to the regulations governing cross-border access to the supply and funding of health-care services and health worker mobility within the Union (see Chapter 9). It highlighted the job creation potential of the care sector, stressing the importance of ensuring that care workers were properly trained and were offered quality jobs. A series of proposals was listed for achieving the three major objectives: ensuring fair and universal access to care based on solidarity; promoting high-quality care as a way of improving health and quality of life; guaranteeing the financial sustainability of accessible, high-quality care. The added value of the OMC lay in the identification of common challenges and support for reforms at national level.

The 2005 green paper on confronting demographic change and the subsequent communication, issued in 2006 [1.25], provided further evidence of the Union's resolve to stimulate a concerted approach to the questions raised by demographic ageing applying the full panoply of instruments at its disposal to develop a life-course strategy [1.25, 2006, p. 8]. In its synthesis report on adequate and sustainable pensions for 2006, the Commission reminded the Council and Parliament that, while contribution years had been decreasing due to later labour market entry and earlier exit, years in receipt of benefits had been increasing. It therefore again stressed the need to address the problems of effective retirement age and to prepare for the impending retirement of the postwar baby-boom generations. The report portrayed pension reform as requiring long-term strategies, with public provision at national level as a central plank. It acknowledged that no one-size-fits-all solution existed, but implicitly recognized the continued importance of the Commission's monitoring, mediating and coordinating roles, recommending that 'adequacy, sustainability and modernisation should be considered jointly' [7.19, p. 14].

THE DEMOGRAPHIC CHALLENGE FOR EU MEMBER STATES

In the 1980s and 1990s, all EU member states were facing rising levels of public expenditure on pensions, health and social care for a growing proportion of the population, as medical advances, better living and working conditions and improved social protection contributed to greater life expectancy. A legal age of retirement had been implemented across the Union. Occupational pension schemes were being extended to all categories of former workers, at the same time as the number of economically inactive older people was increasing. Despite longer compulsory schooling and the more widespread development of vocational training and later labour market entry (see Chapter 3), the combination of falling birth rates (see Chapter 5), greater life expectancy, enforced and early retirement had shifted the balance in the dependency ratio away from younger towards older people. A dwindling labour force was being called upon to bear the cost of supporting a growing proportion of economically inactive older people. Not all member states were affected to the same extent by the consequences of population ageing. This section examines different conceptions of ageing and the differential impact of the ageing process on member states.

Common characteristics of population ageing in the Union

From the mid-1980s, as a result of falling mortality rates in member states, the absence of new waves of immigration or a universal rise in the birth rate, the Union's population was beginning to stagnate and, in several member states, to decline [5.8, 2006, table B-2]. The trend towards an ageing and declining population had intensified by the end of the century, presenting a common challenge for EU member states [1.25]. In 2004, 16.5 per cent of the Union's population was aged over 65. Using a baseline scenario, Eurostat estimated that, by 2030, this age group would represent 24.7 per cent of total population and 29.9 per cent by 2050 [2.5, 3/2006, tables 1, 4]. Irrespective of any upturn in the birth rate or an increase in migration, if life expectancy continued to grow, the number of older people over 80 in the Union was set to rise from 18 million in 2004 to 50 million in 2051, with the impact becoming most visible from the mid-2020s [2.5, 3/2006, p. 2, figure 3]. These predictions of population ageing during the twenty-first century located EU25 below Japan but above the United States [1.25, 2005, graph 3].

Whereas in 2004, the old age dependency ratio (people aged over 65 in relation to the population aged 15–64 theoretically available for work) was 25 per cent in the Union, by 2050, it is expected to have doubled. In other terms, in 2004, approximately four people were of working age for one aged over 65; by 2050, fewer than two people will be of working age for every person over 65 [2.5, 3/2006, p. 2]. The number of actual workers is, in reality, much smaller due to late labour market entry, periods spent out of the labour market, especially for women, and early retirement. The old age economic dependency ratio (population aged over 65 in relation to the population in employment) was 37 per cent in 2005. It was expected to reach 70 per cent in 2050. From three workers for each pensioner, it was predicted that 1.4 workers would be supporting every pensioner [7.19, 2006, p. 9].

Economic dependency is exacerbated by low employment rates among the older working age population. During the 1980s and 1990s, in most EU15 member states early retirement was being encouraged to release jobs, whereas biologically, socially and economically, it would have been more logical to consider postponing the end of working life. Economic activity started to decline as much as ten years before legal retirement age in a process of phased withdrawal from the labour market, which did not necessarily reflect ability to work. While growth in the male working age population was slowing down, actual employment rates for men aged 55–59 fell by seven percentage points in as many years between 1990 and 1997, thereby reducing the size of the labour force contributing to pensions and, at the same time, increasing the number of recipients of benefits [4.14, 1999, pp. 89–90].

In the 1990s, most member states were not yet feeling the full impact of population ageing, since the postwar 'baby-boomers' were still actively contributing to the labour supply. Because young people are also big consumers of services, such as education, health and family benefits, the falling birth rate produced some savings in the short and medium term. In the longer term, however, the economic and social costs of an ageing population were expected to outweigh any advantages that may have accrued initially. The task of supporting these two dependent population groups falls differently: while families meet a considerable share of the economic costs of raising children, seen as an investment for the future, those associated with older people (pensions and health care) tend to be borne largely by society, and, increasingly, to be conceptualized as a burden. At the time when the cost of caring for older people is expected to become most acute in the twenty-first century as the baby-boomers reach retirement age, any savings from raising smaller numbers of young people will have been expended.

The relationship between population ageing and care needs is not straightforward. Statistics measuring demographic ageing in terms of the increase in the proportion of older people in the population generally assume that old age begins at 60 or 65, particularly if this is the legal age for retirement. Chronological age does not, however, take account of the biological phenomenon of individual ageing. In western Europe, biological or physical ageing of individuals is occurring at a much older age than in the early twentieth century: being 60 in the 2000s was very different from what it was in the 1920s or 1930s. Age, when measured solely by calendar years, can therefore be misleading as an indicator of social and physical needs and competences. While medical advances have, undoubtedly, made it possible to prolong the lives of older people with disabilities, they also mean that a large proportion of the population reaching the age of 60 can expect to enjoy many more years of good health. The proportion of older people in need of care in old age will not necessarily increase with population ageing. Rather, the problems of disability and frailty associated with biological ageing will be postponed to a later age.

In combination with greater longevity, the institutionalization of retirement age has created different categories of older people: young or third age older people in the 60–74 age group and what is sometimes referred to as the fourth age for those over 75. Third-age older people are more likely to be in good health and to enjoy a relatively generous pension, particularly if they contributed during their working lives to an occupational scheme guaranteeing a high proportion of former earnings. Their numbers were swollen in the early 1990s due to falling male employment rates between the ages of 55 and 64, exacerbating the imbalance in the dependency ratio [4.14, 2001, p. 110].

Due to the differential impact of armed conflict and the greater incidence among men of health risks associated with smoking, alcohol, road accidents and industrial hazards, women are over-represented among older people. Increasingly, they outnumber men, particularly in the higher age groups. Whereas in 1960, life expectancy at 60 was 15.8 years for men and 19 for women, by 2004 it had increased to 20.1 for men and 24.2 for women [5.8, 2006, tables E-6, E-7]. In the early 2000s in EU15, disability-free life expectancy at birth was estimated to be 64.5 years for men and 66 for women. However, due in part to their larger numbers, more than 54 per cent of women, compared with 48 per cent of men, aged over 65 reported that they were hampered in their daily activities by a physical or mental health problem, illness or disability [5.7, 2003, p. 191, 2005, annex]. Since women usually tend to marry older men, fourth-age older people include growing numbers of women, who are often living alone in poor quality housing, dependent on derived entitlements from the pension of a deceased or separated spouse or partner, or a minimum state pension, contending with failing health, and reliant on family and community support.

National differences in population ageing and dependency

The population ageing process has not taken place at the same rate or to the same extent throughout the Union. In the early 2000s, the shortest life expectancy was being reported for men in the central and east European member states: 66.1 years at birth in Estonia, compared with

78.3 in Sweden. By contrast, women could expect to live only 75.5 years in Romania but to the age of 83.8 in Spain and France. Gender differences in life expectancy were most pronounced in Latvia (11.4 years) and Estonia (11.1 years), and least marked (less than five years) in Sweden, the Netherlands, United Kingdom and Denmark, in that order [5.8, 2006, tables E-4, E-5]. Estimates of healthy life expectancy at birth reinforce the disparities between member states and gender differences: the population in EU15 member states could expect to live for 70 or more years free of disability, compared with 66 years in central and eastern Europe (World Health for All Database, 2006). Women in Italy and Poland could expect to enjoy about five more years than men free of disability, but in the Nordic states, Germany, the Netherlands and United Kingdom, men were living longer than women in good health [6.21, 2005, p. 22].

When different indicators for population decline and ageing are cross-tabulated, for the early 2000s, Austria, Germany, Greece and Italy stood out as the EU member states most affected by the combination of population decline and ageing. They were the first countries to have to grapple with the effects of a declining working age population and a relatively large proportion of older dependants. Countries that had maintained higher than average, albeit declining, birth rates, namely Cyprus, France, Ireland, Luxembourg, Malta and Sweden, were not expected to feel the full impact of population ageing for several decades. Compared with EU15, the central and east European member states were affected more by population decline than by population ageing because of their relatively shorter life expectancy (Hantrais, 2004, figure 2.1). Their old age dependency ratios remained below the EU15 average of 40.7 per cent in 2005, except in Bulgaria and Latvia, falling below 30 per cent in Poland and Slovakia [5.8, 2006, table C-8].

Economic dependency rates also varied between member states. A trend identified in Belgium, France, Germany, Luxembourg, the Netherlands and United Kingdom during the 1980s and 1990s was for men in the 55–59 age group who left the labour force to be classified as disabled rather than unemployed, thereby swelling the figures for disabled older people [4.14, 1999, p. 12]. The 2001 Stockholm European Council set a target for raising average EU employment rates for men and women aged 55–64 to 50 per cent by 2010, and the 2002 Barcelona European Council concluded that coercive efforts should be intensified to delay the age of labour market exit by five years by the end of the decade [1.20]. By the early 2000s, EU25 employment rates for this age group were rising at a faster rate than for the working age population. In

2005, eight countries had met the 50 per cent target, including 16 for men, but only the Nordic states and Estonia for women. Poland recorded the lowest overall employment rate for the 55–64 age group at below 30 per cent. Rates for women fell below 20 per cent in Malta, Poland, Slovenia and Slovakia [4.14, 2006, pp. 260–86]. The average exit age from employment for EU25 was 61 in 2004, but this figure concealed important differences between the countries with the earliest age (56.2 in Slovenia) and the latest age (64.4 in Ireland) [4.14, 2005, pp. 58–60]. The timing and intensity of the challenges associated with the impact of population ageing on the workforce, therefore, differed markedly from one member state to another.

NATIONAL PROVISIONS FOR OLDER AND DISABLED PEOPLE

By the late 1990s, the hitherto silent revolution in the ageing structure of the European population was becoming increasingly audible. Population ageing was already putting pension systems and health services under strain, raising doubts about their sustainability and quality, and the need for alternative methods of funding and delivery. Before the issue rose up the EU agenda, some countries had begun seeking solutions to the problem of long-term care, and national social protection systems were undergoing reform in an attempt to meet the financial and care needs of dependent older people [2.2, 1997, pp. 141–51].

Despite the stated objective in the EEC Treaty of promoting harmonization of national social protection systems, the Union has not used its legislative powers to eliminate disparities in formal national provisions for older and disabled people. Although some convergence may have taken place over time as social security arrangements have been adapted to meet the common challenges facing member states, important conceptual and practical differences remain in this area of social policy. Just as several models of social protection could be identified within the Union (see Chapter 2), arrangements for old age, retirement and invalidity pensions, disability allowances and long-term care can be analysed with reference to different national approaches.

Retirement age

Variations in demographic ageing are not necessarily closely reflected in policy responses, as indicated by the discrepancies between legal and actual retirement age. In 2006, the most common legal retirement age across EU25 was 65 for men and women, in most case coinciding with the age of entitlement to the standard basic pension. France operated the lowest age for men and women at 60, and Denmark the highest at 67. Finland, Italy and Sweden had introduced more flexible systems, with the level of pension varying according to age of retirement (from 57 in the case of Italy). The central and east European countries generally operated a lower age, most often of 62. They also tended to differentiate between men and women. As in the EU15 member states, they were generally increasing the age for women, but not always with the intention of achieving parity with men. In the Czech Republic, retirement age for women depended on the number of children raised, with a minimum for five or more of 55 years 8 months [2.4, 2006, table VI].

In practice, as already suggested, legal retirement age offers no more than a guide to the date at which most people leave the labour market. Since the legal age does not, in most cases, take account of the physical and mental state of the individual, except where early retirement is permitted on health grounds, the age chosen to mark the end of working life is determined more by political and economic considerations than on the basis of fitness for work. Although Denmark reported the highest retirement age, the life expectancy of Danish men and women at age 60 was below the EU25 average in 2004. Denmark was also below the EU25 average for the old age dependency ratio. France with its low retirement age fell below the EU25 average for the proportion of the population aged 20–59. Estonia and Latvia, with their relatively low retirement ages were above the EU25 average for the old age dependency ratio [5.8, 2006, tables C-4, C-8, E-6, E-7].

Social protection expenditure on population ageing

Taken together, differences in the proportions of the population over retirement age and, effectively, out of the labour force help to explain national variations in the resources devoted to older people. By the early 2000s, spending on old age and survivors was the largest item of public expenditure on social benefits across EU25, accounting for almost 46 per cent of spending on benefits in 2003. Only Ireland spent more on health. In Italy, the old age and survivors' function accounted for nearly 62 per cent of total spending on social benefits. Greece, Latvia, Malta and Poland devoted nearly 50 per cent of their social protection budget to this function. Everywhere in EU25, expenditure on health and disability amounted to at least 30 per cent of the total, and to over 40 per cent in 12 of the EU25 member states [2.5, 2006/14, table

4]. In combination and adjusted to take account of their proportion in the population, spending on older people amounted to more than twice the expenditure on total population in 2003 [8.15, 2006, pp. 113–14].

Income security in old age

Continental countries that followed the corporatist or conservative model of welfare, as developed initially by Germany, based their pension schemes on the principle of income maintenance, financed by employers, employees and the state. Although Belgium, France and Italy originally established old age pension schemes using subsidized voluntary insurance, they later adopted the German occupational scheme making old age insurance compulsory. According to this 'industrial achievement-performance' (Titmuss, 1974, p. 31) or 'income security' model (Ginn and Arber, 1992, p. 259), social needs are met in proportion to work performance through mandatory social insurance. Basic disability allowances, invalidity and old age pensions were income related, ensuring that workers with the highest incomes from earnings continued to receive higher benefits when they ceased work. Differences occurred within the continental income maintenance model with respect to the number of years that must be worked to qualify for a full pension. In the early 2000s, in the corporatist member states where the concept existed, the qualifying condition for a full pension was most often 40 years for both men and women [2.4, 2006, table VI].

The income security system had the disadvantage that non-earners and many low earners were excluded and could only gain entitlements in their capacity as dependants either of a spouse or the state. Individuals who were prevented from working because of family responsibilities or disability might have no chance of qualifying for full pensions in their own right, or of being able to achieve the high level of income that would guarantee a substantial pension on retirement. This issue was recognized in the income security member states by taking account of the number of years spent out of the labour market caring for young children or disabled relatives (see Chapters 6 and 8).

Basic security and residual state welfare

Member states with socialist or social democratic welfare regimes initially provided a basic state pension for all citizens, regardless of their employment record, funded from general taxation and with only a weak link to earnings. Denmark was one of the first member states to decide to introduce an old age pension scheme in 1891. Sweden followed suit in 1913 and Finland in 1937. The Danish scheme was based on a very different principle from that in Germany: it was entirely funded from taxation, with entitlements on the basis of citizenship and universal services provided according to need. The same principle applied for invalidity pensions. In 2006, a full basic, or social, pension was paid from the age of 67 to all citizens with 40 years of residence, supplemented by a compulsory employment-related scheme. Flat-rate supplementary pensions were funded from employer and employee contributions. Finland and Sweden also operated a 40-year residence requirement for the guaranteed basic pension. Both countries had developed supplementary employment-related contributory schemes [2.4, 2006, table VI]. For women, the basic security model had the advantage of enabling them to draw adequate pensions in their own right. The disregard for employment record in the universal flat-rate pension meant that women were not penalized as in earnings-related schemes.

The 'institutional-redistributive' or 'basic security' model of welfare was initially followed by Britain. In his plan for pensions, William Beveridge opted for a basic state scheme that maintained flat-rate benefits on the grounds that the state should not be involved in making provision for income maintenance. This principle continued to be applied for invalidity pensions in Ireland and the United Kingdom in the 1990s, although the British pension system moved towards the residual state welfare model for the basic state pension. Both countries required a high level of contributions to qualify for a full state pension – 48 years in Ireland, and 44 in the United Kingdom for men and 39 for women – with provision for years spent out of the labour market caring for family members [2.4, 2006, table VI].

The Netherlands also followed the basic security model, by instituting a first-tier pension scheme based on residence but funded by employee contributions. While pension arrangements ensured a basic income for women in their later years, irrespective of their employment record, the extensive private occupational pension schemes that were put in place tended to work against women due to their predominantly part-time status, with no provision being made for crediting time spent out of the labour market [2.4, 2006, table VI].

Despite the original intention, the British basic state pension scheme served essentially to alleviate poverty in old age and thus corresponds to what has been described as 'residual welfare' (Titmuss, 1974), characteristic of a 'liberal' welfare regime approach (Esping-Andersen, 1990). In such a system, state provision is minimal, while the market provides for privately funded earnings-related pensions. In the United Kingdom, non-earners had no guaranteed pension and depended on an earner or a means-tested safety net. The United Kingdom was the first member state to operate a statutory supplementary scheme, but those in better paid jobs could opt out in favour of earnings-related occupational and private individual pension schemes, offering more generous earnings-related benefits. By the 2000s, Britain had developed one of the most extensive second-tier pension schemes in the Union.

Women were at a particular disadvantage under the conditions operating in the British residual system (Ginn and Arber, 1992, pp. 261–3). Because of their interrupted employment histories and low part-time hours, which often fell below the earnings threshold for insurance contributions, many women were excluded from benefits that were dependent on employment record and level of earnings. The British social security scheme, as conceived by Beveridge, treated women as dependants on the understanding that male earnings should be sufficient to support a wife and children. Despite the provision of Home Responsibility Protection in 1978 and the disregard of contributions, granting credits to carers for years spent looking after children, sick or disabled persons, relatively few older women had acquired a sufficient contributions record to enable them to claim a full pension of their own.

Rudimentary or formative welfare

The member states that joined the Community in the 1980s – Greece, Portugal and Spain – had less developed social protection systems. Although their social security arrangements largely followed the continental model, in the 1990s their highly inequitable pension schemes were still far from providing the average level of benefits enjoyed by most older people in northern member states. Comparisons of income inequalities between generations suggest, however, that the material differences in living conditions between older people aged 65–84 and the 45–64 generation remained smaller in Greece, Italy, Portugal and Spain than elsewhere in EU15, due largely to the sharing of resources in extended households (Vogel, 1997, p. 153) (see also Chapter 8).

As in other EU member states, older women may suffer from having shorter periods of contribution to pension schemes. In Portugal, for example, despite their relatively high employment rates, women were twice as likely as men to have belonged to the non-contributory pension scheme, rather than the general contributory scheme. They were, therefore, entitled to lower benefit in retirement. In addition, women aged 65 or over in Portugal, and also in Greece, Italy and Spain, were twice as likely as men in the same age group to be living alone, whereas the gender difference was small in the other EU15 member states (4.15, 2002, table 9). The challenge in these countries was, therefore, how to improve the level of the minimum old age pension.

Transitional welfare

Despite the fact that population ageing was still seen as less of a threat than in EU15 member states, governments in the central and east European countries devoted considerable attention to reforming pension systems during the transitional period of the 1990s. Under the Soviet system, pension schemes were centralized and funded by employers or state agencies, creating a direct link with public finances. Because male and female employment rates were very high, most people qualified for pensions. Retirement age was generally low at 55 for women and 60 for men. When pension systems were being reformed, everywhere the pay-as-you-go principle was retained for the basic compulsory pension, although the concept of a full pension was not generally applied.

In response to falling employment rates and increasing dependency ratios, retirement age was raised, bringing it closer to the EU15 level [2.4, 2006, table VI]. Additional pension tiers were introduced involving the private sector. Evidence from several of the central and east European countries suggests that older people were not the biggest losers from transition. In Estonia, for example, they were relatively successful in focusing attention on their demise and in lobbying for pension reform. Pensions therefore followed inflation more closely than other social transfers. However, many retired people still lived on the verge of poverty in a context where family bonds were weakening at the same time as care for older people was, increasingly, seen by government as the responsibility of families (Hantrais, 2004, pp. 129–30).

Towards common objectives for national pension systems

The exchange of information through the European observatory's work and its efforts to develop policy for older people were expected to 'contribute to some convergence in national policies' (Walker, 1993, p. 1). Although their ideological and cultural origins and administrative structures differed, the future viability of pension systems in member states, as in other areas of social protection, created common concerns. In the early 2000s, one of the factors encouraging the exchange of information and experience, if not convergence, was the shared objective of containing the cost of pensions in the face of growing pressures from population ageing at a time when member states were striving to ensure their sustainability. The countries that initially made provision only for a flat-rate universal, national or state pension based on residence or citizenship had introduced second-tier earnings-related, occupational or supplementary pensions. Most member states were operating an earnings-related insurance-based scheme, increasingly in combination with a supplementary arrangement, which was progressively being made compulsory.

The financial crisis facing pension schemes at the turn of the twenty-first century provided an opportunity for a more thorough review of their rationale than had hitherto been countenanced. Most countries were implementing, or seriously considering, measures designed to reverse the trend towards early retirement by imposing stricter controls on labour market exit, restricting eligibility criteria and reducing pension levels. Retirement age was being raised, and the number of years of contributions needed to qualify for a full pension was being increased. Various forms of partial, phased or progressive retirement were being made available, with provision for accumulating pensions and earnings, and incentives in the form of additional pension contributions for those postponing retirement. The pay-as-you-go principle had been extended across the Union for first-tier pensions, with funding arrangements in place for supplementary schemes, while the involvement of the private sector in managing occupational pensions was an option being streamlined and regulated [2.4, 2006, table I].

Despite the progress made, the issues highlighted in the 2003 joint report on pensions remained priorities in the 2006 report: increasing incentives for working longer; developing a life-cycle approach and strengthening the link between contributions and benefits, while ensuring adequate income replacement and managing increasing longevity; making pension systems more adaptable to structural changes; strengthening the role of minimum pensions and solidarity in pension systems; ensuring secure private pensions complementing and partially replacing public pension provision; and improving the governance of pension systems [7.19, pp. 8–14].

Between informal and formal caring

A closely related issue that national governments were tackling from the 1990s in parallel with the pension problem was how to meet the demand for good quality health and social care for older and disabled people, increasingly under the impetus provided by the Union through the OMC. Most member states had been pursuing policies focusing on community care, while changes in family and employment structures were imposing strains on informal care structures. The issue became more pressing during the 1990s, due not only to the increase in the number of frail and disabled people, but also to the reduction in the number of traditional carers, as a result of the 'shrinkage of the female care taker potential' (Alber, 1993, p. 54) at a time when governments were trying to reduce the cost of formal caring.

Although the full impact of the decline in family size was not expected to be felt until after the turn of the century, in the late 1990s, the general increase in female economic activity rates was already making heavy demands on women at a stage in their lives when they had ageing relatives requiring care. Yet, women were still expected to be the main providers of family care. Because women in the younger generations were more likely to be economically active outside the home, and in the absence of other close relatives able and willing to take on the responsibility for caring, most member states were being faced with the question of how to ensure the most effective level of social care at the lowest cost to the public purse, and how, if appropriate, to provide incentives for informal carers (Daly and Lewis, 2000).

From the 1980s, most member states had been moving towards a policy of community care and de-institutionalization of caring. However, in the early 2000s, wide variations in practices could still be observed. Provision of good quality care services in the Nordic countries was recognized as a responsibility of the state, and more especially of local authorities. At the other extreme, the southern European countries continued to place a clear legal obligation on relatives to care for older people, and formal service provision was made only in cases where no relatives were available to meet these obligations. Whatever the legal responsibilities of the state and of families with regard to care for older and disabled people, during the 1990s all governments had begun confronting the question of how to ensure support for the provision of long-term care [2.2, 2001, pp. 44–5]. Although the instruments used to implement policy differed, member states seemed to agree on a number of objectives. An important policy priority was to ensure the independence of older and disabled people for as long as possible by providing home support or sheltered accommodation. The employment-creating potential of formal subsidized caring was widely recognized, but was limited by financial considerations. Most countries were looking for ways of

174   *Social Policy in the European Union*

making savings, in some cases by rationing care through means-testing, and in others by requiring a contribution from the person concerned or by privatizing services.

Very few countries had introduced a single discrete scheme for long-term care. The solution adopted in Germany in 1995 was to create a new branch of social insurance – *Pflegeversicherung* – to cover the cost of residential care or for care in the person's own home. In 1999, Luxembourg introduced a similar scheme, in the form of dependency insurance, mainly funded from compulsory health insurance contributions. The system applied in Austria since 1993 took the form of a non-means-tested allowance – *Bundespflegegeld* – funded from general taxation and administered at the level of the provinces. Where no discrete scheme was available, most countries had introduced allowances designed to help older people remain autonomous by enabling them to meet the costs of non-medical care. Municipal authorities, in combination with community and non-governmental organizations, were generally required to deliver care services and support family carers. In almost all the member states that joined the Union in 2004, and also in Ireland and the United Kingdom, benefit was paid to family carers. Across the Union, beneficiaries of services such as residential homes were usually expected to contribute to non-medical costs according to their means. Rising costs were being met by increasing taxation and social contributions, and through measures to improve efficiency and relieve the burden on the state, raising issues about the quality of care and individual choice as governments looked, increasingly, to the private and voluntary sectors for solutions [2.4, 2006, table XII].

POLICY IMPLICATIONS FOR GENERATIONAL SOLIDARITY

The emphasis in policy for older and disabled people shifted as awareness grew that the predicted consequences of population ageing were coming closer to realization. Just as demographic concerns had moved family policy onto the agenda in the 1980s (see Chapter 5), the changing age structure of the population across the Union, together with the prospect of the demographic time-bomb exploding, provided an incentive for the Commission to draw the attention of national governments to the social problems associated with the growing imbalance between the generations for the twenty-first century. Generational solidarity became a recurring theme in Union documents during the 1990s. The Commission's 1999 communication, 'Towards a Europe for all ages',

proposed a strategy for effective policy responses to the problems arising from population ageing based on the strengthening of solidarity and
equity between the generations [7.15, p. 4], and the title of the 2005
green paper stressed the link that needed to be made between demographic change and generational solidarity [1.25].

Whereas the Union's institutions did not have a formal remit for
action to promote solidarity between the generations, insofar as it was
limited to intrafamilial relationships and therefore governed by the
subsidiarity principle, action could be initiated when labour market or
equality issues were involved. The preoccupation with employment,
employability and Economic and Monetary Union (EMU) in the 1990s,
culminating in the European employment strategy, formally launched at
the Lisbon European Council in 2000 [1.20], further justified interest in
the contribution that older and disabled people could make to the age
balance of the labour supply. The Council drew attention to the implications of an ageing and declining labour force for international competitiveness. The free movement of labour and capital legitimated interest
in the transportability and comparability of pension arrangements and
was also relevant to the question of family dependency.

The need to contain the cost of funding pensions in the context of
EMU provided an incentive for looking at pension reform to ensure the
longer term viability of pension schemes, while maintaining high standards of care, improving the living conditions of older and disabled
people, and avoiding intergenerational conflicts. It justified the introduction of measures to reverse the trend towards early retirement, as a
means not only of extending the number of years of pension contributions but also of reducing the time during which a pension would have
to be paid, thereby helping to offset the growing imbalance in the dependency ratio.

The reconciliation of employment and family life was also accepted
as a legitimate area for intervention at EU level, since it affected the
availability of women for work (see Chapter 6). Although reconciliation
measures were primarily concerned with childcare, recognition of the
impact of caring for older and disabled people on the contribution of
working age women to the labour supply raised important issues for
equality of treatment. The equality rationale led to calls for the equalization of pension age and the individualization of pension rights between women and men. It also enabled areas of discrimination against
older and disabled workers to be highlighted. For most working age
women, in the absence of external and internal support to relieve the
burden of caring (for young, disabled and older people) and of being

cared for (in the case of frail older women), generational solidarity remained an ambivalent concept. Progress was gradually being made in the early 2000s towards an acceptance of the shift in policy emphasis and in financial resources that was needed if active ageing and collective responsibility for care were to become more positive concepts.

Two other non-labour market issues were raised at EU level in the late 1990s and remained unresolved. Firstly, the attention that had been devoted to the financial needs of older people meant the balance had tipped more strongly towards older and away from younger people, both financially and in terms of policy interest, creating intergenerational tensions. In some countries, policies had been targeted at the most underprivileged groups of older people, often with noteworthy results. Increases in the pension supplement in Denmark in the 1980s were, for example, targeted at pensioners on the lowest incomes. The Spanish government also focused on the level of minimum pensions as a means of raising living standards. In Italy, due to improved pension provision since the 1950s, the growth in living standards of older people was greater than for the population as a whole. The indexing of retirement pensions to wages or prices in France in the 1980s resulted in a marked decrease in the number of older people relying on the minimum pension. Elsewhere, the improvement of living standards could not be directly attributed to social policy for older people but might have been 'a "passive" by-product of increases in the scope and coverage of occupational pensions as a result of collective bargaining and pension scheme maturation' (Walker, 1993, p. 14).

Secondly, the overall improvement in the living standards of older people had not benefited all older people equally. In countries where pensions are earnings related, income inequalities between occupational groups could be greater in retirement than during working life. Where the advantages of supplementary schemes were not equally distributed across age groups, inequalities among older people could also be intensified by widening the differential between those who had recently retired, and who were eligible for generous earnings-related pensions, and fourth-age older people dependent on a minimum state pension.

Although EU level action in the area of old age and disability was largely confined to awareness raising, monitoring, reporting and sharing of experience, the issues addressed by the Commission reflected and foreshadowed the problems being encountered by all member states. They therefore provided opportunities for cross-border learning and the search for common solutions, as promoted through the OMC, which progressively replaced the observatories. During the 1990s, awareness of the impact of population ageing on society and family life prompted the beginnings of the process to reconceptualize old age and generational relations. New challenges were posed for policy makers, who were forced to rethink measures such as early exit from the labour market and their implications for generational equity and solidarity. The concept of active ageing was gradually gaining ground. Awareness was also growing that older people, like children, were subject to abuse both in their own home and in residential care. After half a century, the much enlarged Union could justifiably claim to have expanded its social policy remit, albeit inchoately, to areas that were of little or no concern when the EEC was founded.

Box 7   Secondary legislation and official publications relating to policy for older and disabled people

7.1 Council Resolution of the Representatives of the Member States of the European Community, meeting within the Council of 21 December 1981, on the social integration of handicapped people, *OJ* C 347/1 31.12.1981.

7.2 Resolution of the European Parliament of 18 February 1982 on the situation and problems of the aged in the European Community, *OJ* C 66/71 15.3.1982.

7.3 Council Recommendation of 10 December 1982 on the principles of a Community policy with regard to retirement age, 82/857/EEC, *OJ* L 357/27 18.12.1982; Report from the Commission of 18 December 1992 on the application of Council Recommendation 82/857/EEC of 10 December 1982 on the principle of a Community policy with regard to retirement age, SEC(92) 2288 final.

7.4 Resolution of the European Parliament of 10 March 1986 on services for the elderly, *OJ* C 88/17 14.4.1986.

7.5 Resolution of the European Parliament of 14 May 1986 on Community measures to improve the situation of old people in the Member States of the Community, *OJ* C 148/61 16.6.1986.

7.6 Council Decision of 18 April 1988 establishing a second Community action programme for disabled people (Helios), 88/231/EEC, *OJ* L 104/38 23.4.1988.

7.7 Communication from the Commission on the elderly, Proposal for a Council Decision on Community actions for the elderly, COM(90) 80 final, 24.4.1990; Council Decision of 26 November 1990 on Community actions for the elderly, 91/49/EEC, *OJ* L 28/29 2.2.1991.

7.8 Commission proposal for a Council Directive on minimum requirements to improve the mobility and the safe transport to work of workers with reduced mobility, COM(90) 588 final, 11.2.1991, *OJ* C 68/7 16.3.1991; amended proposal, COM(91) 539 final, *OJ* C 15/18 21.1.1992.

7.9 Commission of the European Communities, 1993: European Year of Older People and Solidarity between Generations, *Social Europe*, 1/93.

7.10 Council Decision 93/136/EEC of 25 February 1993 establishing a third Community action programme to assist disabled people (Helios II 1993 to 1996), *OJ* L56/30 9.3.1993.

7.11 Council Resolution of 30 June 1993 on flexible retirement arrangements, *OJ* C 188/1 10.7.1993.

7.12 Commission proposal for a Council Decision on Community support for actions in favour of older people, COM(95) 53 final, 1 March 1995, *OJ* C 115/6 9.5.1995.

7.13 Communication of the Commission on equality of opportunity for people with disabilities. A new European Community disability strategy, COM(96) 406 final, 30.7.1996.

7.14 European Commission, The outlook on supplementary pensions in the context of demographic, economic and social change. A report by the EU network of experts on supplementary pension provision – 1996, *Social Europe Supplement*, 7/96.

7.15 Communication from the Commission, Towards a Europe for all ages – promoting prosperity and intergenerational solidarity, COM(1999) 221 final, 21.5.1999.

7.16 Communication from the Commission, Supporting national strategies for safe and sustainable pensions through an integrated approach, COM(2001) 362 final, 3.7.2001.

7.17 Council Directive 2000/78/EC of 27 November 2000 establishing a general framework for equal treatment in employment and occupation, *OJ* L303/16 2.12.2000.

7.18 Communication from the Commission, Modernising social protection for the development of high-quality, accessible and sustainable health care and long-term care: support of the national strategies using the 'open method of coordination', COM(2004) 304 final, 20.4.2004.

7.19 Commission staff working document, Synthesis report on adequate and sustainable pensions, SEC(2006) 304, 27.2.2006, based on COM(2006) 62 final.

7.20 European Commission, *Adequate and Sustainable Pensions*, joint and synthesis reports, OOPEC (periodic).

8   From Poverty to Social Inclusion

The emphasis in the Community's and Union's treaties and the 1989 charter on employment-related rights and freedom of movement was motivated either by the need to protect workers against major sources of hardship due to incapacity for work as a result of ill health, disability, unemployment, old age and other contingencies, or by the efforts required to ensure access to social security on equal terms for mobile workers. When the Treaty establishing the European Economic Community (EEC) was signed in 1957 [1.2], member states were experiencing a period of economic expansion. Following the German 'continental' model, their welfare regimes were based on the adequacy principle, namely that earnings from paid employment would be maintained at a sufficiently high level to enable workers and their families to enjoy a decent standard of living (see Chapter 2). Provision was made in member states for those who temporarily 'fell through the net' by instituting non-contributory social assistance schemes, but in the postwar boom years the groups considered to be at risk were relatively limited, and unemployment was not seen as a problem area. When the EEC Treaty was signed, many older people, particularly the self-employed, had not accrued the right to generous earnings-related pensions, and not all occupations were subject to a legal age of retirement. In addition, life expectancy was shorter, and the proportion of old age dependants was therefore relatively small (see Chapter 7). Immigration was helping to sustain the workforce (see Chapter 9), and the postwar baby boom had resulted in the rapid growth of the younger population, who had good prospects for finding employment in a buoyant economy. These attenuating factors did not mean that poverty was non-existent, but rather that it was not a political priority for the EEC founder members.

The centrality of freedom of movement and workers' rights in the EEC Treaty had tended to divert attention away from the social implications of the common market for population groups that were, for one reason or another, excluded from the labour force. It was, however, recognized that industrial restructuring, relocation and centralization, which were vital components in the Single European Market (SEM), might provoke economic dislocation, leading to polarization as the prosperous core areas benefited most, and the less favoured peripheral areas degenerated further. Institutional intervention, according to this logic, was necessary to offset the effects of market forces and curb the growth of 'new poverty' as a result of changing social and economic structures, and rising unemployment. New poverty was recognized as being qualitatively different from the poverty experienced hitherto, since it affected people from a much wider range of socio-economic groups. Whereas, in the 1970s, most of the poor were older people, by the 1990s a more pressing problem was the growing number of working age people falling into poverty, particularly younger never-employed and long-term unemployed people. Increasingly, as a result of changing family structures, lone-parent households were suffering from poverty: lone parenthood was frequently associated with low income and dependence on social assistance for long periods of time. Families with children were over-represented among poor people, but poverty was no longer essentially related to large family size. The threat presented to economic and social cohesion by the growing proportion of people of working age living in poverty served as a powerful incentive for continuing action at EU level.

This chapter examines policy to combat social exclusion and promote social inclusion, firstly with reference to the Union's legislative framework and action programmes. Attention is then given to the problems of defining, measuring and comparing poverty in member states and to assessing its extent and regional characteristics. Variations in national systems for income maintenance and in approaches to policy making for socially excluded individuals and groups are explored to provide a better understanding of the ways in which poverty and social exclusion have been conceptualized and dealt with by member states.

DEVELOPING EUROPEAN POLICY TO COMBAT POVERTY AND SOCIAL EXCLUSION

Concern with poverty and social exclusion at EU level developed in parallel with the growing interest in social affairs in the 1970s and 1980s (see Chapter 1). Due to its limited competence, the Community did not introduce binding legislation as a policy instrument to alleviate poverty, for example by formulating directives imposing minimum income levels for individuals, or harmonizing the provision of social assistance for migrant workers. Rather, from the mid-1970s, the Commission initiated action programmes to combat poverty and social exclusion. Member states were bound by treaty commitments and regulations to operate the structural funds in support of labour market policies in priority regions and for underprivileged groups. During the 1990s, emphasis shifted away from Community poverty programmes under the auspices of the Commission towards (re)integration into the labour market and society (social inclusion) through the disbursement of the structural funds at national and regional level in partnership with the Commission, leading on to the open method of coordination (OMC) [8.9]. An important topic in the debates of the early 2000s was the need to adapt the structural funds in preparation for enlargement to the east.

In this section, the development of Community policy for combating social exclusion and promoting social inclusion is tracked through the different overlapping and interconnected measures that have been introduced in an attempt to resolve what have been recognized as common social problems justifying concerted policy responses.

Towards social inclusion in the Union's treaties and charters

The EEC Treaty [1.2] laid stress on the interests of workers not only in the provisions made for employment-related social protection, as illustrated in previous chapters, but also under the terms of the European Social Fund (ESF). In accordance with the Community's market-oriented objectives, the ESF was not concerned with socially and economically excluded categories, such as older people, lone-parent families or groups living in underprivileged areas. Rather, article 3(i) of the founding treaty established the fund 'in order to improve employment opportunities for workers and to contribute to the raising of their standard of living'. Article 123 on social policy confirmed that the ESF was intended solely for the working population, stating: 'it shall have the task of rendering the employment of workers easier and of increasing their geographical and occupational mobility within the Community'. Member states were to be eligible to receive 50 per cent of expenditure incurred in providing vocational training and resettlement allowances as a means of ensuring productive re-employment of workers following the conversion of undertakings. Funds were to be committed to measures aimed at supporting specific population groups in such a way that a safety net was created for designated regions and categories of the population, while also providing opportunities for the development of poorer areas.

By seeking to relieve the problems of uneven regional development through the ESF, the Community recognized that poverty was structural and could be caused by economic forces over which individuals and local economies have little or no control. The financial support provided was intended to tackle underlying structural problems and was therefore a necessary component for economic integration. Analysts of the possible effects of the completion of the internal market had concluded that its long-term benefits were likely to be unevenly distributed, and that income disparities might not be narrowed (O'Donnell, 1992, p. 25). Regions with industries that were able to make economies of scale and had the capacity to innovate would stand to draw the greatest benefits from freedom of movement of goods, services and workers. The Single European Act (SEA) of 1986 [1.5] thus introduced a new title on economic and social cohesion, reforming the structural funds.

The specific objective of cohesion policy was to reduce disparities in levels of development 'between the various regions and the backwardness of the least favoured regions' (article 130a). In addition to existing instruments, the Community was to achieve its objectives with support from the European Investment Bank (EIB), which grants loans on a non-profit basis, and through the structural funds: European Agricultural Guidance and Guarantee Fund, European Social Fund, European Regional Development Fund (article 130b). The fund established in 1975 to support the Community's regional policy was intended to help redress regional imbalances and enable the structural adjustment of regions that were considered to be 'lagging behind' (article 130c). The laggards were defined as regions whose *per capita* gross domestic product (GDP) for the last three years was less than 75 per cent of the Community average [8.11, 1260/1999, article 3]. The identification of priority regions was based on a common geographical system of classification, the Nomenclature of Territorial Statistical Units (NUTS), set up by Eurostat in conjunction with national statistical offices.

The 1989 Community Charter of the Fundamental Social Rights of Workers [1.12] and the Agreement on Social Policy incorporated into the Treaty of Amsterdam [1.6; 1.7] referred only indirectly to poverty or social exclusion. Article 2 of the agreement sought to promote the 'integration of persons excluded from the labour market', and §10 in the charter assigned to member states the duty to provide assistance to individuals 'who have been unable either to enter or re-enter the labour market and have no means of subsistence', leaving national governments to make their own arrangements. In similar terms, the section on employment and remuneration in the charter recommended an equitable wage as the means of maintaining 'a decent standard of living' (§5). When wages were to be 'withheld, seized or transferred', it stated that provision should be made so that the worker could 'continue to enjoy the necessary means of subsistence for himself and his family' (§5).

Article 130b in the SEA was extended in the Treaty on European Union [1.6], becoming article 159 in the consolidated version of the EC Treaty [1.8]. Article 159 required the Commission to report every three years to the European Parliament, the Council, the Economic and Social Committee and the newly established Committee of the Regions on the progress made towards achieving the cohesion objectives. It gave the Commission the power, if needed, to initiate actions outside the funds. A revised article 130d (article 161 in the consolidated EC Treaty) spelled out the procedure to be used for defining the tasks, priority objectives and organization of the structural funds. The Cohesion Fund was set up in 1993 for projects on the environment and trans-European transport infrastructures in the weaker member states (with GDP of less than 90 per cent of the EU average) to help them meet the convergence criteria for Economic and Monetary Union.

The concept of cohesion, which was intended to correct the most discriminatory effects of economic integration, can be seen as directly contradicting the principle of open competition on which the EEC was founded. The potential conflict between the treaty commitment to the removal of constraints on market forces and the provision made for institutional intervention to prevent regional imbalances thus reflects the underlying tensions between socio-economic, national, sub- and supranational objectives, which have been characteristic of the Community's development (see Chapter 1). From the late 1980s, the structural funds came to represent a strong interstate bargaining counter for member states, as exemplified by the negotiations over enlargement.

While the Commission was observing its treaty remit in taking forward cohesion policy at macroeconomic level, the individual right to a decent standard of living was being secured through a different route. With the aim of combating social exclusion and poverty, article II-34 §3 on social security and social assistance in the Charter of Fundamental Rights of the European Union [1.21], adopted in 2000, made reference to the need to recognize and respect 'the right to social and housing assistance so as to ensure a decent existence for all those who lack sufficient resources, in accordance with the rules laid down by Union law and national laws and practices'. The reference to housing, a rare occurrence in official documents, indicated a potential direction for future social policy development through the human rights channel.

Between secondary legislation and action programmes

One of the most binding forms of secondary legislation, the regulation, has only rarely been used to make provision for regional development through the structural funds. More often, the less binding forms of legislation – decisions, recommendations, resolutions and proposals – have been adopted to implement measures concerned with poverty. This section provides a chronological overview of the role played by secondary legislation from the 1970s in the Community's and Union's policies to combat poverty and promote social inclusion by supporting action programmes and monitoring the structural funds.

By 1974, the impact of the energy crisis on employment and living standards was being felt across the Community, and the baby boom had come to an end. The new member states in 1972 – Denmark, Ireland and the United Kingdom – brought with them different welfare traditions in which social protection was based on universal citizenship rights rather than earnings from employment (see Chapter 2). The nine member states shared a conviction, however, that concerted action was needed to improve national provision for particularly disadvantaged groups (Shanks, 1977, pp. 63–4). Following the 1974 Council resolution on a social action programme [1.11], a proposal for a two-year experimental anti-poverty programme therefore received wide support.

The first poverty programme had to be approved by a unanimous vote of the Council under article 235 of the EEC Treaty, since no special provision had been made for formal action in this area. After a difficult process of negotiation in the context of the oil crisis, with the Germans in particular pressing for retrenchment, a Council decision eventually established the programme for one year: 1975–76 [8.1]. The Commission launched 21 pilot or action proj??ects, including basic research into the 'dimensions and nature of poverty' (James, 1982, p. 6). Two cross-national studies were also funded on attitudes towards poverty and research methods for national sample surveys. The second phase of the programme was approved by another Council decision in 1977 [8.1], this time for a three-year period, extending and adding to the pilot projects. The Commission invited independent research teams in each member state to draw up reports on the nature, causes and extent of poverty and to undertake an assessment of national policies.

The second European poverty programme was approved in 1984 for the period 1985–88. The initial budget was increased in 1986 when Portugal and Spain joined the Community [8.5, p. 10]. The Commission was authorized to undertake activities to promote or provide financial assistance for various types of action-research measures, for the collection, dissemination and exchange of knowledge and comparable data on poverty on a regular basis, the coordination and assessment of anti-poverty measures, and the transfer of innovative approaches between member states. Action was justified by reference to article 2 of the EEC Treaty, which required 'balanced expansion' and 'an increase in stability'. The 65 action research projects selected for support covered lone-parent families, the problems of the long-term unemployed, youth unemployment, second generation migrants, refugees and returning migrants, homeless and older people. Integrated urban action programmes were funded with the aim of providing a comprehensive approach to the needs of targeted groups of deprived individuals, by tackling the underlying problems of the social environment creating the circumstances that define poverty.

In terms of the number of projects selected, Spain and the United Kingdom were by far the greatest beneficiaries from the scheme [8.5, p. 12], raising questions about the extent to which European support was being directed to the regions most in need. The criteria used for evaluating the projects – innovation, participation and cost effectiveness – may well have favoured member states that were already trying out innovatory schemes, where community structures were well developed, and where cost effectiveness of services was routinely monitored.

While the Commission had been taking forward programmes to combat social exclusion, between 1988 and 1999, a series of regulations was introduced, laying down general provisions for the structural funds. Following the signing of the SEA, it had been agreed that the funds should be doubled in size, priority areas should be identified and more streamlined regional development plans should be drawn up. The 1988 regulations, in particular 'parent' Regulation (EEC) No. 2052/88 [8.2], removed national quotas and replaced individual proj??ects by integrated programmes. Its effect was to transfer resources from the wealthier member states to the laggard countries in the south. A further reform was undertaken in 1993 through Regulation (EEC) No. 2081/93 [8.2], as provided for in the title on economic and social cohesion in the Treaty on European Union. The regulations identified priority areas for targeted funding. In the case of Greece, Ireland and Portugal, the entire country was designated as an Objective 1, or priority, region whose development was 'lagging behind'. Ten regions in Spain and eight in Italy were included under Objective 1. Northern Ireland fell within this category for the United Kingdom and Corsica in the case of France [8.2, 2081/93, annex 3]. Objective 1 regions were eligible to receive a larger proportion – around 70 per cent – of the total expenditure, with the aim of redistributing resources in relation to need.

Objective 2 regions were identified as those seriously affected by industrial decline and were allocated about 11 per cent of total expenditure from the structural funds. Objective 3 covered regions targeted for combating unemployment and reintegrating people excluded from the labour market, through training and retraining schemes, the creation of stable jobs and self-employed activities. Long-term unemployed women, migrants, young and disabled people were singled out for special schemes. Provision was made for implementing measures at national, local, regional or sectoral level, with the aim of achieving the best match between the difficulties to be overcome and labour market requirements. Objective 4 focused on the adaptation of workers to industrial restructuring and changes in production systems. Objectives 3 and 4 attracted about 11 per cent of expenditure. Objective 5, with 4 per cent of the funds, aimed at promoting structural adjustment in rural areas. An Objective 6, with 0.5 per cent of expenditure, was added in 1993 to promote development of the thinly populated areas in Finland and Sweden following their accession [8.10, 1996, p. 9].

By the end of the 1980s, the growing awareness of the multifaceted, relative and changing nature of poverty had made it necessary to adopt a new approach. The number of people experiencing poverty had increased, and new forms of poverty were appearing as a result of changes in economic and social structures. In 1989, within the framework of the action programme implementing the provisions of the Community charter, a Council decision established 'a medium-term Community action programme concerning the economic and social integration of the economically and socially less privileged groups in society' [8.3]. An additional reason for the decision was the need to take preventive measures against any short-term negative effects of the completion of the internal market by the end of 1992 for the social groups most at risk. The Poverty 3 programme for the period 1989–94 was to provide corrective measures for marginalized groups, with the purpose of ensuring greater economic and social cohesion, as written into the SEA and the Treaty on European Union. Although representing a substantial increase in relation to previous programmes, the budget was relatively small compared with average expenditure on social security in the wealthier member states or the ESF [8.10, 1996, table 5.1].

In line with developments in other areas of social policy, the Commission sought to give its action against poverty a more formal structure. In 1989, a resolution from the Council established an Observatory on National Policies to Combat Social Exclusion [8.4], designed to promote policy analysis, stimulate the exchange of information and experience and report back annually to the Commission. Like the observatories for family policies, older people and employment, the aim was to develop a common understanding of the policy framework, and monitor and analyse trends in member states. In recognition of the importance of the voluntary sector's contribution in combating poverty, in 1990 the Commission's Directorate-General for Employment and Social Affairs initiated and funded a European Anti-Poverty Network, consisting of non-governmental organizations, with the brief of coordinating efforts across member states and acting as a poverty lobby.

One of the most explicit statements of European policy in relation to poverty is to be found in the Council recommendation, issued four months after the signing of the Treaty on European Union in 1992, 'on common criteria concerning sufficient resources and social assistance in social protection systems' [8.6]. The Council stated that the fight against social exclusion was to be regarded as 'an important part of the social dimension of the internal market' (§7) and conducted 'in a spirit of solidarity' (§8), as announced in the 1989 Community charter. The recommendation recognized the multidimensional nature of social exclusion and 'the basic right of a person to sufficient resources and social assistance to live in a manner compatible with human dignity' (part IA). The implementation of such a right was to be organized by 'fixing the amount of resources considered sufficient to cover essential needs with regard to respect for human dignity, taking account of living standards and price levels in the Member State concerned, for different types and sizes of household' (part IC1a). Although no figure was suggested for the level at which to set such a minimum income, the proposal stressed the importance of taking account of the availability of financial resources, national priorities and disparities between national social protection systems. The right to sufficient resources was to be individual and based on need, but subject to active availability for work or vocational training, or to economic and social integration measures, where appropriate. Such a right was not, however, confined to workers. It was to be extended to individuals unable to enter or re-enter the labour market and to older people not entitled to a pension, with the aim of enabling economic and social integration, while at the same time safeguarding incentives to encourage the search for employment.

In pursuit of the objectives set out in documents such as the recommendation, and to ensure continuity of the poverty programmes, in 1993 the Commission presented a proposal for a new medium-term action programme to combat exclusion and promote solidarity for the period 1994–99 [8.7]. The new programme took account of the fact that social exclusion was continuing to increase and spread due to changes in economic, social and demographic structures. The budget sought for the programme was more than twice the amount for Poverty 3, confirming the Union's commitment to intensifying its effort in this area. Previous programmes had shown that sustained targeted action over several years could produce positive results, but that welfare systems needed modernizing. The Commission therefore called for greater cooperation between different agencies in the public and private sectors. While upholding the view that individual member states were responsible for combating social exclusion, the Commission presented its role as contributing to the development and transfer of methods and expertise, identifying good practice and setting up and maintaining networks for sharing experience and deepening understanding of the problem, foreshadowing the approach subsequently developed through the OMC.

To further understanding of social exclusion and find ways of controlling it, the programme sought to promote model actions at local, national or regional level, transnational networks of projects, the collection of information and comparative studies. The Commission proposed to focus on three keywords: namely partnership, active participation and a multidimensional strategy. By partnership and participation, it was referring to collaboration between government bodies, associations and the individuals concerned, since past experience had shown that integrated actions were most effective. The multidimensional strategy underlined the complexity of situations of social exclusion and the processes involved. An attempt was to be made to formulate policies that adopted a global approach to the problem of social exclusion.

At a Council meeting in 1994, the German delegation opposed the proposal for a new action programme on grounds of cost and because the Union had no competence to act in the area of poverty. In anticipation of the programme's approval, the Commission had continued to fund projects under the relevant budget line. The United Kingdom took the Commission to the European Court of Justice on the basis that it had no legal competence to take such action. A ruling in 1996 confirmed the case [8.8]. At the same time, further funding was withheld from the Observatory on National Policies to Combat Social Exclusion, indicating that member states were reigning in on the Commission's power to initiate action at Community level in this policy area.

In preparation for enlargement to the east, a series of regulations was introduced further reforming the structural funds. Regulation (EC)

No. 1260/1999 [8.11] laid down the general provisions for the funds. Together with the accompanying regulations, which were adopted jointly by the European Parliament and Council in 1999, it replaced earlier legislation. In pursuance of articles 146 on the ESF and 159 on economic and social cohesion in the consolidated version of the EC Treaty [1.8], the 1999 regulations redefined the scope of the funds, and restructured and simplified their objectives.

According to the 1999 regulation, the ESF was to be concerned with encouraging action at national level to promote social integration into the labour market and equality between men and women as part of the mainstreaming approach, while also combating social exclusion. Unlike the 1992 recommendation, the target population was confined to people of working age. For example, assistance was offered for schemes designed to promote the reconciliation of family and working life and to enable 'older workers to have a fulfilling occupation until retirement' [8.11, 1262/1999, article 3 §2]. The financing of early retirement schemes was explicitly excluded, although accompanying measures could cover provision of care services and facilities for dependants. The regulation also provided for Community initiatives, such as Equal, a new human resources initiative, to combat discrimination and inequalities in the labour market, but the main emphasis was on action at regional level to underpin the national action plans for employment (article 2). The relationship between the Commission, member states and regional or local authorities, economic and social partners or other competent bodies was to be founded on partnerships between parties pursuing a common goal. Following the principle of additionality, the funds provided could not be used to replace public or equivalent structural expenditure. Any operations financed either by the funds or by the EIB had to be compatible with the treaty provisions and the Community's policy instruments. The regulation thus confirmed the tone that had been set for the twenty-first century by making sure that the onus was placed on national governments to propose innovative plans for labour-market integration measures, which were being promoted as the main route to social inclusion.

Solidarity in enlargement

Successive waves of membership of the Community and Union, particularly to the south in the 1980s and the east in 2004, brought with them major challenges to intra-European solidarity, justifying the development of regional policy in support of weaker members. The 1988 reform of the structural funds had significantly increased the transfer of resources to the less prosperous member states. The impact of the 1993 reform was less concentrated, since the coverage of Objective 1 was extended to take in the new German *Länder* and other regions to the north [8.10, 1996, p. 96]. In relation to gross domestic product (GDP), the countries with some of the lowest *per capita* incomes – Greece, Portugal and Ireland – were the main beneficiaries of the structural funds in the periods 1989–93 and 1994–99, with the addition of Germany in the later period [8.10, 1996, table 5.2a–5.2b]. In relation to the total budget and gross national product (GNP), Germany was by far the largest contributor to the structural funds in the late 1990s, followed by France, the United Kingdom and Italy [8.12, vol. 1, table 6].

Enlargement to the east in 2004 brought an increase in the Union's population of over 19 per cent to almost 460 million, while total GDP increased by less than 10 per cent [4.14, 2005, table 1]. By the time the Union had expanded to 25 members in 2004, more than a third of the EU population was living in a member state with a *per capita* income of less than 90 per cent of the Union average, compared with one sixth in EU15 [8.10, 2001, p. V]. In the run-up to enlargement, the European Council in Berlin allocated 213 billion euros for structural operations in the EU15 member states for the period 2000–06 (at 1999 prices). Additional pre- and post-accession aid was set aside for new member states, equivalent to 0.45 per cent of the enlarged Union's GDP in 2006. Transfer payments were to be limited to 4 per cent of national GDP *per annum* for all member states [8.10, 2001, p. XXXVII]. The Council also decided to reduce the number of objectives from seven to three, and the percentage of the population covered by Objectives 1 and 2 was cut from 51 to 35–40 per cent. Objective 2 was redefined to bring together all measures covering regions with structural problems, and to support programmes favouring economic diversification. A new Objective 3 was designed to help member states adapt and modernize their systems of education, training and employment to make their economies competitive and safeguard the European model of society as part of the European employment strategy. Programmes were simplified and concentrated on geographical zones, through a process of direct (defined by the Commission) and indirect (decided by national governments) zoning [8.10, 2001, p. XXX].

The number of Community initiatives was reduced from fourteen to four. The Commission retained those that had proved to be most successful in translating intentions into effective action: Equal, for combating discrimination and inequality in access to labour markets; Leader, for rural development; Interreg, for cross-border, transnational and interregional cooperation; and Urban, for urban regeneration [8.10, 1999, p. 111; 8.12, vol. 1, pp. 16–20]. Enlargement can thus be seen as having provided an incentive for rationalizing the structural funds and improving their efficiency through the enforcement of decentralization and the promotion of partnerships.

The second cohesion report in 2001 identified three main groups of countries in the enlarged Union, using economic indicators: the most prosperous group, comprising all the EU15 countries, except Greece, Portugal and Spain, with *per capita* income above the EU27 average; an intermediate group comprising the three excluded EU15 member states, the Czech Republic, Cyprus, Malta and Slovenia, with *per capita* income of about 80 per cent of the EU27 average and 13 per cent of total EU27 population; and the six remaining central and east European countries, plus Bulgaria and Romania, with *per capita* income around 40 per cent of the EU27 average, accounting for 16 per cent of EU population [8.10, 2001, p. V].

Greater social cohesion was one of the key components in the Commission's social agenda for 'shaping a new Europe' in the period 2000–04 in preparation for enlargement [1.22, p. 5]. In keeping with the social values of solidarity and justice, member states were charged with building an inclusive Europe by mainstreaming social inclusion and streamlining the OMC [8.13]. The social agenda for 2005–10 [1.24, p. 4] predicted that, in member states eligible for funding under the 'regional competitiveness and employment' heading, the ESF would serve as a catalyst and support the exchange of experience, alongside other policy instruments, including the social dialogue and the OMC. Social inclusion was set to remain a major component in the Union's solidarity and equality objectives for the enlarged Europe, providing the opportunity to develop a concerted policy strategy.

Through employment to the open method of coordination

In addition to providing targeted resources through the structural funds to help regions undergoing economic restructuring, during the 1980s the Commission had responded to the growing problem of long-term unemployment by launching a number of active labour market initiatives, including the establishment of an Employment Observatory, documentation systems on employment and a series of action programmes supported by the structural funds. The observatory's brief was to conduct and publish annual surveys on employment trends [4.14].

The Network of Employment Coordinators (Nec) was charged with producing research reports on different themes relating to unemployment. The European System of Documentation on Employment (Sysdem) and the Mutual Information System on Employment Policies (Misep) reported on the measures adopted in member states, which, since the signing of the Treaty of Amsterdam, were required to prepare annual national action plans, foreshadowing the OMC.

Progressively during the 1990s, the focus on employment became stronger, as the structural funds were used to support the Union's employment strategy and the national action plans for employment, while also helping to prepare for enlargement. This active approach to labour market policy was reinforced in the 1994 white paper on European social policy, in which the Commission described three priority themes for the ESF: access to and quality of initial training and education, designed to promote the labour market integration of young people, particularly those with no basic qualifications or training; increasing competitiveness and the prevention of unemployment through a systematic approach to training; and the improvement of employment opportunities for long-term unemployed people [1.15, p. 27].

A communication from the Commission in 1996 on 'Community structural assistance and employment' [8.9] clearly established the role the structural funds should play in promoting employment in the context of economic and social cohesion. The funds were to provide support for job creation and stimulate demand for goods and services, while promoting 'balanced territorial development of the priority regions' [8.9, p. 2]. Although funding had been blocked for the Commission's action programme, in 1996 agreement was reached on the allocation for Community initiatives on employment. A package adopted for the period 1995–99 contained two human resources initiatives (Employment and Adapt). The four strands of Employment targeted disaffected young people (Youthstart), people with disabilities (Horizon), socially excluded people (Integra) and women (Now).

The new title VIa in the Treaty of Amsterdam [1.7] reinforced the importance of employment activation. This message was reiterated in the preamble to the 1998 employment guidelines, which stressed the need for 'active employability measures rather than passive support measures' [1.18, p. 2]. The Lisbon European Council's [1.20] formal adoption in 2000 of the OMC in the area of social inclusion brought further confirmation of the tight association between employment integration and social cohesion. The OMC was able to build on well-established practices for developing indicators, monitoring trends in poverty rates and exchanging information and experience. Drawing on two rounds of the OMC, the first joint report on social protection and social inclusion reiterated the Union's resolve to adopt an integrated approach to social policy [8.15, 2005, pp. 7–8]. It stressed the positive interaction between economic, employment and social policies, and reinforced the Commission's conviction that social inclusion and protection policies should be seen not as a drain on resources but as a productive factor contributing to a dynamic and sustainable workforce.

DEFINING AND MEASURING POVERTY AND EX/INCLUSION

The Commission's aim in requiring member states to produce national reports on levels of poverty and policies to combat exclusion was to monitor and compare the situation, and develop its own action programmes, a task subsequently pursued through the OMC. Definitions and concepts of poverty and social ex/inclusion have evolved over time and space as have methods of data collection and analysis. Despite the large amount of information assembled by the Commission, in the early 2000s, the Union was still looking for robust definitions and measures that could be operationalized in different national contexts and would yield comparable data. This section considers some of the definitions applied and a selection of the materials used over the years as a basis for comparisons across EU member states.

Defining poverty and ex/inclusion

The Commission initially defined poverty in terms of income and spending. Any individual with a disposable income falling below a specified level could be considered to be living in poverty. In the first poverty programme, the line was drawn at less than 50 per cent of the national average disposable *per capita* income in the relevant member state. Definitions of poverty as determined by an income poverty line are, however, problematic for both practical and ideological reasons. In practice, low income is a very crude measure of poverty, particularly from a comparative perspective. For example, services in kind, such as social housing and health care, represent a considerable proportion of income but they are unevenly distributed both within and between countries. Households vary markedly in their ability to manage their budgets. Ideological factors are important because the level at which a poverty line is set can be interpreted as 'a highly political act' (Brown,

1986, p. 49), raising issues about tax and social security benefit scales, definitions of low wages and minimum wage levels, as well as eligibility for assistance with education or housing costs.

Poverty is not only relative, it is also cumulative: people on low incomes generally also experience poor housing, educational facilities, transport and communications. Poverty can therefore be defined more broadly in terms of individuals and groups whose resources are so far below the average that they are excluded from the living conditions and amenities that are widely available in the society concerned (Townsend, 1979, p. 31). The concept of exclusion was present in the first poverty programme. Article 1 §2 [8.1] of the Council decision setting up the programme in 1975 provided a definition of 'persons beset by poverty' as 'individuals or families whose resources are so small as to exclude them from the minimum acceptable way of life of the Member State in which they live'. Resources were defined as 'goods, cash income, plus services from public and private sources'.

The evaluation made of the first poverty programme pointed to a number of inadequacies in the Council's definition (Room, 1982, pp. 159–61). The focus on individuals and families obscured wider societal processes and structures. The Council recognized that the 'minimum acceptable way of life' would differ from one member state to another, but did not take account of variations within societies. The focus on resources concealed the way in which poor people are excluded from social participation and the need for structural changes in society.

While the definition used in the second poverty programme was close to that of the first, it was extended to include 'material, cultural and social' resources [8.5, p. 11]. By not being confined to income poverty, this definition had the advantage that it introduced the concept of social exclusion, thereby recognizing that poverty brings with it a sense of powerlessness and marginalization, or exclusion from society, and engenders dependence. It did not resolve the question of how to determine what might be considered as a 'minimum acceptable way of life' or how to apply such a minimum across Europe.

The Observatory on National Policies to Combat Social Exclusion went on to define social exclusion in relation to social rights with reference, for example, to the right to employment, housing and health care. It asked questions about the effectiveness of national policies in ensuring access to such rights, and the barriers that exclude people from them. The observatory's second annual report studied the evidence that, 'where citizens are unable to secure their social rights, they will tend to suffer processes of generalised and persisting disadvantage and their social and occupational participation will be undermined' (Room, 1991, p. 17). It found that, although the manifestations of relative poverty may not have changed significantly, since the standard of living and access to resources for poor people are by definition well below the average for the population as a whole, the nature and determinants of poverty have undergone substantial change since the mid-1970s. The term 'new poverty' was coined to record the way in which poverty was affecting a much broader cross-section of the population, spanning different age groups, social and economic categories, ethnic groups and geographical areas, and threatening people who had previously been in stable employment and well-paid jobs with sporadic and recurrent periods of poverty and social exclusion.

The terms 'polarization', 'dualization' and 'marginalization' entered into the vocabulary of poverty analysts to describe the growing rift between those able to take advantage of the social and economic systems and those excluded from them. These terms signalled that the gap had been growing between people in work covered by generous social insurance and those without work, between urban and rural populations, core and periphery, the able bodied and those with disabilities, and between men and women. Categories of individuals were identified who were living on the margins of society and required special help: long-term unemployed and young unemployed people, working poor, older people, lone-parent families, migrants and refugees, and under-privileged people living in rural and urban areas.

The 2004 joint report on social inclusion [8.14, p. 10] provided consolidated definitions of poverty, social exclusion and social inclusion. The definition of poverty described income and resources as inadequate if they precluded people from a standard of living considered acceptable in the society in which they live, involving multiple disadvantage and marginalization. The definition of social exclusion emphasized problems of access and participation due to lack of basic competences, lifelong learning opportunities or discrimination. Social inclusion was defined as the process ensuring that those at risk of poverty and social exclusion gain the opportunities and resources necessary to participate fully in economic, social and cultural life, and enjoy a standard of living and well-being considered normal in the society in which they live. It also means that they are able to participate in decisions affecting their lives and that they have access to their fundamental rights. Being at risk of poverty was to become a key concept in the twenty-first century, applied in constructing a set of EU indicators of poverty and social exclusion.

Measuring poverty and social ex/inclusion

Although the first reports on the action proj??ects under the poverty programmes were drawn up using a common framework and an agreed method for calculating poverty lines, the quality of the comparative data was very uneven. Some countries had a long tradition of research on poverty: in France and the United Kingdom, studies of poverty had been conducted for a century or more. Others had only begun to carry out research in this area in the late 1960s. Whereas some member states had available regular data series on topics such as expenditure, earnings, social security provision, education and housing, others had given low priority to collecting and analysing data on indicators of poverty levels. Therefore, the information that could be assembled rarely lent itself to reliable comparisons across countries.

To circumvent issues of non-comparability, the Commission sought to establish a common definition of poverty, according to a European base-line of living (EBL), or the capacity to satisfy a body of needs, either by income from earnings or by other means. Batteries of indicators were used to collate data: the number of people living on an income below a certain percentage of average *per capita* income; what the population regards as a minimum income; what individuals consider as an absolute minimum for them; the degree of deprivation in terms of actual consumption and participation in social life; and the number of persons at or below the social assistance level used in each country.

The application of the OMC to social inclusion from 2000 required a set of reliable and meaningful criteria and indicators that could be used in national and Commission reports to monitor and benchmark social inclusion. In 2001, the Laeken European Council [1.20] endorsed 18 common multidimensional indicators of social exclusion and poverty. The list was subsequently reviewed and refined by the Social Protection Committee. In 2006, the committee agreed on a revised portfolio consisting of 11 primary indicators, eight secondary indicators and 11 'context' statistics (Marlier *et al.*, 2006, table 2.3). The 'at-risk-of-poverty rate' was applied as a lead indicator from the first joint social inclusion report [8.14]. The rate was defined as the share of persons living in households with an income below 60 per cent of national equivalized median income, defined in turn as the household's total disposable income divided by its equivalent size [8.15, 2006, p. 141].

The primary indicators included the at-risk-of-poverty rate (with illustrative values of national poverty thresholds for typical families), the persistence and intensity of poverty risk, long-term unemployment, joblessness in households, early school leaving, the employment gap of immigrants, material deprivation, housing, unmet healthcare needs and the well-being of children. The secondary indicators covered the at-risk-of-poverty rate broken down by individual and household variables such as household type, work intensity, activity status and accommodation tenure; the dispersion of the poverty risk rate around the threshold; educational attainment and literacy performance of pupils. Context information took account of regional cohesion, life expectancy, at-risk-of-poverty rates, social transfers and the in-work poverty risk.

The authors of an independent study exploring the further development of the common indicators advocated a multidimensional approach combining monetary and non-monetary indicators. They underlined the need to strengthen policy analysis through modelling, embedding the OMC in domestic policies and improving its effectiveness, while remaining sensitive to contextually determined national characteristics and being wary of drawing conclusions to support policy from simple correlations. They also called for statistical capacity building at EU, national and subnational level (Marlier *et al.*, 2006).

Comparing indicators of poverty and social ex/inclusion

Applying the Commission's earlier definition of a poverty line – those persons whose disposable income is less than half of average equivalent *per capita* income in their country – the final report of the first poverty programme estimated that in the mid-1970s the number of poor people in the nine member states was about 30 million or almost 11 per cent of population. When the southern European member states were included, the level of poverty across the Community rose to 38 million, or just over 11 per cent [8.5, p. 5]. By the late 1980s, about 52 million people, or 15 per cent of total population, were considered to be living at or below the 50 per cent poverty threshold [8.7, p. 82].

Using the 60 per cent threshold of median equivalized income, which had by then been widely adopted within the Union, the first joint report on social inclusion estimated that, in 1997, some 18 per cent of the population in EU15, or 67 million people, were at risk of poverty [8.14, 2002, table 3c]. By 2003, again applying the 60 per cent threshold, an assessment of the situation in EU25 member states suggested that 16 per cent, or 73 million people, were living below the at-risk-of-poverty threshold in 5 (Marlier *et al.*, 2006, p. 64).

If the poor are defined as the population suffering from material, cultural and social deprivation, which is even more difficult to measure, a larger proportion of the population can be identified as living in poverty. European Community Household Panel (ECHP) data on subjective poverty for the mid-1990s suggested, for example, that about 20 per cent of the EU15 population aged 16–84 years had difficulty in 'making ends meet', and identified unemployed persons and lone parents as the categories experiencing the greatest problems. The countries where it was most difficult to 'make ends meet' were Greece, Portugal and Spain. Luxembourg and Germany were at the other end of the scale (Vogel, 1997, tables 9.1, 9.4). Despite data limitations, ECHP surveys would seem to confirm the national differences identified in *per capita* GDP that had justified cohesion policy: the southern European member states fell far below the EU15 average for most indicators of living standards, whereas the Nordic states were generally above the average. ECHP data did not cover fifth-wave member states. Compared with EU15, under socialism the central and east European countries had experienced very low levels of income inequality. Their GDP per capita in purchasing power standards was forecast to remain well below the EU15 level. When they joined the Union, it was less than half the EU25 level in Latvia, Lithuania and Poland [8.15, 2006, table 1]. The collapse of their economies and of the labour-centred welfare systems that had prevented extreme forms of poverty resulted in a sharp fall in living standards, particularly exposing young people, families with children and other vulnerable groups to the risk of poverty [2.3, pp. 243–4].

Despite their common welfare legacy, the central and east European countries did not share the same outcomes over the period of transition. When they joined the Union, they were found to display marked disparities in their rankings on selected dimensions of the Laeken indicators for at-risk-of-poverty, long-term unemployment, jobless households and early exit from education (Marlier *et al.*, 2006, box 3.2). According to 2003–04 data sources, the Czech Republic and Slovenia recorded the lowest at-risk-of-poverty rates, well below the EU25 rate, followed by the Nordic states and Luxembourg. Slovakia was the member state with the highest at-risk-of-poverty rate, at the same level as Ireland and Portugal. None of the central and east European member states was among the nine countries with the lowest long-term unemployment rates, whereas Slovakia, Poland and Latvia (with Greece) displayed the highest rates. Across the Union, over 10 per cent of adults aged 18 to 59 were living in jobless households. Slovenia was among the five countries with the lowest rates, whereas Poland displayed the highest rate, followed by Belgium and Hungary. Sixteen per cent of young people aged 18 to 24 in EU25 had left education early without pursuing training, potentially exposing themselves to the risk of poverty in later life both in and out of work. Here, Slovenia [8.15, 2006, table 5], Poland, the Czech Republic and Slovakia were the best performers; the worst were Malta, Portugal and Spain with twice the EU25 rate.

The proportions of children and older people living in households at risk of poverty are of particular concern for national governments. In 2003, at-risk-of-poverty rates for children aged 0–15 varied to a considerable extent between countries: from 11 per cent or less in the Nordic states, Cyprus and Slovenia to over 25 per cent in Italy and Slovakia. Children in lone-parent households were especially prone to high at-risk-of-poverty rates, with an average of 34 per cent across EU25, but over 50 per cent in Ireland and Malta, and less than 20 per cent in the Nordic states and Hungary [8.15, 2006, table 5]. The available time series data suggest that child income poverty increased in the new member states in the 1990s and declined in EU15, due in the latter case to a combination of delayed fertility, lower unemployment rates and more targeted social transfers. In north western Europe, however, young adults were less likely to be living with other family members in work than in southern, central and eastern Europe.

For the population aged 65 or over, the Czech Republic, Denmark Hungary, the Netherlands, Poland and Luxembourg reported at-risk-of-poverty rates of 10 per cent or less. Rates in Greece, Portugal and Spain reached 28 to 30 per cent, in Ireland 40 per cent and in Cyprus 52 per cent. Rates for women in the older age group rose to even higher levels in these last five countries [8.15, 2006, table 5]. Variations in the risk of poverty among older people can be attributed to a number of factors, including differences in life expectancy and living arrangements, women's employment patterns and their ability to accrue pension entitlements. People aged over 65 living alone were particularly prone to poverty. More women than men are likely to find themselves in this situation due to their greater life expectancy (see Chapters 6 and 7).

When indicators for at-risk-of-poverty data are combined with information about purchasing power, in the early 2000s, Estonia, Greece, Italy, Latvia, Poland, Portugal, Slovakia and Spain combined an above-average poverty risk with a below average purchasing power. A below-average poverty risk and purchasing power were found together in the Czech Republic, Hungary, Lithuania, Malta and Slovenia. The only countries with an above-average poverty risk and an above-average purchasing power were Ireland and the United Kingdom. The remaining nine EU15 countries and Cyprus combined a below-average poverty risk with an above-average purchasing power. Since, in calculating the overall population at risk of poverty rate, countries are weighted according to size, individual rankings obscure the fact that over half the at-risk-of-poverty population is living in France, Germany, Italy and the United Kingdom. Contrary to expectations, enlargement to the east did not produce a marked increase in the poverty risk, but it did extend the range for some of the key structural social cohesion indicators by adding low and high performers (Marlier *et al.*, 2006, pp. 65, 68–9). These examples of variations in rankings across different indicators give the lie to straightforward causal factors and confirm the need to resort to multivariate analyses of poverty and social exclusion.

NATIONAL POLICY RESPONSES TO SOCIAL EXCLUSION

Although changing economic conditions intensified the need for greater solidarity between member states, by the 1990s no legally binding rights and obligations had been generated at EU level for common social assistance provisions. The growing recognition by the Union that poverty and social exclusion were a result of the inadequacy of cultural and social as well as material resources helps to explain why official statements continued to emphasize the subsidiarity principle in formulating measures to combat social exclusion. The 1992 Council recommendation on sufficient resources and social assistance [8.6] left member states to institute their own schemes to provide the necessary financial aid to bring resources up to an unspecified minimum level in accordance with national conditions. Subsequent reports commented on the importance of social transfers in reducing household poverty [8.6, 1999, p. 8]. In the mid-1990s, for example, transfer payments were found to be the main source of income for some 37 per cent of households; without income maintenance payments, an estimated 40 per cent of households would have fallen below the poverty level [2.2, 1997, pp. 8, 79]. Although it was becoming more difficult to distinguish between the provisions made in different welfare systems, Commission reports on social inclusion/protection indicate the extent to which the impact of transfer payments still varied from one country to another [8.15, 2006].

By the early 2000s, all member states operated unemployment insurance systems. Most countries organized both basic and insurance-funded schemes. All except Greece and Hungary had instituted provision for general guaranteed income maintenance for individuals not entitled to insurance benefits. Just as it is possible to identify different national models of retirement and invalidity pension schemes or health services in member states due to differences in their welfare traditions (see Chapters 4 and 7), diversity is also found in arrangements for income maintenance during unemployment or other contingencies [2.4, 2006, tables I, X, XI]. This section examines in more detail the organization of social insurance and social assistance provisions within different welfare systems, and looks at how transfer payments affect the living standards of low-income groups.

Income maintenance in continental welfare states

Most of the EEC founder member states had instituted corporatist welfare regimes, derived from the Bismarckian employment-related social insurance model of social protection (see Chapter 2). Their governments were more concerned with protecting and compensating workers through the insurance principle than with providing national minimum standards for all citizens. Unemployment benefit was insurance based and earnings related, thereby reinforcing the conceptual link with work. In the 1990s, progressively, benefit became more closely tied to availability for work and efforts made to find employment in accordance with the distinction made between unemployment and inactivity.

In the early 2000s, the duration of insurance-based benefit was unlimited in Belgium but elsewhere dependent on contributions record and age. Claimants who had exhausted their insurance rights moved on to a form of unemployment assistance or basic resources for jobseekers at a fixed rate in France, Germany and the Netherlands. Italy followed the corporatist approach as far as contributory social insurance was concerned. Benefit was, however, paid at a relatively low level of 50 per cent of average earnings over the previous three months for six months and then at 40 per cent, in contrast to Luxembourg where it reached 80 per cent of reference earnings [2.4, 2006, tables I, X].

For young never-employed or disabled people not eligible to receive employment-related benefits, and for those who had exhausted all other rights and whose parents or partners were unable to support them, the founder member states and Austria had all introduced social assistance schemes that were not related to social insurance contributions and were funded from taxation. Entitlements to means-tested benefit were granted on the basis of the right to reside, and payment was of unlimited duration, except in Italy where a renewal could be granted, and in France where the integration allowance was limited to three months with a possible extension. Austria, Germany and Italy did not apply a minimum age condition. Belgium and the Netherlands set the age of entitlement at 18, and France and Luxembourg at 25, with some exceptions, for example for pregnant women or those with young children. The rate was generally determined at national level, but was subject to regional variations in Austria, Germany, Italy and the Netherlands.

In the absence of a national health service (except in Italy), the corporatist welfare states made provision to cover health care for those without insurance rights. Heating and housing costs were also taken into account. By the early 2000s, willingness to work for those capable of doing so was a condition for benefit. Most countries had introduced incentives in social assistance schemes to stimulate (re)integration into the labour market, reflected in the titles of the Belgian and French schemes. Incentives could take the form of an earnings disregard or the possibility of combining earnings and benefit.

Income maintenance in Nordic and Anglo-Saxon welfare states

The three Nordic countries had shifted in the opposite direction from the continental welfare states. From a system founded on the principle of universal provision for all residents of a guaranteed income in return for a high level of general taxation, by the early 2000s they had all introduced employer and employee earnings-related insurance contributions, opening entitlement to unemployment benefit calculated according to former earnings for a defined period. Denmark paid benefit of up to 90 per cent of reference earnings, and Sweden up to 80 per cent for the first 100 days; in both cases a maximum amount was stipulated. Rates were much lower in Finland. The basic unemployment benefit granted in Finland and Sweden was paid at a fixed rate.

All three countries operated social assistance schemes of unlimited duration, based on residence. No age condition was imposed, but in practice children under the age of 18 were considered to be the responsibility of their parents. Benefit rates were set and administered at national level, with some provision for local differentiation.

Ireland and the United Kingdom had also moved towards a combination of insurance and tax-based unemployment compensation schemes. The job-seeker's allowance, instituted in 1995 in the United Kingdom to replace unemployment benefit, was designed to ease the return to work, thereby enabling beneficiaries to escape from the poverty trap. An insurance–based allowance was dependent on contributions and was paid for a maximum of 182 days in any job-seeking period. A tax-funded income-based jobseekers' allowance operated in parallel as a social assistance scheme for those not entitled to benefit based on contributions. In both cases, benefit was paid at a flat rate. In the early 2000s, the United Kingdom and Ireland belonged to the small number of EU25 member states where contributory schemes paid unemployment benefit with no reference to former earnings.

In 1988, social assistance in the United Kingdom was reorganized into two separate state-financed schemes – income support and family credit – providing a means-tested, guaranteed minimum income for nationals, and a few other categories residing in the country, aged 18 or over, for an unlimited period. Family credit was replaced in 1999 by a working family tax credit, designed to guarantee a minimum income for families on low earnings, thereby lifting them out of poverty. In 2006, support for children, which was previously included in the income-based jobseekers' allowance, was transferred to child tax credit.

Unemployment benefit and social assistance schemes in Ireland shared some features with the United Kingdom. Unemployment insurance gave entitlement to a non-means-tested flat-rate benefit of limited duration. Beneficiaries were also eligible to receive means-tested unemployment assistance for an unlimited period. The supplementary welfare allowance was paid to individuals without other resources for an unlimited period from the age of 18, at a rate set at national level and with incentives to encourage beneficiaries to return to work.

It has been argued (Lødemel, 1992, p. 16) that, where the social insurance principle was not originally adopted as the basis for social protection, as in the Nordic states, Ireland and the United Kingdom, reforms of social assistance have gone in two different directions. In the United Kingdom, emphasis was on creating a rights-oriented scheme to meet the needs of the large number of individuals and groups excluded from occupational insurance schemes. In the Nordic states, by contrast, state-financed social insurance was extended in such a way that social assistance was confined to a relatively small section of the very poorest groups in society. By the early 2000s, the distinction between the insurance principle and tax-funded benefits had become increasingly blurred in Ireland and the United Kingdom, whereas it had become more marked in the Nordic states. All five countries had in common, however, the priority they gave to ensuring that those capable of work were integrated into the labour force and not reliant on welfare provision.

Income maintenance in rudimentary welfare states

The social security systems in the southern European countries that joined the Community in the 1980s largely followed the corporatist employment-related insurance model of social protection with emphasis on entitlements derived from employment. In the early 2000s, they all had in place insurance-based schemes for unemployment. Portugal and Spain both operated means-tested, flat-rate unemployment assistance schemes for those who had exhausted their entitlements. Greece applied a different rate for white collar and manual workers. All three countries provided supplements for dependent children.

Greece was the only EU15 member state not to guarantee a minimum income, but young people who had never worked were entitled to receive unemployment benefit, and an additional benefit could be claimed once insurance-based unemployment rights had expired. In the early 2000s, the minimum age of entitlement for social assistance was 18 in Portugal and 25 in Spain, except in special circumstances. No national rates were set in Spain, and the autonomous communities could use discretion to vary payments according to resources and needs. In both countries, social assistance was associated with labour market integration. Compared with the Nordic states, where households were reliant on universal state provision of benefits and services, the southern European countries continued to rely more heavily on intergenerational solidarity than on state welfare policies. The domestic unit for the calculation of resources in Spain explicitly included relatives by marriage or an analogous relationship, and biological or adopted children between the second and fourth degree (see also Chapters 5, 7).

Income maintenance in transitional welfare states

For the central and east European member states that joined the Union in 2004, unemployment had been almost unknown under Soviet rule. The economic restructuring of the 1990s brought with it the experience of labour market disruption and, in some cases, high levels of long-term unemployment, particularly in Poland and Slovakia. By the early 2000s, all the fifth-wave member states, including Cyprus and Malta, had put in place schemes to compensate for unemployment. Generally, they were based on insurance contributions from employers and employees, with the state providing subsidies to offset deficits, but in Latvia and Poland only employers contributed to the scheme. The level of benefit and its duration were dependent on age and contributions record. Hungary, Poland and Slovenia operated unemployment assistance schemes. Rather than introducing specific non-contributory schemes for those not entitled to unemployment benefit or who had exhausted their rights, in the other new member states, claimants moved on to social assistance, a guaranteed minimum or subsistence income, in most cases with no age restrictions and of limited duration, but often with the possibility of short-term renewal. Only Hungary did not operate a general income maintenance scheme, although it did provide a means-tested housing benefit. Sustaining willingness to work was a primary concern. Measures designed to stimulate social and professional integration included career counselling, training, activation subsidies as well as rehabilitation programmes for alcohol and drug addicts.

The contribution of welfare spending to social inclusion

The examples quoted in this chapter show how the arrangements for paying unemployment and social assistance benefit vary substantially from one member state to another in a relationship that does not necessarily correspond closely to need. In the early 2000s, two of the countries with the highest *per capita* incomes – Denmark and Luxembourg – also provided some of the most generous earnings-related unemployment and assistance benefits, while several of the southern, and central and east European countries with the highest at-risk-of-poverty rates could afford only limited provision.

Estimates of the number of beneficiaries of social assistance are unreliable and problematic for comparative purposes, since the criteria for gaining access to social assistance and the level of benefits differ from one country to another. Take-up rates may vary too in accordance with social attitudes and the stigma attached to means-tested welfare: in the early 1990s, in the United Kingdom, 80 per cent of those eligible to claim social assistance did so, compared with 50 per cent in Germany (Lødemel, 1992, p. 16). Take-up of the integration allowance in France and the social assistance pension in Spain was said to be 100 per cent, but only a third of those eligible to receive family income support in Ireland were claiming benefit (Room, 1991, figure 2). Studies during the 1990s suggested that non take-up of benefits was probably more widespread than had been anticipated but remained difficult to measure with any precision (van Oorschot and Math, 1996). Data from the 2004 labour force survey indicated that less than 10 per cent of those reporting that they were unemployed said they were receiving unemployment benefit in Italy, Lithuania and Poland, compared with over 70 per cent in Belgium and Germany [8.15, 2006, figure 3.5].

Analysis of expenditure on social welfare is further complicated by the lack of reliable data on benefits in kind and the effect of taxation. Data on relative income poverty reflect inequalities in earnings and cash benefits, but they say nothing about housing conditions or the impact on living standards of social services and benefits in kind. The provision of low-cost housing may substantially improve the spending power of households at risk of poverty [2.2, 1997, p. 97; 8.6, 1999, table 2]. In countries where home ownership is widespread among older people, at-risk-of-poverty rates may be reduced if imputed housing costs are taken into account. The available data on this indicator are problematic, even if progress is being made in improving them (Marlier *et al.*, 2006, p. 149). Benefits in kind in the form of care services and self-provisioning can also mean that at-risk-of-poverty rates based on income measures alone are overstated. Where means-testing is widely used, the redistributive effect of benefits generally appears to be greater, but taxes on benefits may reduce their anti-redistributive effect (see also Chapter 5). In addition, governments may handle the trade off between minimum wages, tax bands and minimum income guarantees in different ways to encourage labour market participation.

For all these reasons, data tracking the extent to which social insurance payments and benefits designed to support individuals and households may reduce the risk of income poverty must be treated with caution. Figures for the at-risk-of-poverty rate before and after social transfers, using the 60 per cent threshold, suggest that, in 2003, the EU25 countries experiencing the largest overall reduction in risk following social transfers, whether or not pensions are taken into account, were the three Nordic states and the Czech Republic, with a reduction of over 60 per cent. The smallest reduction (less than 25 per cent) was recorded in the four southern European countries when pensions were excluded. Including pensions, Ireland was found to experience the smallest reduction with around 45 per cent [8.15, 2006, figure 2.7].

CONCERTED ACTION FOR SOCIAL INCLUSION

Even if agreement could be reached on how to define and measure poverty and social exclusion across member states, it does not follow that the same solution could, or should, be adopted throughout the Union to deal with the problem. Until the 1990s, the main policy choice was often between concentrating resources on raising the incomes of the poorest of the poor through transfer payments and spreading resources more thinly to reduce the hardship of a larger number of individuals and households. By supporting projects that targeted specific groups at risk in the poverty programmes, and through the selective distribution of the structural funds, the aim was specifically to channel resources towards some of the most problematic regions and categories. In pursuance of this policy objective, the recommendation on common criteria for sufficient resources and social assistance in social protection systems [8.6] set out to combat exclusion, primarily by encouraging the improvement of existing national benefit schemes.

During the 1990s, as confirmed by the Treaty of Amsterdam [1.7], attention shifted decisively from passive measures for unemployed people towards active labour market policies, designed to promote social inclusion through employment and incentives to work, supported by employment-friendly social protection systems. The danger inherent in the employment-centred approach was that it tended to reinforce the divisions between work-rich and work-poor households, sidelining those who remained excluded from the labour force for whatever reason. Just as new forms of exclusion were appearing for young people unable to obtain academic or vocational qualifications, or for those unable to benefit from the information society, the criterion of employability engendered the risk that resources would be diverted away from measures to deal with urban deprivation and other areas of social exclusion where different policies were required, but where they were more difficult to justify within the Union's legal remit. After 50 years of EU social policy, member states had not lost sight of the objectives written into the original EEC treaty, but they had become more aware of the need to monitor and evaluate the effectiveness of social policies in an attempt to close the gap between objectives and implementation [8.15, 2006, p. 5].

Box 8　Secondary legislation and official publications relating to poverty and social ex/inclusion

8.1　Council Decision of 22 July 1975 concerning a programme of pilot schemes and studies to combat poverty, 75/458/EEC, *OJ* L 199/34 30.7.75, amended by Council Decision of 12 December 1977, 77/779/EEC, *OJ* L 322/28 17.12.1977.

8.2　Council Regulation (EEC) No. 2052/88 on the tasks of the structural funds and their effectiveness and on coordination of their activities between themselves and with the operations of the European Investment Bank and the other existing financial instruments, *OJ* L 185/9 15.7.1988; Council Regulation (EEC) No. 2081/93 amending Regulation (EEC) No. 2052/88, *OJ* L 193/5 31.7.1993.

8.3　Council Decision of 18 July 1989 establishing a medium-term Community action programme concerning the economic and social integration of the economically and socially less privileged groups in society, 89/457/EEC, *OJ* L 224/10 2.8.1989.

8.4 Council Resolution of 29 September 1989 on combating social exclusion, *OJ* C 277/1 31.10.1989.

8.5 Commission of the European Communities, The fight against poverty, *Social Europe Supplement*, 2/89.

8.6 Council Recommendation of 24 June 1992 on common criteria concerning sufficient resources and social assistance in social protection systems, 92/441/EEC, *OJ* L 245/46 26.8.1992; Report from the Commission on the implementation of the Recommendation 92/441/EEC of 24 June 1992 on common criteria concerning sufficient resources and social assistance in social protection systems, COM(1998) 774, 25.1.1999.

8.7 Commission of the European Communities, Medium-term action programme to combat exclusion and promote solidarity: a new programme to support and stimulate innovation (1994–1999), COM(93) 435 final, 22.9.1993.

8.8 Cases C–239/96 and C–240/96 United Kingdom of Great Britain and Northern Ireland v Commission of the European Communities [1996] ECR I–4475. Application for interim measures – Social Policy – Community measures to assist the elderly – Community measures to combat poverty and social exclusion.

8.9 Communication from the Commission on Community structural assistance and employment, COM(96) 109 final, 20.3.1996.

8.10 Commission of the European Communities, First cohesion report, COM(96) 542 final, 6.11.1996; Second report on economic and social cohesion, COM(2001) 24 final, 31.1.2001.

8.11 Council Regulation (EC) No. 1260/1999 of 21 June 1999 laying down general provisions on the structural funds, *OJ* L 161/1 26.6.1999; Regulation (EC) No. 1262/1999 of the European Parliament and of the Council of 21 June 1999 on the European Social Fund, *OJ* L 161/48 26.6.1999.

8.12 Commission of the European Communities, Agenda 2000, vol. 1, For a stronger and wider Union; vol. 2, The challenge of enlargement, COM(97) 2000 final, 15.7.1997.

8.13 Communication from the Commission, Working together, working better: a new framework for the open coordination of social protection and inclusion policies in the European Union, COM(2005) 706 final, 22.12.2005.

8.14 European Commission, *Joint Report on Social Inclusion*, OOPEC, 2002; COM(2003) 773 final, OOPEC, 2004.

8.15 European Commission, *Joint Report on Social Protection and Social Inclusion*, OOPEC (annual from 2005).

9 Social Policy and Mobility

The Treaty establishing the European Economic Community (EEC) [1.2] was not intended to provide a fully developed framework for social policy across member states. A major reason for promoting the social dimension and for seeking to harmonize national social protection systems was to remove obstacles to intra-European mobility. The treaty firmly endorsed the policy aim of creating the necessary conditions so that persons, services and capital could move freely between member states. This continued to be a primary objective as membership of the Community was extended from the 1970s. The Single European Act (SEA) [1.5], Maastricht and Amsterdam Treaties [1.6; 1.7], Community Charter of the Fundamental Social Rights of Workers [1.12] and social policy agendas [1.22; 1.24] reaffirmed that employment, adaptability, training and mobility were to be the keywords for the Single European Market (SEM), Economic and Monetary Union (EMU) and the enlarged Europe in the twenty-first century.

Mobility of labour is determined by a whole range of factors operating at the level of the socio-economic environment. If mobility is to be encouraged, incentives are therefore needed through company law, taxation, wage systems and employment law, supported by qualifications, education, training and by transferable social protection rights. Either directly or indirectly, the Community's and Union's treaties and charters have addressed all these issues. Less attention has been paid in official documents to social and cultural factors that may also impede mobility, and to non-workers.

This chapter begins by analysing the principle of freedom of movement of persons, as embodied in primary and secondary legislation. An attempt is then made to assess the impact of Community law on intra-European migratory flows. Both formal and informal obstacles to mobility help to explain why only relatively small numbers of nationals across the European Union (EU) have become mobile since the establishment of the common market. At the same time as the Community was formulating policies to promote freedom of movement between member states, it was limiting immigration flows from non-EU countries. Immigration from outside the Union is also discussed with reference to the Union's social policy and the concept of 'fortress Europe'.

EUROPEAN LEGISLATION ON FREE MOVEMENT OF PERSONS

The EEC was premised on the assumption that the free movement of labour was necessary if the common market was to become a reality. The Community's and Union's treaties and charters have all reiterated this objective, and binding legislation has been implemented to remove formal obstacles to mobility. This section examines the development of the Union's social law on migration and its underlying assumptions.

Freedom of movement in the treaties and charters

In the 1960s, migration within the Community was mainly of unskilled workers moving north from the Italian regions. In combination with non-EEC immigrants, many of whom came from Greece, Portugal and Spain, this mobility was a response to the needs of the labour market for low-paid manual workers. Intra-European migration served a dual purpose: for the host countries, it answered the demand for manpower at a time of economic expansion and labour shortages; for the provider countries, it offered job opportunities for unskilled workers from areas of high unemployment. Italy, as the only EEC founder member with a persistent unemployment problem, had a particular interest in ensuring that unemployed workers within the Community were given preference over recruits from elsewhere (Collins, 1975, p. 99).

Articles 48–51 of the EEC Treaty [1.2], which became 39–42 in the consolidated EC Treaty [1.8], contained the main clauses establishing the right to freedom of movement of workers. Article 48 [1.2] reiterated the principle of non-discrimination set out in article 7: all discrimination based on nationality was prohibited with regard to 'employment, remuneration and other conditions of work and employment'. The same article confirmed the right of workers to accept an offer of employment in another member state, to take up employment, except in public service, under the same conditions as nationals and, subsequently, to remain in the territory of another member state. Article 49 contained the measures required to ensure freedom of movement of workers, covering close cooperation between employment services, the elimination of administrative procedures and practices, and of qualifying periods that had previously been concluded between member states. It also referred to the need for 'appropriate machinery' to facilitate a balance between supply and demand in the employment market. Article 50 made specific reference to the need to encourage the exchange of young workers. Article 51, which was subject to unanimous voting, focused on the measures required in the field of social security, covering arrangements for aggregation of all periods taken into account under the laws of the countries concerned 'for the purpose of acquiring and retaining the right to benefit and of calculating the amount of benefit', as well as 'payment of benefits to persons resident in the territories of Member States'. Article 121 (144 in the EC Treaty) under the section on social provisions assigned to the Commission the task of implementing common measures for the social security of migrant workers.

The Single European Act (SEA) [1.5] of 1986 expressly excluded the use of qualified majority voting for matters relating to free movement of persons (article 100a). However, the revised EC Treaty prepared the ground for concerted action by member states over policies relating to free movement, by gradually introducing alternative procedures avoiding the need for unanimity [1.8, articles 62, 67, 251].

In the Community Charter of the Fundamental Social Rights of Workers [1.12], the priority attributed to the free movement of workers was indicated by its position at the beginning of the document. The right of workers to freedom of movement throughout the Community was reiterated. Equal treatment was to be promoted in 'access to employment, working conditions and social protection in the host country', implying 'harmonisation of conditions of residence in all Member States, particularly those concerning family reunification; elimination of obstacles arising from the non-recognition of diplomas or equivalent occupational qualifications; and improvement of the living and working conditions of frontier workers' [1.12, §§1–3]. The Commission subsequently brought forward implementation initiatives including actions to ensure the rights of workers in frontier regions and to coordinate supplementary social security schemes [9.10; 9.11].

The Treaty on European Union [1.6] marked an important stage in the development of European policy on freedom of movement. A new article 8 was inserted under title II establishing the principle of 'citizenship of the Union'. In addition to freedom of movement within the territory of member states, citizens of the Union were afforded the right to vote and stand as candidates at municipal and European Parliament elections under the same conditions as nationals. It has been argued, however, that the concept of citizenship of the Union is a flag that fails to cover its cargo, on the grounds that Union citizenship cannot exist separately from national citizenship for so long as the Union is not a federal state and has no legal personality. The granting of citizenship remains a matter for the state concerned (Gormley, 1998, p. 174). The Treaty of Amsterdam [1.7] retained article 8, which became article 17 in the consolidated EC Treaty [1.8], but amended the wording to state that citizenship of the Union complemented and did not replace national citizenship. A paragraph was also added to article 8d in the Maastricht Treaty (article 21 in the revised EC Treaty) to the effect that citizens may write to the Union's institutions in any of its 12 official languages and receive a reply in the same language. Article 238 of the original EEC Treaty and article 310 in the revised EC Treaty gave the Community the power to conclude association agreements with other states or international organizations involving reciprocal rights and obligations. Between 1991 and 1996, ten such agreements were signed with central and east European countries, in principle ensuring free movement of workers under conditions similar to those pertaining between the EU member states, thus preparing the way for enlargement.

The Treaty of Amsterdam repeated the extension introduced by the SEA to the prohibition of discrimination on grounds of nationality (EEC Treaty article 7; article 12 in the consolidated EC Treaty), empowering the Council to adopt rules by qualified majority voting to prevent such discrimination. The Charter of Fundamental Rights of the European Union [1.21], signed in Nice in 2000, reiterated the prohibition of discrimination (article II-21) and confirmed that 'Everyone [not just workers] residing and moving legally within the European Union is entitled to social security benefits and social advantages in accordance with Union law and national laws and practices' (II-34).

Secondary legislation regulating freedom of movement

In the years immediately following the signing of the EEC Treaty, action with regard to freedom of movement was primarily concerned with administrative procedures, the easing of restrictions on mobility (work permits, visas, labour and residence permits), and the transfer of wages and social security rights. A number of regulations – the most binding form of Community legislation – were adopted, and subsequently amended, to implement the treaty obligations, thereby gradually creating a strong body of legislation.

Some of the earliest EEC legislation, Regulations Nos 3/58, 4/58, addressed the question of social security for migrants [9.1]. A spate of preliminary measures during the 1960s culminated in Regulation (EEC) No. 1612/68 [9.2], which laid down the conditions for freedom of movement for workers within the Community, and Directive 68/360/EEC on 'the abolition of restrictions on movement and residence within the Community for workers of Member States and their families' [9.3]. The intention was to outlaw discrimination on grounds of nationality. Member states were to recognize the fundamental right of workers and their families to choose where they wished to work and reside. They could not demand visas or other entry requirements from Community nationals. Equality of treatment in gaining access to work, housing and social protection was to be ensured, as was the social integration of migrant workers and their dependants (see Chapter 5). The regulation also covered the arrangements for bringing together potential applicants and information about job vacancies through the European system for the international clearing of vacancies and applications for employment (Sedoc), which was set up in 1989 and supplanted in 1993 by the European employment service (Eures) [9.25].

The EEC Treaty had established the principle that workers should be suitably equipped to conduct their business in another member state, and that the conditions of employment should be at least as good as those in the country they were leaving. Therefore, accrued social security rights needed to be transferable. The coordination and application Regulations (EEC) Nos 1408/71, 574/72 [9.1] replaced the 1958 regulations, providing for equal treatment in matters of social security. These regulations laid down rules determining the member state whose legislation applied to a mobile person, the rights accrued through aggregation (and proratization) of periods of insurance, employment and/or residence spent in different member states, and the right to export benefits. Originally, the regulations applied only to workers, their families and dependants, stateless persons and refugees. The scope was extended in 1982 to the self-employed, in 1998 to civil servants and in 1999 to students and some other categories not in gainful employment. In 2003, provision was made for the rights of nationals of third countries under Regulation No. 859/2003 [9.1].

As the number of member states increased, and as more nonworkers became mobile, the original regulations were replaced in 1996 by a consolidated version, Council Regulation No. 118/97 [9.1]. Council Directive 96/71/EC 'concerning the posting of workers in the framework of the provision of services' [9.13] extended the guarantee of social protection and employment rights to workers posted to another member state for limited periods. Council Directive 98/49/EC [9.17] closed a remaining loophole in social security matters by making survivors' benefit and some disability benefits payable net of any taxes and transaction charges throughout the Union.

The aim of European law was not harmonization of social security systems but coordination, so that workers would not be discouraged from moving within the Community. Member states were legally bound to observe the principle that workers should be free to move from one country to another without prejudicing their right to employment and employment-related benefits. Over time, the rules became more complicated due to changes in national social security legislation, the introduction of new categories of benefit and changing working patterns. Between the adoption of the Community's social security provisions and 2004, the European Court of Justice (ECJ) delivered more than 500 judgements interpreting the regulations [9.24, 2004, pp. 46–7].

In the period prior to enlargement eastwards, in April 2004 the Council and European Parliament adopted Regulation No. 883/2004 on the coordination of social security systems [9.1]. This revised regulation was designed to reform and simplify the rules and regulations for coordinating national social security arrangements. The target date set for the implementation regulation was initially 2008. To facilitate the movement of workers and ensure their social and economic integration, the regulation required member states to supply information on job availability, recognize professional qualifications and experience (see Chapter 3), and transfer earned social security entitlements between member states. In 2004, Directive 2004/38/EC [9.22], brought into force in 2006, replaced nine previous directives and provided legal recognition of European citizenship. The revised legal framework was thus in place in time for enlargement. However, most EU15 member states announced that they would be availing themselves of the transitional period, allowing them to delay formally opening their borders to mobile workers from accession countries for up to seven years.

THE IMPACT OF UNION POLICY ON MOBILITY

It is difficult to assess the extent to which European social policy encouraged the movement of workers between member states. In the first 25 years of the postwar period, the impact of Community policy, whether social or economic, on labour mobility is thought to have been limited (Collins, 1975, p. 114). In practice, the labour shortage was such that the preference to be given to EEC nationals probably had little effect on mobility. Despite the lack of evidence of increased migration due to the provisions of the EEC Treaty, the need to promote freedom of movement was used constantly as a justification for policy developments in areas such as education and training, the improvement of living and working conditions, and social protection (see Chapters 3 and 4). In the context of the 1990s, when the Union's social priority was to reduce unemployment, intra-European mobility became more difficult to promote [1.15, 1994, pp. 35–6]. It was subordinated to the aim of creating jobs by stimulating economic growth and competitiveness.

In the early 2000s, issues of intra-European mobility had moved up the agenda in the context of population decline and ageing, enlargement and the search for ways of bolstering the labour force and sustaining economic growth (Niessen and Schibel, 2002). In recognition of the multidimensional aspects of migratory phenomena, the complexity of managing migration and the continuing responsibility of member states for implementing migration policy, in 2001 the Commission brought forward a proposal to apply the OMC to migration [9.20]. The aim was to develop a coordinated approach to migration management at national level, to improve information on legal arrangements for admission, to deal with the consequences of using illegal channels and to reinforce the fight against illegal immigration, smuggling and trafficking. The debate took account of fears about the threat of competition for jobs in countries with high levels of unemployment and the potential burden on their social protection systems [5.7, 2002, p. 38]. For their part, the central and east European countries were expressing concern about the effect mobility would have on their skilled labour, which they could not afford to lose. This section examines the possible impact of efforts to promote free movement of labour within the Union and analyses the attempts made to measure intra-European mobility.

The impact of the internal market and enlargement on migration

The completion of the internal market, following the signing of the SEA, was expected to provide an incentive to accelerate existing trends, such as the flow of Portuguese workers to France. Due to the changing nature of the labour market in the Community, by the end of the 1980s, the demand for unskilled workers had fallen to a low level and was expected to remain so as further automation was introduced. The assumption that the completion of the internal market would bring an increase in migration from the south (Greeks, Portuguese and Spaniards) to the north was also offset to some extent by the displacement of the industrial core through the withdrawal of manufacturing to peripheral areas outside the Union with lower labour costs. Some growth was recorded in non-labour migration, due to student mobility (see Chapter 3), and the attraction of warmer climates in the Union's sun belt for pensioners and migrants with a private income.

Demographic factors were also expected to have an impact on migratory movements. Already in the 1980s, due to the slowing down of the birth rate and population ageing (see Chapters 5 and 7), a gradual fall was being predicted in the number of young people entering working life, provoking skill shortages in most member states, particularly in high technology industries with rapid staff turnover. In the short term, the expectation was that the problem would be offset to some extent by the increase in the number of women becoming economically active. In the longer term, however, non-EU migrants, or previously inactive women, were unlikely to compensate for the shortfall in the labour supply. Since younger unattached and often lower paid workers tend to be the most mobile, a possible implication of an ageing workforce was upward pressures on labour costs, leading to the reduction of geographical and occupational mobility. These predictions were largely premised on the assumption that skill shortages would continue to be a major factor influencing labour markets (see chapter 3). As these shortages led to greater staff turnover and increased competition among employers for professional workers and managers, future migration between member states was expected to involve short-stay resettlement of mainly highly qualified workers in multinational companies [4.14, 1989, p. 153], encouraging the brain drain or brain migration.

Even before 1 January 1993 when the internal market was to come into force, forecasts of increasing levels of intra-European labour mobility were being revised downwards, except insofar as border areas were concerned. During the 1990s, although the Commission continued to advocate active measures to encourage intra-European mobility, free movement of workers was not a prominent issue in the run-up to monetary union. The completion of EMU was expected to increase demand for workers and to have a particularly strong impact on labour in cross-border regions by simplifying economic transactions [9.14, p. 7]. Geographical labour mobility between regions within countries was given more attention as one of the possible ways of adjusting labour markets to changing economic conditions and, more especially, to differences in regional growth rates. It was recognized that, if controlled, such movements could contribute to higher rates of growth and a more balanced development. Union policy was not, however, intended actively to promote inter-regional migration because of the negative multiplier effect it could have on income in the regions from which people were moving [4.14, 1997, p. 67].

By the early 2000s, the expectation was that the combination of EMU, enlargement to the east, population ageing and the changing nature of working life would provide a new impetus for mobility by skilled workers in a single European employment market. The positive view of enlargement was that it was extending opportunities for workers to find jobs and for employers to find people with adequate skills, thereby enhancing employment and economic growth [9.21].

Measuring intra-European mobility

Until the mid-1980s, little information about intra-European migration was available. Subsequently, the Community labour force survey (LFS) monitored migratory flows between member states on an annual basis by asking a small non-representative population sample where they were living one year previously. Data from this source are of limited value since they do not record short-term mobility and rely on individual recall. Nor do they show how many intra-European migrants are living in another country having taken up its nationality and citizenship. The cross-national comparability of data collected by other means is also restricted due to measurement problems and the non-compatibility of national sources (Poulain *et al.*, 2006). Such data do, however, provide an indication of trends within countries over time.

Before the Union began monitoring intra-European mobility using the LFS, one means of assessing movement was by counting the number of labour permits delivered. Between 1958 and 1968 when labour permits were issued for Community nationals, the proportion taken by Italy, the country that had insisted on the need for freedom of movement for labour and stood to gain most from it, actually decreased. By the early 1970s, about 1 million Community nationals were believed to be working in another member state, compared with 2.5 million non-EEC migrants. About 2 million EEC nationals were estimated to be living in another member state (Collins, 1975, pp. 114–15).

During the 1980s, annual mobility was on average equivalent to less than 0.1 per cent of the Community's population. By the mid-1980s, it was estimated that fewer than 2 million Community nationals were working on a more or less permanent basis in another member state. When family members were included, foreign residents were estimated to number 12.5 million, including almost 5.5 million nationals from member states [4.14, 1989, p. 153]. The entry into the Community in the 1980s of Greece, Portugal and Spain, who were in the past the main suppliers of non-EEC workers, did not coincide with a major increase in internal migratory flows; intra-European mobility may even have decreased by comparison with the level reached in the early 1970s.

By the early 2000s, about 1.5 per cent of EU15 citizens were estimated to be living in another member state, representing some six million people. Figures had remained stable for a number of years. Almost a third of Luxembourg's population was composed of nationals from other EU countries. Elsewhere in EU15, intra-European migrants exceeded 2 per cent only in Germany, Ireland and Belgium, where they reached 5.5 per cent. The lowest levels were found in the southern European member states. In absolute figures, Germany was the country receiving the largest number of EU migrants, with a high proportion from Italy and Greece. France was also a big importer of other EU nationals, with a particularly large influx from Portugal. Citizens from EU member states tended to concentrate in neighbouring countries: Dutch migrants in Germany or Belgium, Finns in Sweden and Irish migrants in the United Kingdom [5.7, 2002, p. 28; 4.14, 2004, p. 53].

Each year, only about 0.1 per cent of working age population, or 170–180,000 workers, report having changed their place of residence within EU15. Much greater numbers go unrecorded, amounting to an estimated 610,000 in 2005. At this time, the United Kingdom was the destination for 27 per cent of mobile workers, followed by Germany. French citizens made up the largest group going to work in another EU15 country [4.14, 2006, p. 216]. Data for the same year suggest that the anticipated large-scale wave of migration from east to west following enlargement in 2004 had not materialized. In the first year following enlargement, among the countries for which comparable data were available, the proportion of workers from EU10 in EU15 countries had increased only in Austria (from 0.8 to 1.4 per cent) and in the United Kingdom (from 0.3 to 0.4 per cent) [9.23, pp. 8–9]. Legal intra-European mobility from the east may have been held in check by the fact that all but three of the pre-2004 member states postponed opening their borders to economic migrants from the accession countries. The registration scheme set up in the United Kingdom, the largest of the three countries agreeing to accept migrant workers (the other two being Ireland and Sweden), approved almost 490,000 new registrations for workers from the eastern accession countries between May 2004 and September 2006. These 'economic migrants' were filling gaps in the labour market, most often in lower paid jobs in the service sector and as process operatives; the largest national group (72 per cent) was predictably from Poland, the most populous of the new member states; 82 per cent of registered workers were aged 18–34; and 7 per cent were accompanied by dependants (Home Office *et al.*, 2006, tables 1–4, 6). In EU25, cross-border commuting seemed to be more attractive than relocation. In 2005, on average 0.4 per cent of the Union's working age population lived in one country and worked in another. A similar proportion commuted to a country outside the Union, the majority to Switzerland. With 5.3 per cent, Slovakia reported the highest proportion of residents working outside its borders, mainly in the Czech Republic and Austria. In EU15, Belgium recorded the highest rate, mainly to the Netherlands and Luxembourg. By contrast, transfrontier mobility was limited in Italy and the United Kingdom [4.14, 2006, p. 241].

Whatever the measures used or categories considered, the striking feature remains the relatively low level of labour movement within EU25. The impact of Community efforts to ensure priority for EU workers appears to be minimal in relation to the scale of immigration and emigration among member states before the EEC was founded.

OBSTACLES TO INTRA-EUROPEAN MIGRATION

Despite the removal of administrative barriers, attempts to harmonize social protection systems and to implement directives on the mutual recognition of qualifications (see Chapter 3), intra-European mobility has not increased at the rate that might have been expected if the main obstacles to freedom of movement were legal restrictions. Analysis of migratory patterns suggests that legislation may be only one of a number of variables influencing decisions about labour mobility. Many of the remaining practical barriers may have little to do with legal restrictions on mobility and establishment. On the eve of enlargement to the east, the Commission listed the principal factors likely to determine the flow of migrants: the income gap, the labour market situation in the host country and the country of origin; the distance between the two countries; migration patterns between the new independent states and the accession countries; and cultural and language barriers [5.7, 2002, p. 38]. Decisions about mobility may also be affected by personal factors such as health, income and qualifications, and by the social and relational context, including the working environment, the availability of affordable housing, acceptance by the host population and household circumstances. This section considers a range of institutional, social and cultural obstacles to mobility, which, cumulatively, may help to explain why the completion of the internal market may not have accelerated migration flows to the extent anticipated by policy makers.

Transferability of social security rights

According to European law, by the early 2000s, a person who exercised the right to move within the Union could not be placed in a worse position with regard to social protection than someone who had always resided and worked in a single member state [9.21, p. 10]. Under the terms of European legislation, EU nationals who moved to another member state to take up employment could expect to be covered by the social security system of the country in which they were residing and pursuing their activity. They were eligible to receive the same insurance-based benefits for sickness, maternity, pensions and unemployment as nationals residing and working in that country [9.1].

In the case of pensions, insurance rights already acquired in another member state were not lost but were preserved until the person concerned reached pensionable age. Pensions were then calculated and paid by each country according to the person's insurance record. Crucially, non-contributory or special benefits, such as minimum or supplementary income, which were often means tested, were usually paid only in the country of residence and were not exportable. Provision therefore varied depending on the national system in place (see Chapter 8). In 2006, entitlement to a basic minimum income was dependent on residence in all member states except Greece and Hungary, which did not operate a general scheme. Only Belgium, Denmark, Germany, France, Ireland, Italy and Malta applied a nationality requirement. Even in these cases, except in Malta, the eligibility criterion could be met after a period of legal residence [2.4, 2006, table XI].

Family benefits were paid by the country in which the insured person and his or her children resided. If the children were not resident in the country where the insured person worked, they were treated as if all the family members concerned resided and were insured in the competent state [9.1, 833/2004, article 67] (see also Chapter 5).

Medical treatment was provided according to the legislation of the member state of residence under the same conditions as for other residents, irrespective of where a person was insured, although posted workers were entitled to benefits in kind in the country of employment. The health insurance institution in that country normally then reimbursed the institution in the country of residence. From 1 January 2006, the European Health Insurance Card had to be used for a temporary stay in member states other than the country of residence to obtain treatment, and costs were subsequently reimbursed by that country. Prior authorization was required for travel to another country specifically to obtain treatment. Rulings of the ECJ have confirmed that such authorization must be dealt with objectively and impartially, and within a reasonable time [9.24, p. 22].

In the case of unemployment, benefit could only be claimed from the country where insurance contributions were paid in the period immediately preceding unemployment. Jobseekers should normally have been looking for work for at least a month in the country in which they were previously employed before going to another member state to seek employment. They were required to register with the employment service in the host country. The member state where the jobseeker was insured then continued to pay unemployment benefit for a period of up to three months, provided the beneficiary returned within that time. An exception was made for frontier workers who were eligible to receive benefit from the country of residence rather than of employment.

Over the years, cases brought before the ECJ showed that unequal treatment resulted from inadequate adaptation of national laws and practices to Union legislation, from the narrow interpretation of regulations concerning pension rights, or the non-recognition of qualifications and skills, and social security benefits [9.21]. A report from the Commission in 1999 revealed that most member states had failed to implement the requirements of Directives 90/364, 90/365 and 93/96 on social security [9.19, p. 9]. The transitional arrangements were extended to 2011 to allow the accession countries to implement fully the social security regulations [9.23].

Education, training and recruitment

The enforcement of agreements over the mutual recognition of diplomas and qualifications, the revised EC Treaty commitment to education, vocational training and youth, and the Commission's action programmes undoubtedly removed many of the formal and practical obstacles to intra-European mobility. They did not, however, eliminate important differences in approaches to education and training or change their relationship with the labour market. Nor did attempts to encourage mobility among students lead to a uniform product from national educational systems (see Chapter 3).

Differentiation in the structure of internal labour markets may be related to disparities in national systems of vocational education and training, in particular between countries with well-developed apprenticeship training schemes for skills acquisition and those where vocational training was less highly valued. National practices followed traditionally in recruitment and training, and in the assessment of competence, skills and abilities are also important in understanding the acceptability and integration of workers who are the products of another educational system. Differences in formal and informal recruitment practices and imbalances in the demand and supply of specialists may serve as exclusionary mechanisms making it difficult for outsiders to enter labour markets in other countries.

Job information and access to employment

Lack of information about jobs is frequently mentioned as a reason why intra-European mobility has been limited. In this area, Community action did not gather momentum until the end of the 1980s when Sedoc was established to enable the matching and clearance of jobs. From the early 1990s, the computerized system for exchanging job vacancies under the Eures project operated in conjunction with public employment services in member states [9.25]. The aim was to provide detailed information on job vacancies and job applications, as well as general information on living and working conditions and labour markets, to assist both individuals looking for work and employers wanting to recruit elsewhere in the Union. Eures also developed cross-border partnerships designed to help people living in one country and commuting to work in another. A network of some 700 appropriately trained Euro-advisers was linked by an electronic mail system. These mobility advisers were required to provide jobseekers with the guarantee of a standard of service at least the equivalent of what they would obtain if they were in the member state to which they were trying to move. The contacts established by Eures with employers and job-seekers tended to be concentrated in the information technology, healthcare and tourism sectors, which attracted the majority of mobile workers.

Public sector employment

Despite general agreement over arrangements to facilitate and encourage freedom of movement among employees and self-employed workers, article 48 of the EEC Treaty [1.2] explicitly excluded public servants from the freedom of movement clause. The revised article 39 in the consolidated EC Treaty [1.8] specified that the provisions did not apply to employment in the public sector. The restriction was intended to safeguard the general interests of the state and did not therefore cover all public sector employment. Posts in the judiciary, police, armed forces and diplomatic service, as well as architects and supervisors in public administration, could be reserved for nationals, whereas access to professional employment, in nursing or teaching for example, could not be restricted. The fact that civil servants might have access to more generous social security arrangements, as in Germany or France, and also a guarantee of employment, may help to explain why governments were reluctant to extend access to public sector jobs to non-nationals in cases where national interest was not paramount. Employment in the public sector was an area where, in the late 1990s, the Commission recognized that action was still needed to open up access across the Union [9.14, p. 6], but it was not until 1998 that Council Regulation (EC) No. 1606/98 brought special schemes for civil servants within Regulation (EEC) No. 1408/71 [9.1]. Access to posts involving the exercise of public authority and responsibility for safeguarding the general interest of the state continued to be subject to restrictions.

Language and culture

Ultimately, the reluctance of employers to recruit senior staff from other member states or for well-qualified labour to move within the Union, except in the case of multinational firms, could be explained by an inadequate knowledge of foreign languages and by cultural differences. Although qualified skilled workers might be able to exercise their occupation in another country without being proficient in the relevant language, fluency was usually essential for professional practice by highly qualified workers. An understanding of other cultures and an appreciation of national mores were important prerequisites for social integration for all categories of workers and their families.

Justifiably, the Community had long seen language acquisition as a key to effective labour mobility and integration. Under Council Directive 77/486/EEC 'on the education of the children of migrant workers' [9.6], member states were obliged to offer suitable tuition in the language of the host state, while being expected to promote teaching of the mother tongue and about the culture of the country of birth, to facilitate the reintegration of migrants returning to their country of origin. Article 149 §§1–2 of the consolidated EC Treaty [1.8] committed the Community to take action to promote the teaching and dissemination of Community languages as a component of quality education. The 1995 white paper on education and training [3.9] advocated proficiency in three EU languages for every European citizen, while Council resolutions in 1997 and 2002 recommended linguistic diversity and early teaching of languages [3.17; 9.15].

Programmes such as Lingua may have had some impact on language proficiency, but the size of the language problem continued to be daunting, and became more so with the addition of nine new languages in 2004, bringing the number of official EU languages to 20. A Eurobarometer survey (No. 54) in 2001, the European Year of Languages indicated that almost half of Europeans knew only their mother tongue. A third spoke English as their first foreign language. English was, by far, the most widespread foreign language taught in secondary schools across the Union. More than 90 per cent of upper secondary school pupils in 15 EU member states in 2001/02 studied English. In the years preceding EU membership, the central and east European countries intensified their efforts to extend English language provision. Only in Hungary did the proportion of upper secondary school pupils studying English in these countries fall below 80 per cent [3.25, 2005, table C8]. Young people from other member states seeking employment in the United Kingdom, therefore, had a linguistic advantage over English native speakers contemplating migrating to other parts of Europe

Language policy is an area where the Union can do little more than make recommendations about what would be desirable, and support programmes to encourage language acquisition. Within member states that are multilingual, such as Belgium, language was already a contentious issue. EU institutions in Brussels, Luxembourg and Strasbourg were prime examples of the difficulties of reaching agreement over working languages, a problem exacerbated by internal power struggles that resurfaced each time new member states joined the Union.

Lack of proficiency in the relevant language was often combined with an insufficient understanding of other national cultures. While the Community was careful to record the need to respect national and regional diversity, it was also attempting to promote a common cultural heritage (article 151 in the consolidated EC Treaty). Interpreted in the broader sense, cultural differences were seen as a source of major problems not only for participants in international negotiations and business undertakings, who needed to understand the assumptions, expectations and cues characteristic of different national and regional communities, but also for migrants wanting to settle in another member state. Understanding time-keeping or what is acceptable social behaviour may, for example, affect the ability of migrants to adapt to life in countries that might be expected to share similar cultural norms.

Personal and family factors

Workers, particularly in dual-career couples, may be constrained by personal and family factors that the completion of the internal market in itself could probably do little to change. Reasons frequently put forward by well-qualified workers for not being mobile were their concern about their children's education or about finding employment for a spouse. The Commission recognized the possible restraining effect on labour mobility of the increased participation of women in the labour force and the reduction of gender imbalances, which meant that couples needed to consider their joint careers [9.14, p. 9]. Despite legislation on equal treatment, the social and economic position of women, attitudes towards female economic activity and the provision of support for families varied from one member state to another (see Chapters 5 and 6). In addition, the much higher cost of living in some member states and problems of finding suitable accommodation in what were often very different labour market conditions could reduce the attractiveness, feasibility and financial viability of moving to another member state.

Many of the personal factors determining the relative stability of the internal labour force were also likely to explain low intra-European mobility rates. Most EU nationals living in another member state were of working age; they were slightly more likely to be men (52 per cent) than women, but the male population aged 35–55 was generally less mobile than the female and younger population. The family size of migrants was usually smaller than in the country of origin. Owner occupation of housing, which increased with age, tended to reduce geographical mobility. Public sector workers, particularly dual earners with children, were more stable than single employees in the private sector and unemployed workers [5.7, 2002, pp. 29, 32–3]. Information about the characteristics of EU10 migrants in the year following enlargement confirmed that women were as mobile as men. They were mostly skilled workers, single, childless, aged 18 to 34, and prepared to move into jobs for which they were overqualified [4.14, 2006, pp. 222–3].

UNION POLICY ON NON-EUROPEAN IMMIGRATION

In the early 1990s, the increasing participation of women in paid employment continued to offset the decline in the size of the working population. Over the decade, male employment rates fell, while female rates were rising, especially in part-time jobs [4.14, 1999, p. 127]. The immediate concern, expressed in the European employment strategy, was how to resolve the problem of unemployment and underemployment by improving employability [1.18]. By the early 2000s, the issue of labour shortages had moved onto the Community's agenda. The Commission was examining policy responses to the predicted longer term downturn in the labour supply (Rubery and Smith, 1999), and to the need to modernize social protection systems to cope with the consequences of accelerated population ageing [1.17]. In the wake of the terrorist attacks and events such as the racially motivated conflicts that flared up in several EU15 member states, measures to encourage non-EU immigration, the solution to labour shortages adopted in the post-war period, were not being advocated. A new wave of immigration was not expected to offer a long-term solution to the problems associated with population ageing. The revised EC Treaty (title IV) confirmed the Union's formal commitment to regulate the flow of migrants from outside its borders, but it also required action to ensure that race and ethnic origins were not a source of discrimination' [1.8, article 13]. The Council was, therefore, seeking to achieve a common approach to immigration and asylum using the OMC [9.20]. This section examines two potentially conflicting objectives: responding to population decline and ageing, and outlawing discrimination against third-country migrants with reference to nationality, citizenship and social protection rights.

Developing policy on non-EU immigration

Freedom of movement, as provided for in the original EEC Treaty, did not apply to non-EEC nationals. While the freedom of movement clause outlawed discrimination based on nationality [1.2, article 48 §2], it said nothing about racial discrimination against non-EEC nationals. The issue of non-EU migration moved onto the social agenda in 1976 when the Council adopted Regulation (EEC) No. 311/76 'on the compilation of statistics on foreign workers' [9.4]. The Commission launched an action programme for migrant workers and their families [9.5]. In 1985, the need was acknowledged for the Community to develop a common policy in a Council resolution 'on guidelines for a Community policy on migration' [9.7], followed by a joint declaration from the European Parliament, Council and Commission 'on attitudes and organisations motivated by racism and xenophobia' [9.8]. The declaration outlawed all forms of discrimination and expressions of racism, calling on member states to adopt measures to protect the identity and dignity of all people, regardless of race, religion, nationality or ethnic group. It went on to advocate action to eliminate discrimination and to raise awareness of the dangers associated with racism and xenophobia.

Provision was made in the Maastricht Treaty [1.6] under the title on justice and home affairs for cooperation in areas of common interest, extending to asylum and immigration policy, and policy regarding nationals of third countries, covering conditions of entry and residence, family reunion and employment, and efforts to combat unauthorized immigration (article K.1). The Treaty of Amsterdam [1.7] gave the Council the power, acting unanimously (subsequently providing for qualified majority voting), to determine the 'third countries whose nationals must be in possession of a visa when crossing the external borders [of the Member States]' (revised EC Treaty article 62 §2). In the negotiations leading up to the signing of the Treaty on European Union [1.6], the Council sought to ease migratory pressure by improving the economic position of developing countries, exemplified by the Lomé Convention with 69 African, Caribbean and Pacific countries, and programmes with southern, central and eastern Europe [9.12].

While the Council seemed unsure about its competence in the area of migration, as indicated by the decision to leave a number of issues concerning immigration in abeyance in the Maastricht Treaty, two agreements were being negotiated independently by member states. The Schengen Agreement on asylum and visas was signed in 1985, initially by the EEC founder members, except for Italy. By the time it was due for implementation in 1994, it had been ratified by all member states except Denmark, Ireland and the United Kingdom. Essentially, the intention of the signatories was to harmonize frontier controls and procedures for asylum-seekers, and to abolish internal border controls. Since questions of drug trafficking and terrorism were also on the agenda, the expectation was that the group would favour tight restrictions and would do little to protect the rights of legal refugees and immigrants (Rex, 1992, p. 116). The Dublin Convention on the right of asylum was signed in 1990 by all member states. As in the Schengen Agreement, one of its objectives was to ensure that an application for asylum could not be submitted in several member states at the same time. Both agreements raised important issues concerning national sovereignty, since they implied that a decision reached in one member state should be accepted in another without renegotiation.

Significantly, the Treaty of Amsterdam [1.7] shifted visa, immigration and asylum policy from the intergovernmental third pillar to the first pillar, which meant that asylum and immigration matters were brought within the competence of the Union's institutions and, more especially, the jurisdiction of the ECJ. Title IV (articles 61–9 of the consolidated EC Treaty) covered visas, asylum, immigration and other policies related to free movement of persons, with the aim of establishing an 'area of freedom, security and justice', by adopting appropriate measures over a five-year period from the entry into force of the treaty (article 61). Ireland and the United Kingdom were not bound by any such measures, and they also remained outside the protocol integrating the Schengen *acquis* into the framework of the Union. Although technically a signatory, Denmark did not accept the integration of the *acquis* into the Union, which meant that it could choose whether or not to adopt any legislation that was binding on other member states.

With the Treaty of Amsterdam [1.7], member states reached what was almost a common position over third-country migrants. A new article 6a (revised EC Treaty article 13) was introduced giving the Council authority, subject to unanimous voting, to take action to combat specified instances of discrimination, including cases concerning racial or ethnic origin. Symbolically, 1997 was designated European Year against Racism. In 1998, the Commission presented an action plan against racism, paving the way for legislative initiatives, mainstreaming the fight against racism, developing and exchanging new models, and strengthening information and communication [9.16]. In 2000, the Charter of Fundamental Rights of the European Union confirmed the right to freedom of thought, conscience and religion [1.21, article II-10], and to asylum (II-18), while outlawing discrimination on grounds of race, colour, ethnic origin, language and belief (II-21).

National policies on non-EU immigration

While the rights to freedom of movement were being actively developed in the 1980s at EU level for migrants within the Community, individual member states were tightening controls over non-EU immigration and extending visa requirements, lending a social justification to the description of the Community as 'fortress Europe'. In the absence of Community jurisdiction for third-country nationals, member states continued to pursue their own immigration policies. Four national policy regimes could be identified across the Union in the early 1990s (Baldwin-Edwards, 1991, p. 203). Belgium, France, Germany, Luxembourg and the Netherlands conformed to the Continental or Schengen model, characterized by a move towards stricter control over immigration in the traditional labour-importing industrialized countries. The United Kingdom had shifted away from its former liberal policy and had also enforced stricter controls. Denmark, and the other Nordic states, continued to pursue more liberal policies. The southern European countries and Ireland represented the semi-peripheral regime. Due to their emigratory histories, they did not need to develop infrastructures to absorb immigrants, but Portugal, Italy and Spain introduced visa controls.

As approaches to immigration vary historically across the Union, this is an area where concerted action is not easy to achieve. France, Germany and the United Kingdom were, for example, all major importers of non-EU immigrants, but each developed its own ideology and approach. France, which became a country of immigration in the mid-nineteenth century, sought to assimilate its immigrants. It therefore made French nationality relatively easy to obtain. The French approach to citizenship has been described as illustrating the 'inclusionary republican or civic model', whereby all residents were entitled to citizenship, whatever their ethnic origin (Mitchell and Russell, 1998, pp. 84–5). Since French policy left little room for cultural diversity, the major tensions in French society were ethnic and cultural rather than narrowly racial. The riots in the suburbs in 2005 could, therefore, be interpreted as signalling a policy failure. Germany had developed a combination of 'the ethnic nationalist and the guest-worker ideologies' (Rex, 1992, pp. 110–11), whereby its foreign workers were considered as temporary guest workers who would return home in due course. They did not therefore need to be assimilated and were excluded from many citizenship rights. A liberal policy was adopted towards asylum-seekers, especially with respect to ethnic Germans (*Aussiedler*), at least until 1991 when a bill was drawn up to end automatic right of entry following unification. The United Kingdom pursued a policy of encouraging and absorbing immigration from its colonies, particularly after the Second World War, and demonstrated its intention to create a multicultural society, accommodating cultural and ethnic differences, by setting up a Commission for Racial Equality in 1976. Following a series of racially motivated confrontations in the early 2000s and the London bombings in 2005, multiculturalism was, however, also being called into question.

Under the terms of the consolidated EC Treaty, nationality and citizenship rules remained within the competence of member states, but were subject to any bilateral international agreements that they may have concluded. In the 1990s, as a result of different national traditions, practices varied considerably across the Union. In the United Kingdom and France, nationality had been attributed traditionally on the basis of the place of birth (*jus soli*). In 1983 and 1993 respectively, the British and French governments moved to make their national legislation more restrictive. German and Italian law favoured the acquisition of nationality on the basis of descent (*jus sanguinis*) or parental nationality, but Italy applied the *jus soli* rule in exceptional cases, and a shift in that direction was under consideration in Germany. Where *jus sanguinis* applies and naturalization is difficult to achieve, second and third generation 'migrants' may be prevented from obtaining the nationality of their country of birth and the rights that flow from it, thereby reinforcing the distinction between insiders and outsiders with regard to social protection (Ferrera, 2005, p. 39).

The number of years of residence required before naturalization became possible also varied. In the early 1990s, the requirement ranged from five years in France, Ireland, Italy, the Netherlands and the United Kingdom to ten in Luxembourg and Spain (Baldwin-Edwards, 1991, table 8). Germany reduced its requirement to eight years in 2000 but imposed strict conditions concerning language, attitude and employment before granting naturalization. Policy in the Netherlands was much more liberal. The United Kingdom gave considerable discretion to officials making decisions. Nationality did not, therefore, necessarily coincide with citizenship. Differences in national law meant that, depending upon the place of birth and country to which they or their parents migrated, the children of immigrants, might or might not, be able to acquire another nationality and the citizenship rights it conferred.

Measuring migratory flows from non-EU member states

Since the mid-1970s, borders have progressively been closed, particularly for unskilled workers. In 1987, Belgium, Denmark, Germany and the United Kingdom introduced legislation to impose fines on airlines carrying passengers without the necessary papers. France and Germany also tried to reverse the flow of migrants by providing incentives to encourage them to return home, sometimes in the form of forced repatriation for unemployed immigrant workers. Policies such as these seem to have slowed down the flow of non-EU migrants. Precise figures are difficult to obtain for a number of reasons. Many immigrants were not legally registered. Variations in arrangements for attributing and recording nationality and citizenship made comparisons unreliable. The extent of intra-European mobility was obscured when migrants became citizens of the country in which they resided, if the place of birth and ethnicity of naturalized foreign-born residents was not recorded. Italy, did not, for example, make available information about people born in another country, and French population censuses were prohibited from asking questions about country of birth or ethnicity.

Analysis of the demographic situation in the mid-1980s suggested that, following decisions taken in 1973 and 1974 by the main host countries, formal immigration into the Community had been halted, although residual immigration was continuing through reunion of families, the arrival of political refugees and illegal entry [9.9, p. 6]. Family reunion thus became a dominant source of immigration, while the number of asylum-seekers rose, particularly towards the end of the decade following German unification. Meanwhile, illegal immigration into southern Europe, especially from North Africa, increased largely due to demographic pressures in the countries supplying immigrants and to the inadequate control of some of the Union's external borders.

Despite restrictions, between 2000 and 2004, net migration increased from 1 to nearly 2 million persons per annum in EU15, whereas the impact in central and east European member states was negligible [5.8, 2006, table F-1]. Corrected net immigration, calculated on the basis of the difference between population change and natural increase, was estimated to be 5.1 per 1000 population across EU15 and 4.3 in EU25 in 2002. Cyprus was attracting the largest number of immigrants in relation to population size (17.1 per 1000), followed by Spain (14.9) and Italy (10.6). Most of the central and east European countries were displaying very low and, in some cases, even negative rates [5.7, 2005, annex 2.3]. By 2003, it was estimated that some 14 million third-country nationals were living in EU15 member states, excluding those who had acquired citizenship of the country in which they were residing [4.14, 2004, p. 53]. During the period 1990–2004, the total number of asylum applications received in EU25 reached almost 6 million, the vast majority being to EU15 member states. The German figure for asylum applications fell significantly from 193,000 in 1990 to 35,600 in 2004. By that time, France had become the country receiving the largest number of asylum applications, with close to 64,500, most of which were from Africa and Asia. In the same year, it was estimated that the United Kingdom received 40,200 applications, after peaking at 86,000 in 2002. According to the limited data available for 2004, France also recorded the largest number of citizenship acquisitions (165,100), followed by the United Kingdom (140,700) and Germany (127,200). During the period 1990 to 2004, Germany granted citizenship to a total of over 1 million immigrants, compared with almost 850,000 for the United Kingdom. Germany recorded particularly large numbers of new citizens in the 1990s [5.8, 2006, tables F-12, F-13, F-14].

In the early 2000s, the contribution of third-country nationals to the working age population was of growing interest in the context of an ageing EU workforce. Non-EU citizens and foreign-born nationals were estimated to make up 3.4 and 4.1 per cent, respectively, of EU25 working age population. Estonia and Spain reported 8.4 per cent for non-EU citizens. Sweden recorded 11.5 per cent and Latvia 10.9 per cent for foreign-born nationals. Austria, Germany, Estonia and Sweden all displayed combined figures of over 13 per cent, indicating the heavy reliance of their workforces on non-EU labour. Mobile workers from third countries tended to possess lower educational and skill levels than the EU25 workforce [4.14, 2006, pp. 21, 222–3]. Their contribution to employment also varied with the country of origin: whereas migrants from North America or Australia displayed higher employment rates and lower unemployment rates than EU nationals, those born in North Africa reported lower employment rates and higher unemployment rates. Non-EU women migrants had most difficulty in finding employment that fully utilized their skills [4.14, 2004, p. 54]. With the exception of Greece, EU10 migrants were more likely than non-EU migrants to find employment in EU15 member states in 2005 [9.23, p. 11].

FREEDOM OF MOVEMENT IN AN ENLARGED UNION

The Treaty of Amsterdam confirmed that EU policy on freedom of movement was engaged simultaneously on several different and potentially conflictual tracks. Prompted by the need to meet EMU convergence criteria, efforts were made to complete the regulatory framework removing barriers to the free movement of workers and their families within the Union, and to grant EU citizenship. The treaty reinforced the commitment of member states to securing agreement on controls over the entry of non-EU migrants while outlawing discrimination on grounds of race and ethnicity. The numerous loopholes in the regulations governing social protection rights for intra-European migrants were being closed, but legislation designed to secure the rights of nationals of EU member states served as an exclusionary mechanism insofar as it limited access to benefits and services for non-EU nationals, at least until Regulation No. 859/2003 came into force [9.1].

The EU15 member states managed to reach agreement on Regulation No. 883/2004 [9.1] just two days before the new members joined the Union, albeit with provision for transitional arrangements and without requiring the harmonization of national systems. It had taken almost

50 years of negotiations during five waves of enlargement for the Union to put in place the legal framework needed to operationalize articles 49–51 of the EEC Treaty [1.2; 1.8, articles 39–42] for EU nationals moving from one member state to another. In 2002, the Commission admitted that many practical, administrative and legal barriers were still preventing citizens of the Union from exercising the right to free movement [9.21, p. 3]. The analysis carried out in this and earlier chapters suggests that access to social protection may not be the main reason why intra-European migration, insofar as it can be accurately measured, remained relatively limited, raising questions about the added value of the effort expended over the years at national and EU level.

In the 1990s, the Union was characterized as 'an emergent European immigration regime', which was far more complex than implied by the term 'fortress Europe' (Mitchell and Russell, 1998, pp. 75–6). Despite the introduction of restrictive measures, immigration from third countries had not ceased, mainly due to the limited effectiveness of border controls, and many member states continued to depend on migration to meet the demand for unskilled labour. In the early 2000s, the argument still held that a passport conferring citizenship of a country in the Union was a valued possession for immigrants from third-world countries, because it brought 'relatively generous safeguards of existence' (De Swaan, 1990, p. 19). Amid concern that economic refugees might take advantage of the situation to profit from welfare provision in member states where access was more readily granted, demographic concerns and the Union's enlargement to the east gave a renewed impetus to the search for a common approach at EU level to the problems of accommodating refugees and asylum-seekers [9.18]. The varied nature of the reasons explaining why population groups seek to cross international borders meant, however, that the practical and political issues raised were not easily amenable to EU-level policy solutions.

A dual approach was also pursued at national level, as most member states sought a balance between policies designed to tighten up controls on entry for 'undeserving', illegal, uninvited, low-skilled economic migrants or bogus refugees, and the promotion of socio-cultural, political and economic integration for 'genuine' migrants and refugees on liberal, economic and humanitarian grounds. The terrorist acts of the early 2000s highlighted the dilemma faced by governments and the pressures exerted by public opinion. In a context of population decline and ageing, they also heightened the debate about the possible benefits to be gained from a selective policy on economic migration and a common approach to asylum and refugees.

Box 9   Secondary legislation and official publications relating to social policy and mobility

9.1 Regulations Nos 3/58, 4/58 of 25 September and 3 December 1958 on social security for migrant workers, *OJ* 561/58 16.12.1958, 597/58 16.12.1958; Council Regulation (EEC) No. 1408/71 of 14 June 1971 on the application of social security schemes to employed persons, to self-employed persons and to members of their families moving within the Community, *OJ* L 149/2 5.7.1971; Council Regulation (EEC) No. 574/72 of 21 March 1972 laying down the procedures for implementing Regulation (EEC) No. 1408/71, *OJ* L 74/1 27.3.1972; Council Regulation (EC) No. 118/97 of 2 December 1996, amending and updating Regulation (EEC) No. 1408/71 and Regulation (EEC) No. 574/72, *OJ* L 28/1 30.1.1997; amended by Council Regulation (EC) No. 1606/98 of 29 June 1998 to cover special schemes for civil servants, *OJ* L 209/1 25.7.1998; Council Regulation No. 859/2003 of 14 May 2003 extending the provisions of Regulation (EEC) No. 1408/71 and Regulation (EEC) No. 574/72 to nationals of third countries who are not already covered by those provisions solely on the ground of their nationality, *OJ* L 124/1 20.5.2003; Regulation No. 883/2004 of the European Parliament and of the Council of 29 April 2004 on the coordination of social security systems, *OJ* L 200/1 7.5.2004.

9.2 Regulation (EEC) No. 1612/68 of the Council of 15 October 1968 on freedom of movement for workers within the Community, *OJ* L 257/2 19.10.1968.

9.3 Council Directive 68/360/EEC of 15 October 1968 on the abolition of restrictions on movement and residence within the Community for workers of Member States and their families, *OJ* L 257/13 19.10.1968.

9.4 Council Regulation (EEC) No. 311/76 of 9 February 1976 on the compilation of statistics on foreign workers, *OJ* L 39/1 14.2.1976.

9.5 Council Resolution of 9 February 1976 on an action programme for migrant workers and members of their families, *OJ* C 34/2 14.2.1976.

9.6 Council Directive 77/486/EEC of 25 July 1977 on the education of the children of migrant workers, *OJ* L 199/32 6.8.1977.

9.7 Council Resolution of 16 July 1985 on guidelines for a Community policy on migration, *OJ* C 186/3 26.7.1985.

9.8 Joint Declaration by the European Parliament, the Council and the Commission on attitudes and organisations motivated by racism and xenophobia, COM(85) 743 final, 19.12.1985.

9.9 Economic and Social Consultative Assembly, Demographic situation in the Community: information report, CES 602/84 fin, 1986.

9.10 Communication from the Commission on the living and working conditions of Community citizens resident in frontier regions, with special reference to frontier workers, COM(90) 561 final, 27.11.1990.

9.11 Communication from the Commission on supplementary social security schemes: the role of occupational pension schemes in the social protection of workers and their implications for freedom of movement, SEC(91) 1332 final, 22.7.1991.

9.12 Commission of the European Communities, Background report: immigration, ISEC/B26/93, 29.10.1993, London.

9.13 Directive 96/71/EC of the European Parliament and of the Council of 16 December 1996 concerning the posting of workers in the framework of the provision of services, *OJ* L 18/1 21.1.1997.

9.14 Communication from the Commission, An action plan for free movement of workers, COM(97) 586 final, 12.11.1997.

9.15 Council Resolution of 16 December on the early teaching of European Union languages, *OJ* C 1/2 3.1.1998.

9.16 Communication from the Commission, An action plan against racism, COM(1998) 183 final, 25.3.1998.

9.17 Council Directive 98/49/EC of 29 June 1998 on safeguarding the supplementary pensions rights of employed and self-employed persons moving within the Community, *OJ* L209/46 25.7.1998.

9.18 Proposal for a Council Decision establishing a Community action programme to promote the integration of refugees, COM(1998) 731 final, 16.12.1998.

9.19 Report from the Commission to the Parliament and the Council on the implementation of Directives 90/364, 90/365, 93/96 (Right of residence), 17.3.1999.

9.20 Communication from the Commission on an open method of coordination for the Community immigration policy, COM(2001) 387 final, 11.7.2001.

9.21 Communication from the Commission, Free movement of workers – achieving the full benefits and potential, COM(2002) 694 final, 11.12.2002.

9.22 Council Directive 2004/38/EC of the European Parliament and of the Council of 29 April 2004 on the right of citizens of the Union and their family members to move and reside freely within the territory of the Member States, *OJ* L 158/77 30.4.2004.

9.23 Communication from the Commission, Report on the functioning of the transitional arrangements set out in the 2003 Accession Treaty (period 1 May 2004–30 April 2006), COM(2006) 48 final, 8.2.2006.

9.24 European Commission, *The Community Provisions on Social Security: your rights when moving within the European Union*, OOPEC. http://ec.europa.eu/employment_social/free_movement/docs_en.htm

9.25 European Employment Service, home page: http://eures.europa.eu

10 Assessing 50 Years of European Social Policy

After 20 years of operation of the Community's founding treaty, Michael Shanks, who had served as Director-General for Social Affairs at the Commission in the 1970s, could still ask: 'does the European Community have a role to play in the social field...over and above that of its member-States? If so, what is it? If not', he wondered, 'what is the degree of social diversity...which the European Community can tolerate and survive?' (Shanks, 1977, p. 9). The next three decades brought many signs that the Community was actively developing a social dimension, but that, with each successive wave of enlargement, social diversity was increasing rather than diminishing.

Fifty years after the establishment of the European Economic Community (EEC), in a much enlarged and further diversified Union, rather than eclipsing social issues, the socio-demographic and economic challenges facing the European Union (EU) in the twenty-first century provided a new impetus for social action and for a concerted strategy at EU level to adapt and modernize social protection systems. The Commission had by no means become complacent; it was calling for the Union's social dimension to be strengthened, but with due respect for existing national policies and practices [1.24].

In this concluding chapter, the materials and policy areas discussed throughout the book are drawn together in an attempt to unravel four complex and interrelated questions. Firstly, during its 50 years of development, to what extent have the parameters of European social policy been shaped by questions concerning economic integration and workers' rights? Secondly, how has competence in the formulation and implementation of social policy been shared between different policy actors? Thirdly, to what extent has national sovereignty been placed under threat as the Commission has used its competence to seize the initiative in the social policy area? Finally, how has the European social model been configured, and what are its prospects in the twenty-first century, in light of the demographic and institutional challenges confronting the Union?

CHANGING PARAMETERS OF EUROPEAN SOCIAL POLICY

Opinions as to whether or not the Union has progressively established a coherent social policy of its own depend to a large extent upon definitions. If a broad definition of social policy is applied, it would probably be difficult to deny that EU institutions have developed a social policy competence, although, as argued below, doubts could still be expressed about its coherence, autonomy and redistributive powers. Social policy broadly defined can be described in terms of the principles governing actions directed towards achieving specified ends, through the provision of welfare, minimum standards of income and some measure of progressive redistribution in command over resources, in such a way as to shape the development of society (Titmuss, 1974, pp. 23–32). Attempts to ground social policy more firmly in social theory have also needed a broad definition encompassing 'those social arrangements, patterns and mechanisms that are typically concerned with the distribution of resources in accordance with some criterion of need' (Mishra, 1977, p. xi). Social policy is generally understood to mean that the state ensures provision is made to meet major welfare needs. Quite how this role is interpreted has been constantly subject to variation over time and space, resulting in the development of concepts such as welfare pluralism and the welfare mix (see Chapter 2). Whether the growing interest in the social dimension of the internal market over the years and the extension of the Union's competence in social affairs are sufficient to justify calling its actions in the social area a 'social policy' is a matter for academic debate. By the same token, whether the Union can, or should, be a provider of welfare remains a much disputed question.

In this section, the parameters identified by the broad definitions presented above, and widely adopted in the social policy literature, serve as a framework for retracing the themes that recur throughout the book. The relationship between social and economic policy is reviewed, as is the scope of EU-level institutions in establishing and implementing welfare principles. The theme of redistribution is considered both in this context and with reference to the citizenship versus worker's rights debate over welfare provision and delivery.

European social policy as an emerging concept

Despite the use of the title 'Social Policy' in the Treaty establishing the EEC in 1957 [1.2], in the 1950s no clear consensus existed about the need for social intervention, the form it might take and the instruments that might be used for delivery (see Chapter 1). The objectives of the EEC Treaty were therefore defined in economic terms, implying that any harmonization of social policies between member states could be justified only insofar as it was likely to support and strengthen economic policies. Reference was made in the founding treaty to harmonization of social protection systems on the grounds that disparities in provision might impede freedom of movement and distort competition (see Chapter 2). Despite the subsequent name change to the European Communities (EC) under the 1967 Merger Treaty [1.4], the European Council's priorities remained resolutely focused on economic concerns and the rights of mobile workers. Categories of the population that were not full-time members of the indigenous labour force, or undergoing training or retraining for employment, were totally neglected under the terms of the EEC treaty.

From the early 1970s, awareness was growing that economic developments were resulting in regional inequalities. 'Social' intervention was called for at supranational level as a means of redressing the balance. At the same time, differences in approaches to social protection among the founder members were exacerbated as new countries joined the Community in the 1970s (see Chapter 2). The social problems with which member states were beginning to grapple were brought to the fore by the oil crises of the mid-1970s. They were further intensified as the less economically and socially developed states of southern Europe became members of the Community in the early 1980s.

The social action programmes of the 1970s had been introduced in response to the problems of poverty and the needs of disabled people, marginalized and socially excluded groups who had not benefited from the postwar economic boom, and whose interests had been neglected in the drive for efficiency, increased productive capacity and competitiveness. The late 1970s and early 1980s saw a burgeoning of new action programmes, together with binding legislation to promote equal opportunities between men and women. A number of national observatories and networks were created with responsibility for collecting and coordinating information about trends and for monitoring the social situation, so that policy makers would be in a stronger position to recommend appropriate measures, providing a prototype for the open method of coordination (OMC) of the late 1990s. The deepening of the process of integration was premised on the principle of economic and social cohesion, whereby high levels of social protection and support were to be ensured across the Union, so that no people or region would be left behind.

The 1989 Charter of the Fundamental Social Rights of Workers [1.12] can be seen as the logical outcome of many years of monitoring and negotiation, affording the Community an opportunity to make a clear statement of its social policy aims and objectives, and to raise the social dimension to a more elevated status. In the event, the charter was much diluted in its final stages. It took the form of a solemn declaration and was adopted by only 11 member states, a reminder of persisting differences in policy-making objectives and styles.

Three years later, after considerable debate in national parliaments and referenda in Denmark, France and Ireland, the Treaty on European Union [1.6] was signed in Maastricht in 1992, but only after the chapter on social policy had been removed from the main body of the text on the insistence of the United Kingdom. The commitment to social policy had been undermined. The British opt-out, the emphasis in the charter and treaty on the principles of subsidiarity and proportionality, and the need for unanimous voting on legislation regarding social protection, whereas other social areas, such as health and safety required only qualified majority voting, meant that many of the Commission's initiatives on social affairs could still be easily blocked or rendered ineffectual. Doubts about the ability of member states to agree over social policies had been confirmed. The competence of the Union to take policy decisions had been called into question, and member states had demonstrated that they were not prepared to forego national sovereignty in the interests of greater European social solidarity.

Economic and political developments on the eve of the twenty-first century, in particular the implementation of EMU and enlargement to central and eastern Europe, in combination with persistently high levels of unemployment and the prospect of population decline and ageing, created a climate in which the adaptation and modernization of social protection systems moved onto the political agenda. Social issues acquired a new salience, providing an incentive for member states to look for common ground. In 1997, following the British opt-in under the New Labour government, the Agreement on Social Policy was reinstated in the body of the Treaty of Amsterdam [1.7]. The consolidated version of the EC Treaty [1.8] considerably extended the Union's social affairs remit, signalling that, in the 40 years since the signing of the original treaty, member states had agreed that social rights should be protected as an important component of the *acquis communautaire*, setting standards that accessor states would be obliged to adopt if they were to conform to the European social model, a concept that was progressively gaining greater currency.

Although the revisions to the EEC Treaty undoubtedly strengthened the Union's social policy remit, in the early 2000s its competence to act independently from member states continued to be contested and constrained. Most of the social clauses contained a reference to the consultation process and to the requirement that member states should be free to introduce their own measures according to individual circumstances, in conformity with the subsidiarity and proportionality principles (Protocol No. 30). Despite these safeguards and, as argued by political analysts (for example Marks *et al.*, 1996; Leibfried, 2005, p. 243), even though national welfare states appeared to retain their control over the social policy area, their sovereignty had been substantially eroded by market integration; their autonomy had been progressively constrained within the multitiered pattern of governance that had developed. The Charter of Fundamental Rights of the European Union [1.21], signed in Nice in 2000, brought the long awaited confirmation that the Union was ready to encroach into areas where it had hitherto not been involved, but again the charter did not have binding force. Rather than eclipsing social issues, the challenges facing the European Union (EU) at the turn of the twenty-first century provided a new impetus for social action at EU level and for a concerted strategy to modernize social protection systems, even if they made the prospects of achieving harmonization of social protection systems seem ever more unrealistic.

The changing relationship between economic and social policy

In the early years of the EEC, a complementary relationship existed between economic and social policy objectives, but the dominant partner was undoubtedly the economic dimension. The social aspects of the Community were gaining salience in the mid-1980s, as testified by the assertion in the preamble to the 1989 charter [1.12] that, in the context of the internal market, 'the same importance must be attached to the social aspects as to the economic aspects', which were to 'be developed in a balanced manner'. This approach was not, however, substantiated by other statements in the same text that spoke of top priority being given to employment development and creation in the Single European Market (SEM). Reference was made to the action necessary to counter the possible adverse spillover effects for the social area of the completion of the internal market. Measures were advocated to ensure that the SEM resulted in improvements in the social field for workers in the areas that had, long before, been identified in the EEC Treaty: freedom of movement, living and working conditions, health and safety at work, social protection, and education and training. With a view to ensuring equal treatment, member states were enjoined to combat all forms of discrimination on grounds not only of sex, as in the EEC Treaty and 1970s and 1980s directives (see Chapter 6), but also of colour, race, opinion and belief. The fight against social exclusion, which had been pursued since the 1970s through social action programmes, was to be continued 'in a spirit of solidarity' [8.6, §8] (see Chapter 8).

The 1989 charter did not develop these themes. Nor did it reproduce the emotive language of the preamble. The charter did not demonstrate a strong commitment by member states to social affairs on a par with their support for economic cohesion. The social consensus was limited to strengthening the competitiveness of undertakings and contributing to the creation of employment. Social policy was, in sum, to be a pre-requisite and a support for economic integration, rather than an equal partner. It was a facilitator, but also an essential condition for ensuring sustained economic development.

The genesis of the social dimension in the Single European Act (SEA) [1.5] and the Treaty on European Union [1.6] can perhaps best be understood within the context of the debate in the 1980s about the impact of economic dislocation resulting from the completion of the internal market on regions in the less developed areas of the Union. The aims of the Maastricht Treaty were broadened to promote balanced and sustainable economic and social progress by strengthening economic and social cohesion (article B). According to this interpretation, the social dimension was a response (or spillover) to growing concern among member states about the regional imbalance that would stem from the free play of the market and ultimately be to the detriment of the whole Union. Intervention through EU-level social policy was justi-fied to redress the balance, assist labour mobility and maintain the sup-ply of social benefits and services on efficiency grounds.

The relationship between the economic and social dimensions, as presented in the Community's and Union's treaties and 1989 charter, has been aptly summarized in terms of 'the trade-off between equity and efficiency' (Gold and Mayes, 1993, p. 35). By the early 2000s, the issue of how to resolve the tension between these two goals had lost none of its salience (Pestieau, 2006). The equity argument was a recur-ring theme in the debate over the relative importance of the social and economic dimensions of the internal market, and contributes to an un-derstanding of the Union's social policy objectives. Intervention at Community level was advocated on the grounds that, by giving free rein to market forces, the SEM would produce a two-speed Europe with some regions falling behind. Supranational intervention to assist priority areas was, therefore, justified in an attempt to offset the harmful effects of economic dislocation.

Another economic argument used in support of social policies was that disparities between social protection systems would result in social dumping if nations with higher labour costs sought to move production to countries where labour was cheaper. This argument lost some of its force in the early 1990s in a situation where national governments in all member states were looking for ways of containing social spending and reducing unemployment because of their negative effects on productivity and competitiveness *vis-à-vis* non-European markets. Any relocation of industry on the basis of social costs was therefore more likely to be to emerging economies, where labour was still relatively cheap and workers were afforded little or no social protection. Enlargement of the Union to the east in 2004 offered opportunities to recruit skilled labour and to relocate industry to the new member states where labour costs were lower, reviving fears about social dumping.

A cynical view of the reason why social aspects were built into the economic integration package is that the intention was 'to ease the transition into the internal market by reassuring workers that there will be a social dimension; and to assist the casualties of the process of economic restructuring which is at the heart of the whole integration project' (Kleinman and Piachaud, 1993, p. 10). This view found some support in the opening remarks to the 1994 white paper on European social policy in a reference to the vital part to be played by social policy at EU level in underpinning the process of change. Solidarity and competitiveness were juxtaposed as shared values, and high social standards were presented as a 'key element in the competitive formula' [1.15, pp. 9–10]. Assumptions such as these continued to underlie policy statements in the social action programmes and social agendas into the 2000s [1.16; 1.19; 1.22; 1.24]. However, the Commission appeared to be gaining confidence in promoting the social dimension as an essential component of an inclusive social model and as a productive factor, rather than simply an appendage to economic policy. Official documents portrayed economic and social progress as mutually reinforcing [1.17, 1997, p. 1]. The Commission's communication on a 'concerted strategy for modernizing social protection' presented a powerful and unambiguous statement of the principles underpinning the Union's conception of social policy in the twenty-first century:

> [There is] a recognition that strong social protection systems are an integral part of the European Social Model which is based on the conviction

and evidence that economic and social progress go hand in hand and are mutually reinforcing factors. Social protection provides not only safety nets for those in poverty; it also contributes to ensuring social cohesion by protecting people against a range of social risks. It can facilitate adaptability in the labour market and can thus contribute to improved economic performance. Social protection is a productive factor. 'Modernising' social protection means to make best use of its potential as a productive factor. [1.17, 1997, pp. 6–7]

Another term that had entered the Union's vocabulary as part of the integrative and expansive approach to social policy was 'mainstreaming'. Not only did it refer to gender issues (see Chapter 6). A services working paper, issued in 1999 by the Directorate-General for Employment, Industrial Relations and Social Affairs, bore the title 'Mainstreaming disability within EU employment and social policy'. The OMC was proposed as an instrument for mainstreaming employment and social protection [1.24, p.3]. Social inclusion objectives were to be mainstreamed, as was the fight against racism [8.13, p. 5; 9.16, p. 3].

The social agenda for 2005–10 [1.24] reflected the new-found confidence in the ability of the Union's institutions to carry forward the process of mainstreaming social policies, adapting and modernizing social protection systems. Rather than being a handmaiden to economic policies, the aim of 'boosting growth and jobs' was said to go 'hand in hand with promoting social objectives'. Employment had become the Union's mantra to the extent that, without growth and jobs, it would not be possible to deliver on social policy goals. At the same time, employment growth was crucial to ensure financial sustainability of social protection systems, just as having a job and enhancing career prospects by training were the best way to prevent social exclusion [1.24, p. 9].

After 50 years of European social policy development, it could be claimed that the social space had become a wholly legitimate concern of the Union. The social dimension had been consecrated in the revised treaties, and was recognized as more than simply a spillover of market integration. Recognition and acceptance of the need to modernize social protection could be taken to signal that a large degree of consensus was emerging across member states about the justification for a concerted strategy to ensure that high levels of social protection go hand in hand with more efficient public provision of services. The extent to which the shift in emphasis was not solely rhetorical, but an attempt to justify the Union's new-found confidence in its social policy remit, remained to be put to the test in the face of the challenges and opportunities the Union was facing in the early years of the twenty-first century.

Developments in the citizenship *versus* workers' rights debate

The priority given, constantly and justifiably, in the EEC Treaty to economic objectives was accompanied by an emphasis on workers' rather than citizenship rights, reinforced in the late 1990s by the institutionalization of a European employment strategy. If social policy is, by definition, universally applicable and redistributive, the focus on workers could be seen as creating a serious deficit in coverage. It meant that the needs of large sectors of the population were not addressed by the obligations laid down in treaty commitments.

Despite the growing emphasis on employability, in the 1990s, almost a quarter of the male population and nearly half the female population classified as being of working age (15–64) were not in employment. The proportion of men and women aged 15–25 in employment fell from 45 to 42 per cent over the decade [4.14, 2002, p. 173]. Almost two-thirds of the population aged 55–64 were not in employment at the turn of the century. A third of the women in employment were working on a part-time basis. Women were therefore more likely than men to be marginalized by the employment model of welfare (see Chapter 6). In addition, since more women than men were in low-paid precarious forms of employment, they were more likely not only to lack the benefits of a reasonable and secure income from paid work, but also to be denied access to full pensions, sickness benefit and other payments that accrue from long-term employment (see Chapter 6). Their situation was compounded by their caring role (for children, older and disabled people), which also impacted on their eligibility for employment-related benefits (Chapter 7). Non-European immigrants were another group excluded from the provisions of the original EEC Treaty (see Chapter 9). Whereas free movement of workers was laid down as an essential prerequisite for the efficient functioning of the internal market, for the purposes of the Community's and Union's treaties, migrant workers were understood to be nationals of member states.

The 1989 Community charter [1.12] and the action programmes for its implementation [1.13] were not concerned with these categories. The preamble to the charter had suggested that intervention at Community level should extend beyond the needs of workers. At the last minute, however, largely for pragmatic reasons, the term 'workers' had been substituted in the charter for 'citizens'. Accordingly, every section of the charter made reference to workers, working life or employment. Freedom of movement applied to workers (§§1–3). A decent standard of living was to be achieved for workers through equitable wages from employment (§5). Improvements were sought in working conditions for all workers (§§7–9). Social protection was related to labour market activity (§10). Freedom of association applied to workers (§§11–14). Vocational training was to be provided for every worker throughout working life (§15). Equal treatment for men and women applied in the realm of employment (§16). Information, consultation and participation were intended for the working population (§§17–18). Provision for health protection and safety was at the workplace (§19), and even protection of children and adolescents was intended to ensure that they were properly prepared for work and that young workers were provided with suitable working conditions (§§20–3). Workers were to be guaranteed sufficient resources in retirement (§§24–5), and disabled persons were to be assisted in their social and professional integration (§26).

The continued emphasis on workers can be explained by three main reasons. Firstly, the social protection systems in the founder member states were derived from the employment insurance-related model characteristic of continental Europe rather than being based on universal access as of right, such as applied generally in the Nordic states, or in national health services, as operated in the United Kingdom (see Chapters 2 and 4). Social protection rights had therefore been conceptualized with reference to employment and labour markets. Secondly, since the EEC had been established as an economic community, the justification for any interest in human and social rights was contingent on the need to ensure the free movement of labour as an important component in factor mobility. Subsequently, the objectives of creating the conditions for economic restructuring and monetary stability in the context of the SEM and EMU were also premised on criteria that prioritized economic performance and freedom of movement, and hence the working (productive) population. Thirdly, at the political level, in accordance with the subsidiarity principle, national governments were more willing to acquiesce to supranational measures regulating the technical aspects of working conditions than they were to countenance any interference in the provision and delivery of social welfare services that could be dealt with most effectively at local level.

Some account was taken in the Treaty on European Union [1.6] of the need 'to strengthen the protection of the rights and interests of the nationals of its Member States through the introduction of a citizenship of the Union' (article B). Member states also undertook to 'respect fundamental rights, as guaranteed by the 1950 European Convention for the Protection of Human Rights and Fundamental Freedoms (article F). The rights of 'citizens of the Union', as set out in the consolidated EC Treaty [1.8], were limited to political representation and dependent on citizenship of a member state; social citizenship rights did not figure in the treaty. Two new social policy areas were, however, introduced which made no reference to workers. In a section on culture (title XII, article 151), the signatories to the treaty asserted their intention to encourage the 'flowering of the cultures of the Member States, while respecting national and regional cultural diversity and at the same time bringing the common cultural heritage to the fore'. Under the heading for public health (title XIII), article 152 stated that high levels of human health protection and coordination of health policies were to be promoted, but provision and delivery of health services and medical care, and therefore conditions for access, remained the responsibility of member states (see Chapter 4).

The chapter on social provisions [1.8, articles 136–45] continued to focus resolutely on workers as, for example, in article 137 §1, which referred to the 'integration of persons excluded from the labour market', but said nothing about minimum levels of social protection for non-workers. Although the theme of equal treatment was present in the EEC Treaty and was reiterated in the consolidated EC Treaty, emphasis was again on labour market opportunities and treatment at work. The Community charter [1.12] had made reference to the status of women as mothers, by proposing that help should be given to both men and women to enable them to reconcile family and employment responsibilities (§16), but the theme was not pursued in the revised EC Treaty.

In line with the more integrated and inclusive approach to social policy being advocated in the 1990s, the Commission was seeking to demonstrate that the Union was concerned not only with working conditions but also with the quality of life for people outside work and for categories suffering discrimination. The question was how to marry economic imperatives with the image of a Community that cared not only for workers but also for older and disabled people, its youthful population, long-term unemployed people and third-country nationals.

The Treaty of Amsterdam reflected the political climate of the late 1990s by highlighting employment, and thus the population in work, presenting it as the route to greater integration and cohesion. Prompted by the Swedish government, the treaty had introduced a new title on employment, which became title VIII in the consolidated EC Treaty [1.8]. The Swedes were looking for a way of balancing monetary stability with growth and job creation, whereas the Germans, Dutch and British insisted that employment should be coupled with competitiveness, and that the Swedish target of 'full' employment should be modified to 'high' employment (Duff, 1997, p. 63). The guidelines that ensued, as required under article 128 of the consolidated EC Treaty [1.8], made clear that member states should adopt active policies to promote employability, adaptability and integration into the world of work through the creation of more and better jobs [1.18]. Rather than preparing the way for a social policy based on citizenship rights, member states were seeking to draw a larger proportion of the population into the protected labour force for economic and humanitarian reasons. The primary aim was to reduce public expenditure by moving people off welfare and into work. The additional income from payment of social insurance contributions and taxes was expected to sustain social protection systems.

Despite the lip service paid to integration policies, from the 1970s, when external borders were being closed to immigrants, non-workers, and even workers, from third countries were considered as an underclass, often deprived of nationality and citizenship rights. Member states were tightening up their nationality laws, lending weight to the notion of a 'fortress Europe'. The Treaty of Maastricht [1.6] demonstrated that some measure of agreement had been reached by member states over the need for a common asylum and immigration policy for third-country nationals (article K.1). In the consolidated EC Treaty [1.8], the insertion of a combined title on visas, asylum and immigration into the first pillar acknowledged that the issue had become a Union rather than an intergovernmental competence.

In each of the areas examined in this book, the conclusion has been reached that European social policy was designed primarily for EU workers employed in the regular or formal economy. Education and training, and lifelong learning were intended to ensure that young as well as older people were employable and adaptable (Chapter 3). Legislation on living and working conditions was aimed at maximizing the productive capacity of workers (Chapter 4). Equal opportunities between women and men concerned the efficient operation of the workplace. The reference added in the 1999 employment guidelines [1.18] to the importance of an equal sharing of family responsibilities was justified insofar as it meant that women (and men) could continue their participation in the labour market uninterrupted by family obligations (Chapters 5 and 6). Older and disabled people were to be encouraged to remain in employment as a means of reducing the burden on pensions and welfare benefits. In the case of older people, the trend towards early retirement was to be reversed to bolster the labour supply and reduce the cost of pensions (Chapter 7). The route out of poverty was through integration into the labour force and the formal economy (Chapter 8), while the purpose of promoting the mobility of labour lay in its contribution to the efforts needed to enhance the competitiveness of markets for labour (Chapter 9).

The problem with policies based on the assumption that employment and income from paid work are the preferred, if not only, the answer to the challenges facing postindustrial societies is that they leave no place for people who are unable or unwilling to work. For example, young people who 'drop out' of the formal education system before obtaining qualifications tend to be categorized as socially inadequate and are likely to be excluded from mainstream employment. In addition, the attempts to absorb larger numbers of workers into the labour force meant that many of the jobs created did not correspond to the image of work as full-time, long-term, relatively secure employment that the majority of prime-age male workers had previously experienced over the postwar period.

One of the arguments being used in the 1990s to justify public support for the provision of care for children and older people was its job-creation potential [1.15, 1994, p. 43]. The jobs in question were, however, essentially 'peripheral', low status, low paid and often part time, even if they were 'protected' on a *pro rata* basis as a result of European legislation [4.10]. Paradoxically, the active approach to employment policy, with its emphasis on employability and workfare as defining criteria for social inclusiveness, was thus helping to reinforce the divisions within societies between work-rich and work-poor households, and to devalue the contribution made to society and to the economy by unpaid (including parents) and informal workers, former workers and those unable to work. Governments appeared to be opting collectively for an employment-based model of social protection, while reluctantly accepting that provision was needed through residual schemes at national level to ensure sufficient resources for those who were deemed to be 'unemployable' (see Chapters 2 and 8).

The 2000 charter on fundamental rights [1.22, title II] extended the concept of rights beyond the workplace, thereby going some way towards redressing the balance The charter laid down the right to family life (articles II-7, II-9), education (article II-14), reconciliation of family and professional life (article II-33), social security and social assistance (article II-34), and health care (article II-35). It made explicit the rights of children, older and disabled people (articles II-24, II-25, II-26). However, the failure to ratify the Constitutional Treaty [1.10] by the date set on 1 November 2006 meant that the charter did not achieve the legitimacy necessary for it to be binding on member states.

EUROPEAN SOCIAL POLICY AS A SHARED COMPETENCE

The changes introduced in the Treaty of Amsterdam [1.7] not only rein-stated social policy in the supranational core of the treaty, they also removed some of the political, structural and institutional constraints that had hitherto prevented the Union from extending its social policy remit. Common to the analyses by political scientists of European so-cial policy is the interest in the distribution of power and responsibility between member states and Community institutions. In addressing the second and third questions, this section tracks the shifts in competence between supranational and national actors in the social policy area, and seeks to identify the possible implications of supranational intervention for national sovereignty in response to the constraints exercised over the Union's social policy competence. It also examines the added value the Union can bring by coordinating responses to common social prob-lems and needs that cannot be satisfied at national level, while respect-ing the principles of subsidiarity and proportionality.

Social policy as a contested policy area

Political scientists are divided about the extent to which changes in the EEC treaty could lead to a significant development of social policy in the twenty-first century. Intergovernmentalists (for example Moravcsik and Nicolaïdis, 1999) have challenged the view that intergovernmental conferences have become ineffective forums, arguing that the Treaty of Amsterdam did not signal an end to the underlying divergence and ambivalence of national interests. Earlier, structuralists (for example Rhodes, 1995, with reference to the SEA and the Treaty on European Union) reached a similar conclusion on the grounds that the Union did not offer a viable supranational alternative. Social policy was, in any case, still limited to a relatively small number of areas considered cru-cial for market integration. It was only of secondary interest in a con-text where the growth of international capital and the free market ideol-ogy at global level had resulted in the weakening of the nation state and national labour movements. By contrast, neofunctionalists were predict-ing that EMU would have important spillover effects for social policy, while the impact of EMU for social Europe was seen by some critics (for example Teague, 1998) as negative and socially unfriendly. His-torical institutionalists were arguing that the strengthening of EU insti-tutions had helped to consolidate the Union's social policy-making powers. From being simply a multilateral instrument under the control of individual member states, the Union had acquired the characteristics of a supranational entity, capable of developing or modifying policies, justifying its portrayal as 'an emergent multitiered system of governance' (Pierson, 1996, p. 158).

These different theoretical approaches reflect the complexity of the Union's social policy development and the interplay between the many actors involved in the policy process (Geyer, 2000; Pollack, 2005), calling for a mix of conceptual and theoretical tools to analyse European integration (Nugent, 2003, p. 493).

In the search for ways of overcoming the diversity of national welfare systems, it was being argued that, if the sole motivation for including social policy in the EEC Treaty was to make provision for migrant workers, the need could have been met by establishing the Union as a social state in its own right (Leibfried, 1992, p. 108). Another supranational solution, the 'thirteenth state', posited before the accession of Austria, Finland and Sweden, involved superimposing an additional European scheme on top of existing national arrangements, with benefits funded by employers' and employees' contributions and subsidized by the Union (Pieters, 1991, pp. 186–8). To be effective, such a scheme needed to cover all risks and be at least as attractive as national social security systems and as advantageous as the system offering the most favourable arrangements. In the absence of a supranational or federal social protection system, the Union did provide social security entitlements for its own employees, but they represented only a minute proportion of the total population of the Union. No single programme covered all European citizens for any one risk, be it health, disability, old age, unemployment, poverty or family responsibilities.

Analysts (for example Majone, 1996b) maintain that the Community will never be more than a regulatory state for so long as its budgetary powers are held in check, and member states bear the cost of implementing policy. This is not to underestimate the advantages of a supranational regulatory power in terms of social rights, since the Union can insist on more stringent regulation and enforcement than might be politically acceptable at national level. If the Union's social policy competence is judged by the extent of its control over actions designed to achieve specified social ends, clearly the regulatory framework governing the social policy area has expanded considerably over the years. From only 12 articles under the title on social policy in the EEC Treaty [1.2], directly or indirectly, the EC Treaty extended coverage to almost all the areas usually falling within the remit of national ministries for social affairs. In addition to the expanded chapter on social policy, education, vocational training and youth [1.8, title XI, articles 136–50], and on free movement of workers (title III, chapter 1, articles 39–42), the revised treaty contained two articles on discrimination (part 1, articles 12, 13), sections on citizenship of the Union (part 2, articles 17–22), visas, asylum and immigration (title IV, articles 61–9), employment (title VIII, articles 125–30), culture (title XII, article 151), public health (title XIII, article 152), economic and social cohesion (title XVII, articles 158–62) and environment (title XIX, articles 174–6).

The extent to which such a broad remit can be translated into binding legislation and implemented in member states depends on agreement reached between national governments in conjunction with social partners. Where qualified majority voting applied, blocks of legislation were moved forward (see Chapter 4), but important areas of social policy continued to be restrained by the need for unanimous decision making, in particular social security and the protection of workers when their contract is terminated, the conditions of employment for third-country nationals, and the financial contributions for promotion of employment and job-creation [1.8, article 137 §3]. In most of these cases, a caveat was introduced to the effect that national diversity was to be respected, and that governments in member states should be free to apply their own more stringent standards or to implement legislation with regard to national circumstances and practices. The charter of fundamental rights referred explicitly to the subsidiarity principle in the area of social security and social assistance, and to the responsibility of individual member states for implementing Union policies in accordance with national legislation and practice [1.21, article II-34].

Although the Union can impose sanctions for non-compliance with European law, the main reason why it does not qualify as an autonomous social policy actor is that the lack of funds limited its power to redistribute resources directly. An increasing proportion of the EU budget was devoted to priority regions: between 1989 and 1999, the budget allocated through the structural funds doubled, but the funds still accounted for only 0.46 per cent of the Union's total GNP [8.10, 2001, p. XVIII]. It has been argued that, from the outset, the structural funds 'were viewed less as redistributive measures than as side payments to obtain unanimous approval of efficiency-enhancing reforms of the Community system' (Majone, 1996b, p. 131). However, the SEA can also be said to have transformed the funds from side payments into 'an interventionist instrument of regional economic development' (Marks *et al.*, 1996, p. 354). These two interpretations are not incompatible. The structural funds have undoubtedly served as a means of compensating member states for concessions made during intergovernmental negotiations over issues such as enlargement, completion of the internal market and monetary union. They also gave the Union resources of its own, even if the amount involved remained extremely small in relation to national expenditure on social protection and was subject to tight controls. In addition, the resources available for spending on the poverty programmes and other social actions were far too limited to have an enduring and truly redistributive impact on social problem areas and underprivileged population groups.

In defence of national sovereignty and diversity

The substantial social spillover of market integration at Community level is widely acknowledged and documented by economists and political scientists, but so too is the strong resistance of national governments to the erosion of national sovereignty in the social policy area. Constraints on the Union's ability to act do not mean that the sovereignty of national governments has not been placed under threat. The Treaty of Amsterdam further reduced institutional barriers and formalized a process of gradual erosion of national autonomy in the social policy area, which had already been accelerated in the 1980s by the SEA and was prefigured in the 1989 Community charter. However, opinions differ over the extent to which control of social policy has shifted from nation states to supranational institutions. A convincing case has been built in support of the argument that member states have lost more autonomy and control over national welfare policies than the EU has gained in transferred authority. In particular, it can be demonstrated that European law, backed by decisions of the European Court of Justice (ECJ) on the pretext of pursuing market integration, has undermined the authority of national governments (Leibfried, 2005).

The Union's regulatory competence was considerably extended during the 1990s, as were the interventionist powers of its institutions, notably the Commission and the European Parliament. With the introduction of direct elections in 1979 and the extension of its powers under the SEA in 1986, the European Parliament saw its influence in social affairs expand. Although national interests were directly represented at the European Council and the Council of Ministers and, less directly, through the European Parliament, national governments had limited control over the ECJ. Member states were not only taken before the ECJ for infringing European law, but they were also forced to surrender control over their own law-making powers, in some cases where they had themselves pushed for legislation at European level (Lanquetin *et al.*, 2000). Examples abound, particularly with reference to equal treatment for women and men, flexibility in working time or the social security rights of mobile workers, where contentious legislation was able to be passed despite opposition from individual member states (Burrows and Mair, 1996; Shaw, 2000; Búrca, 2005). By providing an expansive interpretation of European social law, the ECJ consolidated its influence, thereby further impinging on national autonomy in the social area.

At the same time, national policies and interests, especially those of the more powerful member states, clearly restricted the Union's ability to develop its own social policy. Many examples have been quoted throughout this book of the ways in which proposals to extend the Union's social policy remit, introduce directives affecting working conditions, or initiate action programmes were delayed or shelved due to the veto of individual member states or the court cases that were brought against the Commission. For example, national governments blocked proposals for legislation on living and working conditions or the allocation of funds to the Observatories on Ageing and Older People and National Policies to Combat Social Exclusion (see Chapters 4, 7, 8). With the extension of qualified majority voting, the principle of subsidiarity assumed greater importance and provides evidence of continued resistance to pressures for uniformity in the social area. The effect of the multilevel system of governance may have been to erode national sovereignty, but it can also be argued that '[t]he complex interplay among these contending institutions in a polity where political control is diffuse often leads to outcomes that are second choice for all participants' (Marks *et al.*, 1996, p. 372).

The efforts by national governments to protect their own interests may not be the only reason for their resistance to supranational intervention. The failure of the Union's institutions to take sufficient account of national welfare traditions and the appreciative settings in which the policy process unfolds may also help to explain why the record on implementation and compliance with European law has been uneven, and why a level playing field of minimum standards was still on the agenda in the early 2000s. Numerous examples have been cited in this book of national differences in approaches to policy formation and practice, with the result that an EU citizen moving around the Union could still experience quite disparate living and working conditions between member states. Since one of the two reasons (the other was to enhance competitiveness) for promoting the harmonization of social protection systems was to facilitate freedom of movement within the

Community, the persistence of diversity could be interpreted as signalling the failure to achieve the original EEC Treaty objectives.

In the area of education and training, laborious attempts to align systems were eventually abandoned in favour of mutual recognition, with the effect that arrangements for schooling, higher education and training, curricula and teaching methods continued to create problems for young people transferring from one national system to another and for employers seeking to recruit qualified labour from other member states (Chapter 3). Analysis of policies to improve living and working conditions reveal fundamental disparities in attitudes towards flexibility, the employment relationship and the provision of health services (Chapter 4). All member states adapted their legislation to take account of changing family forms, but the pace and degree of change varied considerably, as did responses to population decline and ageing. Differences in national policy styles meant that ostensibly similar measures, for example child benefit, fiscal or leave arrangements, were not necessarily used in the same way or to achieve the same ends (Chapter 5). All member states were obliged under European law to address issues of equal pay and treatment, and the conceptualization of women as mothers and workers. However, the approaches of national governments to the question of reconciling employment with family life continued to have a differential effect on the labour market opportunities of women (Chapter 6). Despite efforts to reach agreement over pension arrangements at EU level and to address questions of social and medical care, old age and disability could be experienced very differently. National practices depended not only on the regulations in force in the country in which the person concerned had spent most of his or her working life, but also on the strength of intergenerational relationships and their interaction with public provision (Chapter 7). Similarly, different national systems for ensuring sufficient resources meant that being poor or socially excluded did not have the same implications everywhere (Chapter 8). Being a non-EU immigrant was also experienced differently in terms of social citizenship and welfare rights across the Union, which may help to explain some of the variation in the direction and intensity of intra-European migratory flows (Chapter 9).

Many of these differences can be attributed to the principles according to which welfare is funded and organized. The original EEC founder members had in common their preference for an employment-based insurance welfare model, within which harmonization did not appear to be a wholly unrealistic goal. The increasing diversity brought by subsequent waves of membership, not least enlargement to the east, made the goal become ever more distant and unattainable (Chapter 2), leaving the Commission to explore alternative approaches.

The overriding objectives in the social area, as set out in article 136 of the revised EC Treaty [1.8], were to promote employment, improve living and working conditions, ensure proper social protection, dialogue between management and labour and the development of human resources. The instruments to be used to achieve these objectives were to take account of national practices, particularly with regard to contractual relations and the need to maintain the competitiveness of the economy. Although the term still figured in the revised treaty article as a possible outcome, clearly harmonization of national social protection systems was no longer on the agenda. The 1992 Council recommendation 'on the convergence of social protection objectives and policies' [2.1] had already acknowledged that harmonization was an unattainable objective that did not have the support of member states. Subsidiarity had become a key concept by the time the Treaty of Maastricht was signed in 1992 [1.6, article 3b]. It received fuller recognition by being appended to the consolidated EC Treaty in 1997 as a protocol (No. 30), resolutely signalling, once again, that member states were not prepared to relinquish national sovereignty in the social area.

Article 118 of the original EEC Treaty [1.2] had introduced another concept that was not far removed from the position eventually reached in the 1990s: close cooperation in the social field. Although the title of the 1992 recommendation focused on convergence, cooperation might have been a more accurate description of the Council's intentions. The 'convergence strategy' being promoted was aimed at setting 'common objectives able to guide Member States' policies in order to permit the co-existence of different national systems and to enable them to prog??ress in harmony with one another towards the fundamental objectives of the Community' [2.1, p. 50]. In this context, convergence would be *de facto*. Community action was justified on the grounds that comparable trends were leading to common economic and demographic problems: ageing of the population, changing family situations, the persistence of high levels of unemployment and the spread of poverty. These problems required common, or at least coordinated, responses in order to reduce any disparities that might impede freedom of movement. Article 137 in the revised EC Treaty [1.8] empowered the Council to adopt measures to encourage, rather than promote as in the original treaty, cooperation between member states in areas concerned with health and safety at work, working conditions, information and consultation of workers, the integration of persons excluded from the labour market, and equality of opportunity and treatment between men and women at work. The initiatives authorized were to be aimed at improving knowledge, developing exchanges of information and best practice, promoting innovative approaches and evaluating experience. While this form of cooperation might result in some alignment of systems, member states preserved at least a semblance of autonomy by being able to maintain or introduce their own more stringent protective measures.

During the 1990s, the spillover effects from the convergence criteria established for EMU were also creating pressures for member states to cooperate more closely in the social area. The Commission's social action programme for 1998–2000 referred, for example, to the convergence of employment policies as a complement to the convergence process leading to EMU [1.19, p. 5]. Driven by economic imperatives and in their search for ways of curbing public spending, all member states were constantly reviewing the funding and provision of welfare [2.2, 2001]. The reform of social protection systems was of particular concern in the central and east European countries that joined the Union in 2004 as they sought to meet the requirements of the Union's social *acquis* [2.3]. The reforms of social protection they undertook shifted their social policy towards an employment-based social insurance system resembling the continental or Bismarckian model, while the social dialogue remained relatively underdeveloped (Vaughan-Whitehead, 2003). By contrast, the decision to resort to private funding for pensions was more in line with trends in Anglo-Saxon welfare systems [2.3, p. 250]. In terms of expenditure on social welfare in relation to gross domestic product, they fell far below the EU25 average (see Chapter 2).

Whether these policy shifts will, in the longer term, result in greater uniformity between systems and, if so, what sort of European welfare system will emerge are still open to debate. The 1992 Council recommendation on convergence was non-committal on the question of the model towards which systems might move. While it referred to the need to ensure maximum efficiency and effectiveness and to guarantee a minimum means of subsistence, enabling people at risk to maintain their standard of living in a reasonable manner, member states were left to make their own choices about how these objectives could be achieved. The 1994 white paper on European social policy emphasized the need for minimum standards of social protection, which would not overstretch the economically weaker member states. The intention was to avoid any levelling down while not preventing the more developed countries from implementing higher standards [1.15, p. 12]. The many safeguard clauses built into the treaties and secondary legislation meant that, in theory at least, member states could continue to implement European law in accordance with their own national practices. The sheer volume of legislation that emanated from Brussels, most of it at the request of member states, and the diminishing autonomy of national parliaments or governments as law makers (Majone, 1996a, pp. 265–6) implied, however, that their room for manœuvre had been progressively and, on occasions, almost imperceptibly, constrained.

At the same time, after 50 years of operation, the capacity of the Union's institutions to replace national governments in the social policy arena was also constrained when it came to providing a clear mandate for action. Arguably, social policy was, therefore, more likely to evolve as the result of 'mutual adjustment and incremental accommodation than of central guidance' (Leibfried, 2005, p. 273). While conceding that national boundaries have been redrawn and that national sovereignty has been eroded, new forms of subnational and transnational social protection appeared to be emerging, offering an alternative to both national and supranational institutions: policies to support freedom of movement, for example, made it possible for 'denizens' (legal residents) to gain access to jobs and social protection anywhere in the Union and for mobile workers to transport rights and benefits (Ferrera, 2005, pp. 8, 49).

The Commission as coordinator of European social policy

While the Union's institutions were relentlessly encroaching into an area long seen as the preserve of national governments, and the ECJ was becoming a force to be reckoned with, views about the Commission's contribution to the building of social Europe were divided. In the 1970s, Shanks described the Commission's role in the social policy field 'as a catalyst, an educator and influencer, a co-ordinator of research, a data-bank and a standard-setter' (Shanks, 1977, p. 84). The Commission's wide-ranging powers have been usefully summarized under six major headings: 'proposer and developer of policies and of legislation, executive functions, guardian of the legal framework, external representative and negotiator, mediator and conciliator, and promoter of the general interest' (Nugent, 2003, p. 126). Even if the Commission might not have developed quite into the motor force originally intended, its role has been described as 'central and vital to the whole EU system' (Nugent, 2003, p. 149). Another apt term used to describe the Commission in the social area is that of a 'purposeful opportunist' (Cram, 1997, p. 6). The Commission learnt to manage its role skilfully so as to maximize room for manœuvre in the policy process while avoiding direct conflict with member states, thereby extending scope for action without alienating national governments.

This book has relied heavily on the impressive array of reports, policy statements and communications from the Commission, and more especially from the Directorate-General for Employment, Social Affairs and Equal Opportunities (DG Employment), to document and analyse the development of the Union's social policy. Even if the output of binding social policy legislation was relatively limited both in quantity and scope, the Commission exploited the ambiguities and lack of precision in the treaties to take forward non-binding legislation and soft law (Cram, 1997, pp. 28–9; Shaw, 2000). The Treaty of Amsterdam [1.7] further strengthened the Commission's right of initiative by incorporating new provisions, as noted above. In the area of employment, the Commission was given not only a monitoring and reporting role but was also charged with drawing up employment guidelines and ensuring they were implemented by national governments [1.8, article 128], culminating in the development and refinement of the OMC, which was to become a major 'soft law' policy instrument of 'experimentalist governance' in the 2000s (Trubeck and Trubeck, 2005; Zeitlin, 2005).

As demonstrated throughout this book, the Commission was not prevented by the absence of a clear treaty mandate from intervening actively in the areas of education and training, health, living and working conditions, social protection, equal pay and treatment of workers, the protection of children, older and disabled people, regional development and social exclusion. It made policy recommendations, brought forward proposals for legislation, monitored their implementation, and took national governments before the ECJ for non-compliance. It liaised closely with the social partners following Jacques Delors' overtures and, through the social dialogue, strengthened the involvement of management and labour in the Union's social dimension.

In addition to its own programmes in the areas of vocational training, disability, unemployment, poverty and equal opportunities for women, the Commission monitored social developments through its observatories on social exclusion, older people, family policies and employment, its networks on childcare, women in the labour market, education, vocational training, local employment, job vacancies and employment policies, and social protection systems. It set up specialized institutions such as the European Centre for the Development of Vocational Training (Cedefop), the European Foundation for the Improvement of Living and Working Conditions and the European

Agency for Health and Safety at Work, as well as committees and expert groups. Its capacity for data collection and analysis, in conjunction with Eurostat, and for evaluation of its own programmes became prodigious, and prepared the ground for its coordinating role in the OMC. Scrutiny of the social action programmes from the 1970s, the green and white papers on social policy, the network and observatory reports, the Commission's own reports on the demographic and social situations in the Union, the joint reports on the OMC, and the many studies it commissioned from researchers around the Community on social topics, reveals extensive evidence of the way in which the Commission worked within the constraints imposed by the treaties. Often, its operations were behind the scenes, which may help to explain the accusations of lack of transparency, the questions raised about its legitimacy, and why it was discredited in 1999, when the whole Commission was forced to resign.

While member states were agonizing over the wording of the 1989 charter and social chapter, proposals were being drafted for recommendations that went beyond the terms of the Community charter and Agreement on Social Policy. While the 1997 Intergovernmental Conference in Amsterdam was searching for a means of appeasing electorates over the employment issue, and was struggling to reach consensus, the Commission used its data collection and monitoring powers to identify trends and was looking beyond the politicians' horizon for ways of adapting and modernizing social protection [1.17]. In its demographic and social situation reports [5.7], and culminating in 2006 with the communication on the demographic future of Europe [1.25], it had long sought to raise awareness of the implications of an ageing labour force for the sustainability of social protection and the quality of the future labour supply.

Together, the documents issued by the Commission constitute a more comprehensive and coherent statement of the Union's social policy than is to be found in the more widely publicized formal texts, reflecting the Commission's ability to act as the conscience of the Union. The 1974 social action programme, the white paper on European social policy, the Commission's communications on the modernization of social protection and its social agendas for the first decade of the 2000s [1.11; 1.15; 1.17; 1.22; 1.24] provide a coherent overview of the Union's social policy thinking. All commissioners for social affairs were keen to leave their mark on European social policy, but few could identify issues that had not already been addressed by their predecessors. Key themes moved up and down the agenda in tune with the political climate of the day. By acting as the Union's conscience and social policy coordinator, the Commission was able to seize the opportunity to justify supranational intervention, formulating objectives and proposing instruments for achieving them without infringing the principles of subsidiarity and proportionality. The OMC, which can be seen as a logical extension of the Commission's monitoring and evaluation activities, provided not only 'a viable counterweight to at least some of the destabilizing pressures that European integration is exerting on national welfare states' (Ferrera, 2005, p. 247), but also an opportunity for the Commission to grasp the initiative at a time when the much enlarged Union was looking for alternatives forms of governance.

THE FUTURE OF THE EUROPEAN SOCIAL MODEL

This book has shown how, after 50 years of action at EU level, resulting in a proliferation of legislative texts, few areas of social life remain untouched by official regulations, directives, decisions, recommendations, resolutions, communications or memoranda. Negotiations over the Community Charter of the Fundamental Social Rights of Workers [1.12] and the social chapter of the Treaty of Maastricht [1.6] demonstrated that the United Kingdom was not alone in its concern about the pervasiveness of the Union's powers, as confirmed by the national debates surrounding ratification of the Constitutional Treaty [1.10]. The 1994 white paper on European social policy [1.15], the subsequent social action plans and communications on the modernization of social protection [1.17] did not, however, signal that the Commission would be reducing the scope of its action. Rather, they highlighted the continuing need to seek common and coordinated responses to meet the challenges that the Union would be facing in the twenty-first century.

Although no proposals were put forward for a European social union, during the 1990s reference was made increasingly in policy statements to the European social model, which was progressively taking shape, despite the resistance of member states to any convergence of systems. Such a model was presented as one of the achievements of the Community. Rather than simply taking the form of a multitiered welfare system made up of the sum of its parts, the European social model was depicted as embodying core values, to which member states were committed and that they were prepared to nurture and protect. Whether national social protection systems were based on employment-related insurance or universal benefits funded primarily from taxation, and the extent to which they were controlled by, and depended on, central government or the market were largely irrelevant. What mattered was that policies were being pursued with a common objective: 'to promote a decent quality of life and standard of living for all in an active, inclusive and healthy society that encourages access to employment, good working conditions, and equality of opportunity' [1.19, p. 8].

A constant and recurring aim in policy statements prepared by the Commission from the early 1990s was to achieve a broadly based, innovative and forward looking social policy capable of underpinning the process of change, thereby ensuring 'a unique blend of economic well-being, social cohesiveness and high overall quality of life' [1.15, 1994, p. 7]. The shared values that came to form the basis of such a European social model encompassed 'democracy and individual rights, free collective bargaining, the market economy, equality of opportunity for all and social welfare and solidarity' [1.15, 1994, p. 9]. The future challenge outlined in the Commission's communications on 'modernising and improving social protection in the European Union' [1.17] was how to adapt social protection as a core component of this model while sustaining high standards of provision in a context of population ageing, changing family structures, a new gender balance and enlargement, without abandoning the values of solidarity and cohesion.

In the late 1990s, the Commission portrayed the socio-economic changes that were taking place as opportunities creating the need for a concerted strategy [1.17]. The process of deepening economic integration, with the introduction of the single currency from 1 January 1999, was expected to create an environment conducive to monetary stability, economic growth and sustainability of public finances, both demanding and allowing for the restructuring of expenditure on social protection. The agreement reached between governments, and institutionalized through a treaty commitment, about the need for an active and coherent approach to employment was seen as a means of securing the future viability of social protection systems in the context of demographic ageing, while making them more employment friendly. Employment was also to be the instrument for achieving an inclusive society by promoting family-friendly policies, designed to increase the participation of women in the labour market, and age-friendly policies (although the term was not used) to achieve the objective of adding life to years and making active ageing a reality [7.15, p. 21]. To meet the unprecedented challenges created by accelerated demographic decline and ageing, the prime objectives of the Commission's strategy for modernizing social protection [1.17] were to make work pay while providing income security, to make pensions safe while ensuring the sustainability of pension systems, and to promote social inclusion while guaranteeing high quality and sustainable health provision.

The third challenge, enlargement, was also presented as an opportunity, opening up the way to enhanced trade and economic activity, and giving a new impetus to European integration, while also extending the Union's cultural diversity [8.12, vol. 1, p. 6]. Enlargement had always been an important incentive for member states to engage in reflection about the future shape of the Union's institutions and policies. The prospect of enlargement to the countries of central and eastern Europe after the year 2000 was no exception. In preparation for this unprecedented expansion, the Constitutional Treaty [1.10] proposed a thorough reform of the Union's institutions, including, among other changes, the reweighting of votes in the Council, the extension of qualified majority voting to all areas, and a reduction in the number of commissioners to one per member state. Since social policy often proved to be a contentious area, the extension of qualified majority voting was promoted as a more flexible way of integrating further variants of the welfare mix. Coupled with a streamlined version of the OMC, it provided opportunities for (self-) regulatory development and new forms and processes of governance based on an active approach to social policy. The social agenda for 2005–10 confirmed the aim of combining 'the consolidation of a common European framework with the implementation of diversified measure to respond to specific needs' [1.24, p. 19].

The accession of 12 more countries with very diverse welfare trajectories was expected to have a greater impact on social policy than previous waves of membership. Together, the population of the 12 accessor states amounted to over 100 million, equivalent to more than 21 per cent of the Union's population, but their gross domestic product (GDP), measured in purchasing power standards (PPS), was less than 9 per cent of the EU25 level [4.14, 2005, table 1; 5.8, table C-1]. The new member states were expected to bring with them high levels of unemployment, poverty and deprivation [1.17, 1999, p. 11]. They were required to modernize their own social protection systems, while striving to adopt the Union's *acquis* in the social field, raising fears that they might undermine or weaken the European social model by lowering standards (Vaughan-Whitehead, 2003, pp. 162–3). Analysis of data on social protection spending, unemployment and poverty in the early 2000s illustrates the great diversity of situations in the new member states and of their adaptive capacity (see Chapters 2, 8), suggesting that, at least in some cases, these fears were overstated.

After 50 years, European social policy had become pervasive. Market forces and ECJ rulings had contributed to a gradual and irreversible erosion of national sovereignty and autonomy over welfare systems, but without creating a viable supranational alternative at EU level. Although freedom of movement and competitiveness were still being evoked to justify EU legislation and to establish a base line for policy provision, the future of the 'unique multi-tiered system of social policy' (Leibfried, 2005, p. 273) that had emerged after so many years of gestation was proving difficult to predict. It could still be argued that the new modes of governance introduced to meet the challenges of the twenty-first century might result in further convergence through choice and a bottom-up approach, or by the diffusion of national legal standards rather than their imposition through European law (Adnett and Hardy, 2005, p. 198; Sciarra, 2005, pp. 9–10). Much depended on the extent to which the Union's institutions could successfully weave together EU hard law, the social dialogue and active soft law into a hybrid system of regulation capable of accommodating diversity and of gaining the support of both governments and their electorates.

In contrast to the social policy agendas of the early 2000s, the tone of the Commission's communication on the demographic future of Europe [1.25], issued in the closing months of the first 50 years of European integration, was subdued and only cautiously optimistic. The demographic challenge, which had previously been used to justify EU-level intervention in social affairs, had become a major preoccupation for the Union. Transforming the challenge into opportunity was not considered to be impossible, but the Commission estimated that the Union had only a brief window of opportunity of about ten years. For reasons of efficiency and social equity, only the reform of existing institutions was regarded as a viable response. The restoration of confidence in the long-term future of the Union would, it was argued, be dependent on the participation of men and women in working life, meaning 'more jobs and longer working lives of better quality', and on productivity and performance. Cohesion policy and the open method of coordination in the areas of social protection and inclusion were among the instruments to be applied. Adequate social security (rather than the widely adopted, broader concept of social protection) and equity between the generations were to be guaranteed, but under the heading of 'sustainable public finances in Europe' [1.25, p. 13]. No reference was made in the communication to the European social model.

References

Adnett, N. and Hardy, S. (2005) *The European Social Model: modernisation or evolution?*, Cheltenham/Northampton, MA: Elgar.

Alber, J. (1993) 'Health and social services', in A. Walker, A-M. Guillemard and J. Alber (eds), *Older People in Europe: social and economic policies. The 1993 Report of the European Observatory*, Brussels: Commission of the European Communities, pp. 52–68.

Alber, J. and Fahey, T. (2004) *Perceptions of Living Conditions in an Enlarged Europe*, Luxembourg: Office for Official Publications of the European Communities.

Alcock, P. (2001) 'The comparative context', in P. Alcock and G. Craig (eds), *International Social Policy: welfare regimes in the developed world*, London/New York: Palgrave, pp. 1–25.

Arts, W. and Gelissen, J. (2002) 'Three worlds of welfare capitalism or more? A state-of-the-art report', *Journal of European Social Policy*, 12 (2), pp. 137–58.

Baldwin-Edwards, M. (1991) 'Immigration after 1992', *Policy and Politics*, 19 (3), pp. 199–211.

Beretta, D. (rapporteur) (1989) *Social Aspects of the Internal Market: European social area*, Brussels: European Communities, Economic and Social Committee.

Berghman, J. (1990) 'The implications of 1992 for social policy: a selective critique of social insurance protection', *Cross-national Research Papers*, 2 (1), pp. 9–17.

Bergqvist, C. and Jungar, A-C. (2000) 'Adaptation or diffusion of the Swedish gender model?', in L. Hantrais (ed.), *Gendered Policies in Europe: reconciling employment and family life*, London: Macmillan/ New York: St. Martin's Press, pp. 160–79.

Bimbi, F. (1993) 'Gender, "gift relationship" and welfare state cultures in Italy', in J. Lewis (ed.), *Women and Social Policies in Europe: work, family and the state*, Aldershot: Elgar, pp. 138–69.

Bredgaard, T. and Larsen, F. (eds) (2005) *Employment Policy from Different Angles*, Copenhagen: DJØF Publishing.

Brown, J. (1986) 'Cross-national and inter-country research into poverty: the case of the First European Poverty Programme', *Cross-national Research Papers*, 1 (2), pp. 41–51.

Büchel, F., Grip, A. de and Mertens, A. (eds) (2003) *Overeducation in Europe: current issues in theory and policy*, Cheltenham: Elgar.

Buckley, M. and Anderson, M. (1988) 'Introduction: problems, policies and politics', in M. Buckley and M. Anderson (eds), *Women, Equality and Europe*, London: Macmillan, pp. 1–19.

Búrca, G. de (ed.) (2005) *EU Law and the Welfare State: in search of solidarity*, Oxford/New York: Oxford University Press.

Burrows, N. and Mair, J. (1996) *European Social Law*, Chichester: John Wiley & Sons.

Byre, A. (1988) 'Applying Community standards on equality', in M. Buckley and M. Anderson (eds), Women, Equality and Europe, Basingstoke: Macmillan, pp. 20–32.

Clasen, J. and Freeman, R. (eds) (1994) *Social Policy in Germany*, London: Harvester Wheatsheaf.

Collins, D. (1975) *The European Communities: the social policy of the first phase*, vol. 2 *The European Economic Community 1958–72*, London: Martin Robertson.

Corbett, A. (2005) Universities and the Europe of Knowledge: ideas, institutions and policy entrepreneurship in European Union higher education policy, 1955–2005, Basingstoke: Palgrave Macmillan.

Council of Europe (2003) *Recent Demographic Developments in Europe 2003*, Strasbourg: Council of Europe Publishing.

Cram, L. (1997) *Policy-making in the European Union: conceptual lenses and the integration process*, London/New York: Routledge.

Daly, M. and Lewis, J. (2000) 'The concept of social care and the analysis of contemporary welfare states', *British Journal of Sociology*, 51 (2), pp. 281–98.

De Swaan, A. (1990) 'Perspectives for transnational social policy. Preliminary notes', *Cross-national Research Papers*, 2 (2), pp. 7–22.

Deacon, B. (1993) 'Developments in East European social policy', in C. Jones (ed.), *New Perspectives on the European Welfare State in Europe*, London/New York: Routledge, pp. 177–97.

Del Re, A. (2000) 'The paradoxes of Italian law and practice', in L. Hantrais (ed.), *Gendered Policies in Europe: reconciling employment and family life*, London: Macmillan/New York: St. Martin's Press, pp. 108–23.

Delors, J. (1985) 'Preface', in J. Vandamme (ed.), *New Dimensions in European Social Policy*, London: Croom Helm, pp. ix–xx.

Ditch, J., Barnes, H., Bradshaw, J. and Kilkey, M. (1998) *A Synthesis of National Family Policies 1996*, Brussels: European Commission, European Observatory on National Family Policies.

Drake, K. (1994) 'Policy integration and co-operation: a persistent challenge', in OECD (ed.), *Vocational Education and Training for Youth: towards coherent policy and practice*, Washington: OECD, pp. 143–68.

Duff, A. (ed.) (1997) *The Treaty of Amsterdam: text and commentary*, London: The Federal Trust.

Dumon, W. (ed.) (1991) *National Family Policies in EC-Countries in 1990*, Brussels: Commission of the European Communities/European Observatory on National Family Policies, V/2293/91-EN.

Dumon, W. (ed.) (1994) *Changing Family Policies in the Member States of the European Union*, Brussels: Commission of the European Communities/European Observatory on National Family Policies.

Edwards, N., Hensher, M. and Werneke, U. (1998) 'Changing hospital systems', in R.B. Saltman, J. Figueras and C. Sakallarides (eds), *Critical Challenges for Health Care Reform in Europe*, Buckingham/ Philadelphia: Open University Press, pp. 236–60.

Esping-Andersen, G. (1990) *The Three Worlds of Welfare Capitalism*, Cambridge: Polity.

Esping-Andersen, G. (1999) *Social Foundations of Postindustrial Economies*, Oxford: Oxford University Press.

European Commission (1997) *Tableaux de Bord*, Luxembourg: Office for Official Publications of the European Communities.

European Commission (1998) *National Transposition Measures: situation at 1ˢᵗ January 1998*, Luxembourg: Office for Official Publications of the European Communities.

European Commission (2004) *Development of a Methodology for the Collection of Harmonised Statistics on Childcare*, Luxembourg: Office for Official Publications of the European Communities.

European Commission (2005) *Reconciliation of Work and Private Life: a comparative review of thirty European countries*, Luxembourg: Office for Official Publications of the European Communities.

European Commission and Eurostat (2004) *Work and Health in the EU: a statistical portrait, data 1994–2002*, Luxembourg: Office for Official Publications of the European Communities.

European Commission Childcare Network (1990) 'Childcare in the European Communities 1985–1990', *Women of Europe Supplements*, No. 31.

European Commission Network on Childcare and Other Measures to Reconcile Employment and Family Responsibilities (1994) *Leave Arrangements for Workers with Children: a review of leave arrangements in the Member States of the European Union and Austria, Finland, Norway and Sweden*, Brussels: European Commission Directorate General V, Equal Opportunities Unit, V/773/94-EN.

European Commission Network on Childcare and Other Measures to Reconcile Employment and Family Responsibilities (1996) *A Review of*

Services for Young Children in the European Union 1990–1995, Brussels: European Commission Directorate General V.

Eurostat (2006) *Structures of the Taxation Systems in the European Union, data 1995–2006*, Luxembourg: Office for Official Publications of the European Communities.

Fagnani, J. (1996) 'Family policies and working mothers: a comparison of France and West Germany', in M.D. García-Ramon and J. Monk (eds), *Women of the European Union: the politics of work and daily life*, London/New York: Routledge, pp. 126–37.

Ferge, Z. (2001) 'Welfare and "ill-fare" systems in Central-Eastern Europe', in R. Sykes, B. Palier and P.M. Prior (eds), *Globalization and European Welfare States: challenges and change*, Basingstoke/New York: Palgrave, pp. 127–52.

Ferrera, M. (2005) *The Boundaries of Welfare: European integration and the new spatial politics of social protection*, Oxford: Oxford University Press.

Figueras, J., Saltman, R.B. and Sakallerides, C. (1998) 'Introduction', in R.B. Saltman, J. Figueras and C. Sakallarides (eds), *Critical Challenges for Health Care Reform in Europe*, Buckingham/Philadelphia: Open University Press, pp. 1–19.

Flora, P. and Alber, J. (1981) 'Modernization, democratization, and the development of welfare states in Western Europe', in P. Flora and A.J. Heidenheimer (eds), *The Development of Welfare States in Europe and America*, New Brunswick/London: Transaction Books, pp. 37–80.

Geyer, R.R. (2000) *Exploring European Social Policy*, Cambridge: Polity Press.

Ginn, J. and Arber, S. (1992) 'Towards women's independence: pension systems in three contrasting European welfare states', *Journal of European Social Policy*, 2 (4), pp. 255–77.

Gold, M. and Mayes, D. (1993) 'Rethinking a social policy for Europe', in R. Simpson and R. Walker (eds), *Europe: for richer or poorer?*, London: CPAG, pp. 25–38.

Gormley, L.W. (ed.) (1998) *Introduction to the Law of the European Communities: from Maastricht to Amsterdam*, 3rd edn, London/The Hague/Boston: Kluwer Law International.

Guillén, A. and Álvarez, S. (2001) 'Globalization and the Southern welfare states', in R. Sykes, B. Palier and P.M. Prior (eds), *Globalization and European Welfare States: challenges and change*, Basingstoke/New York: Palgrave, pp. 103–26.

Hannequart, A. (1992) 'Economic and social cohesion and the Structural Funds: an introduction', in A. Hannequart (ed.), *Economic and Social Cohesion in Europe: a new objective for integration*, London/New York: Routledge, pp. 1–18.

Hantrais, L. (2004) *Family Policy Matters: responding to family change in Europe*, Bristol: The Policy Press.

Hantrais, L. (2006) 'Living as a family in Europe', in L. Hantrais, D. Philipov and F.C. Billari, *Policy Implications of Changing Family Formation: study prepared for the European Population Conference 2005*, Population Studies, no. 49, Strasbourg: Council of Europe Publishing, pp. 117–82.

Hantrais, L. (ed.) (2000) *Gendered Policies in Europe: reconciling employment and family life*, London: Macmillan/New York: St. Martin's Press.

Heclo, H. (1981) 'Toward a new welfare state?', in P. Flora and A.J. Heidenheimer (eds), *The Development of Welfare States in Europe and America*, New Brunswick/London: Transaction Books, pp. 383–406.

Hervey, T. (1998) *European Social Law and Policy*, Harlow: Addison Wesley Longman.

Holloway, J. (1981) *Social Policy Harmonisation in the European Community*, Farnborough: Gower.

Home Office (1998) *Supporting Families: a consultation document*, London: Home Office.

Home Office, Department for Work and Pensions, HM Revenue & Customs and Department for Communities and Local Government (2006) *Accession Monitoring Report May 2004–September 2006*, Joint on-line report.

Hoskyns, C. (1996) *Integrating Gender: women, law and politics in the European Union*, London/New York: Verso.

James, E. (1982) 'From Paris to ESCAP', in J. Dennett, E. James, G. Room and P. Watson, *Europe against Poverty: the European Poverty Programme 1975–80*, London: Bedford Square Press/NCVO, pp. 3–13.

James, P. (1993) 'Occupational health and safety', in M. Gold (ed.), *The Social Dimension: employment policy in the European Community*, London: Macmillan, pp. 135–52.

Jones Finer, C. (1999) 'Trends and developments in welfare states', in J. Clasen (ed.), *Comparative Social Policy: concepts, theories and methods*, Oxford/Malden MA: Blackwell, pp. 15–33.

Jones, H. (1990) 'New European challenges for education – the impact of 1992', IBM Annual Lecture 1990, London, 11 July.

Kamerman, S.B. and Kahn, A.J. (eds) (1978) *Family Policy: government and families in fourteen countries*, New York: Columbia University Press.

Kleinman, M. (2002) *A European Welfare State? European Union social policy in context*, Basingstoke/New York: Palgrave.

Kleinman, M. and Piachaud, D. (1993) 'European social policy: conceptions and choices', *Journal of European Social Policy*, 3 (1), pp. 1–19.

Kokko, S., Hava, P., Ortun, V. and Leppo, K. (1998) 'The role of the state in health care reform', in R.B. Saltman, J. Figueras and C. Sakallarides (eds), *Critical Challenges for Health Care Reform in Europe*, Buckingham/Philadelphia: Open University Press, pp. 289–307.

Lanquetin, M-T., Laufer, J. and Letablier, M-T. (2000) 'From equality to reconciliation in France?', in L. Hantrais (ed.), *Gendered Policies in Europe: reconciling employment and family life*, London: Macmillan/ New York: St. Martin's Press, pp. 68–88.

Leibfried, S. (1992) 'Europe's could-be social state: social policy in European integration after 1992', in W. J. Adams (ed.), *Singular Europe: economy and polity of the European Community after 1992*, Ann Arbor: University of Michigan Press, pp. 97–118.

Leibfried, S. (2005) 'Social policy: left to courts and markets?', in H. Wallace, W. Wallace and M.A. Pollack (eds), *Policy-making in the European Union*, 5th edn, Oxford: Oxford University Press, pp. 243–78.

Leibfried, S. and Pierson, P. (1992) 'Prospects for social Europe', *Politics and Society*, 20 (3), pp. 333–66.

Lindley, R.M. (1991) 'Interactions in the markets for education, training and labour: a European perspective on intermediate skills', in P. Ryan (ed.), *International Comparisons of Vocational Education and Training for Intermediate Skills*, London/New York: The Falmer Press, pp. 185–206.

Lister, R. (1997) *Citizenship: feminist pespectives*, London: Macmillan.

Lødemel, I. (1992) 'The poor and the poorest in European income maintenance', *Cross-national Research Papers*, 2 (7), pp. 13–23.

Majone, G. (1996a) 'A European regulatory state?', in J.J. Richardson (ed.), *European Union: power and policy-making*, London/New York: Routledge, pp. 263–77.

Majone, G. (1996b) 'Which social policy for Europe?', in Y. Mény, P. Muller and J-L. Quermonne (eds), *Adjusting to Europe*, London: Routledge, pp. 123–36.

Marks, G., Hooghe, L. and Blank, K. (1996) 'European integration from the 1980s: state-centric v. multi-level governance', *Journal of Common Market Studies*, 34 (3), pp. 341–78.

Marlier, E., Atkinson, A.B., Cantillon, B. and Nolan, B. (2006) *The EU and Social Inclusion: facing the challenges*, Bristol: The Policy Press.

Masson, J-R. (2003) *Thirteen Years of Cooperation and Reforms in Vocational Education and Training in the Acceding and Candidate Countries: what are the lessons to be learned from the perspective of the Lisbon objectives?*, Report for the European Training Foundation, Luxembourg: Office for Official Publications of the European Communities.

Meehan, E. (1993) 'Women's rights in the European Community', in J. Lewis (ed.), *Women and Social Policies in Europe: work, family and the state*, Aldershot: Elgar, pp. 194–205.

Merle, V. and Bertrand, O. (1993) 'Comparabilité et reconnaissance des qualifications en Europe: instruments et enjeux', *Formation emploi*, No. 43, July–September, pp. 41–56.

Milner, S. (1998) 'Training policy: steering between divergent national logics', in D. Hine and H. Kassim (eds), *Beyond the Market: the European Union and national social policy*, London/New York: Routledge, pp. 156–77.

Mishra, R. (1977) *Society and Social Policy: theoretical perspectives on welfare*, London/Basingstoke: Macmillan.

Mitchell, M. and Russell, D. (1998) 'Immigration, citizenship and social exclusion in the new Europe', in R. Sykes and P. Alcock (eds), *Developments in European Social Policy: convergence and diversity*, Bristol: The Policy Press, pp. 75–94.

Moravcsik, A. and Nicolaïdis, K. (1999) 'Explaining the Treaty of Amsterdam: interests, influences, institutions', *Journal of Common Market Studies*, 37 (1), pp. 59–85.

National Statistics (2006) *Health Statistics Quarterly*, No. 29, Spring, Basingstoke: Palgrave.

Nielsen, K. (1996) 'Eastern European welfare systems', in B. Greve (ed.), *Comparative Welfare Systems: the Scandinavian model in a period of change*, London: Macmillan/New York: St. Martin's Press, pp. 185–213.

Niessen, J. and Schibel, Y. (2002) *Demographic Changes and the Consequence for Europe's Future: is immigration an option?*, Brussels: Migration Policy Group.

Nugent, N. (2003) *The Government and Politics of the European Union*, 5th edn, London/New York: Palgrave Macmillan.

O'Donnell, R. (1992) 'Policy requirements for regional balance in economic and monetary union', in A. Hannequart (ed.), *Economic and Social Cohesion in Europe: a new objective for integration*, London/ New York: Routledge, pp. 21–52.

Pascall, G. and Manning, N. (2000) 'Gender and social policy: comparing welfare states in Central and Eastern Europe and the former Soviet Union', *Journal of European Social Policy*, 10 (3), pp. 240–66.

Pestieau, P. (2006) *The Welfare State in the European Union: economic and social perspectives*, Oxford: Oxford University Press.

Pierson, C. (1991) *Beyond the Welfare State? The new political economy of welfare*, Cambridge: Polity Press.

Pierson, P. (1996) 'The path to European integration: a historical institutionalist analysis', *Comparative Political Studies*, 29 (2), pp. 123–63.

Pieters, D. (1991) 'Will "1992" lead to the co-ordination and harmonization of social security?', in D. Pieters (ed.), *Social Security in Europe:*

Miscellanea of the Erasmus-programme Social Security in the E.C., Brussels: Bruylant/Antwerp: Maklu, pp. 177–90.

Pieters, D. (ed.) (1998) *Social Protection of the Next Generation in Europe*, London/The Hague/Boston: Kluwer Law International, EISS Yearbook 1997.

Pollack, M.A. (2005) 'Theorizing EU policy-making', in H. Wallace, W. Wallace and M.A. Pollack (eds), *Policy-making in the European Union*, 5th edn, Oxford: Oxford University Press, pp. 13–48.

Poulain, M., Perrin, N. and Singleton, A. (eds) (2006) *European Migration Statistics*, Louvain: Presses Universitaires de Louvain.

Quintin, O. (1988) 'The policies of the European Communities with special reference to the labour market', in M. Buckley and M. Anderson (eds), *Women, Equality and Europe*, London: Macmillan, pp. 71–7.

Rees, T. (1998) *Mainstreaming Equality in the European Union: education, training and labour market policies*, London/New York: Routledge.

Renoy, P., Ivarsson, S., van der Wusten-Gritsai, O. and Meijer, E. (2004) *Undeclared Work in an Enlarged Union. An analysis of undeclared work: an in-depth study of specific items*, Brussels: European Commission, Directorate General for Employment and Social Affairs, CE-V/1-04-021-EN-C.

Rex, J. (1992) 'Race and ethnicity in Europe', in J. Bailey (ed.), *Social Europe*, London/New York: Longman, pp. 106–20.

Rhodes, M. (1995) 'A regulatory conundrum: industrial relations and the social dimension', in S. Leibfried and P. Pierson (eds), *European Social Policy: between fragmentation and integration*, Washington, DC: The Brookings Institution, pp. 78–122.

Rhodes, M. (1997) 'Southern European welfare states: identity, problems and prospects for reform', in M. Rhodes (ed.), *Southern European Welfare States: between crisis and reform*, London/Portland, Oregon: Frank Cass, pp. 1–22.

Roberts, I. and Springer, B. (2001) *Social Policy in the European Union: between harmonization and national autonomy*, Boulder/London: Lynne Rienner.

Room, G. (1982) 'The definition and measurement of poverty', in J. Dennett, E. James, G. Room and P. Watson, *Europe against Poverty: the European Poverty Programme 1975–80*, London: Bedford Square Press/NCVO, pp. 155–62.

Room, G. (1994) 'European social policy: competition, conflict and integration', in R. Page and J. Baldock (eds), *Social Policy Review 6*, Canterbury: Social Policy Association, pp. 17–35.

Room, G. (co-ordinator) (1991) *Observatory on National Policies to Combat Social Exclusion*, Second annual report, Brussels: Commission of the European Communities, Directorate General V.

Rubery, J. and Smith, M. (1999) *The Future European Labour Supply*, Luxembourg: Office for Official Publications of the European Communities.

Rubery, J., Smith, M. and Fagan, C. (1999) *Women's Employment in Europe: trends and prospects*, London/New York: Routledge.

Sardon, J-P. (2006) 'Recent demographic trends in developed countries', *Population-E*, 61 (3), pp. 195–266.

Sciarra, S. (2005) *The Evolution of European Law (1992–2003)*, vol. 1 *General Report*, Luxembourg: Office for Official Publications of the European Communities.

Shanks, M. (1977) *European Social Policy, Today and Tomorrow*, Oxford/New York: Pergamon.

Shaw, J. (ed.) (2000) *Social Law and Policy in an Evolving European Union*, Oxford/Portland, Oregon: Hart.

Soisson, J-P. (1990) 'Observations on the Community Charter of Basic Social Rights for Workers', *Social Europe*, 1/90, pp. 10–13.

Spicker, P. (1991) 'The principle of subsidiarity and the social policy of the European Community', *Journal of European Social Policy*, 1 (1), pp. 3–14.

Teague, P. (1989) *The European Community: the social dimension. Labour market policies for 1992*, London: Kogan Page in association with the Cranfield School of Management.

Teague, P. (1998) 'Monetary union and social Europe', *Journal of European Social Policy*, 8 (2), pp. 117–37.

Teague, P. and McClelland, D. (1991) 'Towards "social Europe"? Industrial relations after 1992', *Cross-national Research Papers*, 2 (5), pp. 8–22.

Titmuss, R.M. (1974) *Social Policy: an introduction* (edited by B. Abel-Smith and K. Titmuss), London: George Allen & Unwin.

Townsend, P. (1979) *Poverty in the United Kingdom: a survey of household resources and standards of living*, Harmondsworth: Penguin.

Trubek, D.M. and Trubek, L.G. (2005) 'Hard and soft law in the construction of social Europe: the role of the open method of co-ordination', *European Law Journal*, 11 (3), pp. 343–64.

United Nations Statistical Commission/Economic Commission for Europe (1998) *Recommendations for the 2000 censuses of population and housing in the ECE region*, Statistical Standards and Studies, No. 49, New York: United Nations.

van Oorschot, W. and Math, A. (1996) 'La question du non-recours aux prestations sociales', *Recherches et prévisions*, No. 43, pp. 5–17.

Vaughan-Whitehead, D.C. (2003) *EU Enlargement versus Social Europe? The uncertain future of the European social model*, Cheltenham/ Northampton, MA: Elgar.

Vogel, J. (1997) *Living Conditions and Inequality in the European Union 1997*, Eurostat Working Papers, Population and Social Conditions, E/1997-3.

Walker, A. (1993) 'Introduction', 'Living standards and way of life', in A. Walker, A-M. Guillemard and J. Alber (eds), *Older people in Europe: social and economic policies. The 1993 Report of the European Observatory*, Brussels: Commission of the European Communities, pp. 1–6, 8–34.

Walker, A. (1998) *Managing an Ageing Workforce: a guide to good practice*, Luxembourg: Office for Official Publications of the European Communities.

Walker, A. and Maltby, T. (1997) *Ageing Europe*, Buckingham/Bristol, PA: Oxford University Press.

Wilson, R.A. and Briscoe, G. (2004) 'The impact of human capital on economic growth: a review', in P. Desay and M. Tessaring (eds), *Third Report on Vocational Training Research in Europe*, vol. I *Impact of Education and Training: background report*, Thessaloniki: CEDEFOP, pp. 3–70.

Zeitlin, J. (2005) 'Social Europe and experimentalist governance: towards a new constitutional compromise', in G. de Búrca (ed.), *EU Law and the Welfare State: in search of solidarity*, Oxford/New York: Oxford University Press, pp. 213–41.

Index

Numbers in square brackets indicate box references to official documents at the end of chapters.